C000137061

EVERY CLOUD

EVERY CLOUD

CLOUD

How Leeds City Became United

GARY EDWARDS

First published by Pitch Publishing, 2019

Pitch Publishing
A2 Yeoman Gate
Yeoman Way
Worthing
Sussex
BN13 3QZ
www.pitchpublishing.co.uk
info@pitchpublishing.co.uk

A CIP catalogue record is available for this book
from the British Library.

ISBN 978 1 78531 508 4

Typesetting and origination by Pitch Publishing

Printed and bound by TJ International Ltd, Padstow, UK

Contents

Dedication

For the past couple of years, my dear wife Lesley has ignored – most of the time – the stacks of papers, documents, photographs and other stuff that has occupied much of our house. Thank you Wub for your patience and understanding.

Acknowledgements

THIS book was reliant on information and personal accounts from several different sources and to that end I am deeply appreciative of the invaluable input from: Antony Ramm and Josh Flint at Leeds Central Library; Tony Hill, Dave Tomlinson, Neil Roche and the team at ozwhiteslufc.net.au and www.mightywhites.co.uk; Steve Riding, Robert Endeacott, West Yorkshire Archives, Neil Sibson and Yorkshire Amateur AFC, Tony Winstanley, Andrew Varley Official Leeds United Photographer, Neil Jeffries, Mark 'Skippy' Ledgard, Michael Hewitt Programmes, Martin 'Slugger' Jackson, Steve Studd, Keith Barber, Ken Radcliffe, Darren and Ben Coolican.

I am particularly indebted to the following for allowing me into their homes and sharing memories of some of the players and supporters of both Leeds City and Leeds United in the early 1900s; it was truly an honour for me to meet: Mary 'Molly' Hewitt, the daughter of

City player John 'Jack' Hewitt; Luke Griffiths and his grandmother Vera, the daughter of the City goalkeeper Walter Cook; Jon Dodsworth, great grandson of Herbert Dodsworth, Leeds United right-back 1919/20; Mick Duffield, the great nephew of United's Bert Duffield who played in the first ever Leeds United team in 1920. Also in that team was Merton 'Matt' Ellson and I'd like to thank Trevor Chorley, Alice Beesley and Les Harrison for their memories of the man who scored Leeds United's first ever league goal. Huge thanks to Mike Oldfield and the lovely family of Harry Duggan, a Leeds United favourite of the 1930s. I am very grateful also for the contributions by Kathleen Thornton, Michael Gibson and James Mattison, the family of Joe Adams, and Hilary Thompson, the granddaughter of Harry Bennett. And finally, especial thanks to my daughter Vicky Wooldridge.

Introduction

THE story of how Leeds City became Leeds United in the early 1900s is a fascinating and gripping true story of blackmail, threats, underhandedness, intrigue and enough cloak and dagger activity to rival any blockbuster – and all set to the backdrop of World War One. The story begins 18 years earlier in late Victorian Leeds.

Foreword

IT is a fantastic honour to be asked to provide the foreword for *Every Cloud*. I've had the great pleasure of knowing Gary for, well, shall we say a very, very long time.

Gary is not only a fanatical supporter of our club, he is a great lad as well. If you love our club like we do, then this is a must read. Starting with the demise of Leeds City, it goes on to tell the story of the club right up to the birth of Leeds United, but it is not just Leeds fans who this book will appeal to. As I say on stadium tours, it is so important that we know our roots and understand just what we are all about and this book has all that, and more – including some of the lesser known history that ultimately led to the formation of LUFC as we know it today.

Gary's dedication was recognised by the club in February 2018 when a plaque was unveiled at Elland Road Stadium to commemorate him attending every

United game, anywhere in the world, for a remarkable 50 consecutive years.

Marching on Together
Peter 'Stix' Lockwood
The Players' Liaison Officer
Leeds United Football Club

Chapter One

A Menace to the Rugby Game

LEEDS, 12 February 1896. It is dusk as two shrouded figures emerge from a dark alley; they stand beneath a gas lamp totally engulfed in dense fog. The taller of the two men leans towards the cupped hands of the more diminutive one, his face instantly illuminated by a struck match as deep shadows dance around the wrinkles on his face, highlighting his furrowed brow.

His Woodbine sparks to life, and he draws down the smoke before exhaling a long stream that disappears into the night. Joe Adams will be 41 in a month's time, but his face hides his age – he looks 20 years older than he is. The taller man, John Bennett, who is three years senior to Joe, uses the still-lit match to light his lamplighter's pole as he reaches up to bring the lamp to life, revealing a decrepit and fading pub sign – 'Green Dragon Hotel'.

The outline of Leeds Town Hall stands just 200 yards further down The Headrow, just visible through the mist, but the clock which John was hoping to see was engulfed.

Inside, through the orange glowing windows of the Green Dragon, silhouetted figures can be seen… 'Wonder what's going on in there?' asks Joe Adams.

'It's some sort of a football meeting,' John replies. 'They're trying to bring the game up here from down south. There's more chance of 'em catching Jack the Ripper! This is rugby territory, always will be.'

Joe looks at him, 'What do you mean, "football"? Do you mean that association football that some people are talking about? Round ball thing?' He simulates a circle with both his hands. 'I've heard that they're already playing it somewhere in Yorkshire.'

'Aye,' says John. 'Remember when we were watching Holbeck Rugby week 'afore last and people were saying that some big-wigs are coming up from London to try and get association football played around here, "socker" they call it.' He laughs. 'My nephew, Harry, plays soccer as a half-back, whatever that means. His team is called Leeds Northern, they play up near the tram depot at Chapeltown, but to my shame, I've never seen him play. But I will, I need to,' he says, then he remembers he is supposed to be against the round ball sport, and points to a shop adjacent to the Green Dragon, which was at No 15 Guildford Street. 'That shop there is for the southern softies.' It was called Brown, Carson & Co. Wine Merchants.

'We've just about finished here,' says Bennett looking down the dark alley still shrouded in the thick smog caused by the combination of fog rising from the River Aire and smoke from coal fires. Small pools of glowing yellow light disappear into the distance. It is now 6.45pm. 'Why don't we go in and see what they're on about?'

'What do you mean? Can anybody go in?' asks Adams.

Bennett has laid his extinguished pole down in the alley and is already trying the door handle when the door opens. 'Let's go in and find out,' he says.

'Good evening gentlemen, come in. Sit down, we're just about to get started,' says James Spittle, sitting behind a large table that faces a congregation of around 30 men, hunched around tables glugging ale. Many of them are facing away from the speaker.

Spittle is a rather imposing figure, easily over 6ft. His bushy greying side whiskers extend to his moustache, that bears the yellowing inflicted upon it by a clay pipe which he clutches in his right hand. Alongside Spittle to his left is William Hirst and to his right, W. H. Shaw. All three men, from Huddersfield, have been pioneering association football in that area; three weeks earlier they had presided over a similar gathering at the White Swan Hotel in nearby Halifax and they had left suitably encouraged by the outcome. This evening's meeting was to assess the interest and gauge the opinion of football in Leeds and the possibility of forming an official West Yorkshire Association before taking their proposal to the Football Association in London for permission.

It is believed that the first ever association football match in Leeds took place at Holbeck Recreation Ground on Boxing Day, 1877. It had been organised by Mr Fred Sanderson, who was president of the Sheffield New Association. He brought two teams from Sheffield who came with their own kit, goalposts, a ball and even umpires. Despite freezing cold temperatures and vicious high winds, a good crowd gathered. At that time there was no penalty area as the penalty kick hadn't yet been introduced and the goal area was marked off with a semi-circle. There were no nets and the two-handed throw-in was, as yet, unheard of. The crowd weren't overly impressed, being mainly rugby followers, and more disappointment came for the Sheffield Association when after the match they discovered that almost all the spectators had been season ticket holders of Holbeck Rugby Club and had therefore not paid to watch the game, leaving the Association without a single penny in payment. Football in Leeds was certainly going to be a slow process.

Spittle lights and puffs on his clay pipe, 'Gentlemen, my colleagues and I have been greatly impressed with the progress this city has made in its endeavour to establish association football in Yorkshire; last month we met with the same enthusiasm in Halifax and we are supremely confident that we can take the required criteria to London with great expectation of a favourable result.'

There had been several teams in areas of Leeds since 1880 and amongst them two different teams called Leeds FC, both of which had disbanded due to lack of interest, and a club called Leeds Albion that lasted four years before folding in 1892. However, in February 1894, the West Yorkshire League was established with a new team, Leeds AFC, winning the first ever league by eight points. It had been this renewed interest in football and Leeds AFC's success in particular that had alerted Spittle and his men to the idea of expanding soccer across West Yorkshire.

John and Joe have found two chairs at a small table near the back and close to the door. 'I don't think we'll be long here,' whispers John. 'We'll just slip out unnoticed. I don't want to be too late anyway. I'm famished.' He lights up another Woodbine and passes one to Joe. John looks around, the brass of the rails and pumps at the bar are in need of a good polish and some of the damp air from outside has infiltrated the room, but it is homely and has a good feel. 'It's a while since we were in here, eh?' he whispers to Joe who nods and whispers back, 'Aye, about seven or eight years I'd say.'

This gathering was a direct result of that meeting chaired by the three men from Huddersfield at the White Swan Hotel in Halifax the previous month; the first known instance of an interest from Huddersfield in soccer.

This particular meeting in Leeds lasted for over two hours, resulting in Spittle being appointed as the Association's divisional representative with Hirst filling the post of president and Shaw becoming vice president. Overall it was a very positive meeting and the three men left feeling sufficiently armed with enough interest and enthusiasm to take their findings to the Football Association's headquarters in London.

Forty minutes later, John Bennett had walked back to his home two miles away in Holbeck, and now sat alone in his kitchen, his wife Mary having retired to bed hours earlier, but not before she had left his supper on the kitchen table. As he sat and ate his cold offal he reflected on the evening's meeting. There seemed to be a possibility of first-class football in Leeds; but he still maintained in his mind that it would never replace rugby, which had dominated northern England, particularly Yorkshire and Lancashire, for around 30 years. Besides, both John and Joe were rugby men; although John's nephew had started playing 'socker' a couple of years ago, he wasn't sold on the idea. But John admitted to himself that Spittle and his associates had been very convincing at the Green Dragon meeting. Bennett pondered this as he pulled a small crumpled leaflet from his pocket that he had picked up at the pub earlier. 'Association Football in Leeds. Meeting at Green Dragon Wednesday, February, 12. 7 o'clock.' He then poked around at the remains of the sheep's brain and heart on his plate before picking up a tankard of ale, which he drank quickly before resting his head on his kitchen table and lapsing into a deep sleep.

Meanwhile Joe, who lived with his wife Myrtle in a small dwelling close to the Crooked Billet public house in Hunslet, sat down to his table and opened a bottle of beer: he had to be back on the streets of Leeds with John at 6.30 the next morning to put out those gas lamps. He reflected on whether or not 'socker', which was rapidly being branded by the oval ball fraternity as 'a menace to rugby', could really happen.

Although the early form of the official Football Association came about in 1863, rugby, and cricket, were by far the most popular sports with the working class of the north of England. The English Rugby Union had always been staunchly pro-amateurism, but in Yorkshire and Lancashire they believed that the large sums of money coming in the way of gate receipts and such could only lead to one thing – professionalism. In the summer of 1895, 22 clubs resigned from the English Union and the Northern Union was founded with the following clubs: Bradford, Brighouse Rangers, Batley, Broughton Rangers, Halifax, Hunslet, Hull, Huddersfield, Liversedge, Leeds, Leigh, Manningham, Oldham, Rochdale Hornets, Runcorn, St Helens, Stockport, Tyldesley, Wakefield Trinity, Warrington and Widnes. After the first season, however, Tyldesley, Liversedge and Stockport dropped out. But the Northern Union quickly expanded and further clubs such as Salford, Swinton, Morecambe, Castleford, Bramley, Heckmondwike, Holbeck and Leeds Parish Church joined. To accommodate the increasing influx of new clubs the league was reconstructed and also the Challenge Cup competition was inaugurated.

After the introduction of professionalism in 1898 payment for time lost through playing was followed by the legalisation of compensation in the form of wages, but restricted by a stipulation of a supplementary occupation. In 1901, around the time of the death of Queen Victoria, the Northern League was formed and this was to have far-reaching consequences for the world of rugby, and indeed, association football.

The reconstruction of the league and the forming of two divisions would result in a conflict between the union and league bodies. The union had rendered the interests of the richer clubs identical to that of the less fortunately placed. The league on the other hand provided the opportunity for leading clubs to play each other irrespective of their geographical position and so the subsequent two-tier league system was introduced, placing the elite of the crop in the top tier and the less effective teams into the second tier. Eventually, they split the leagues into Yorkshire and Lancashire.

Bradford club Manningham, who only the year before had become the world's first ever rugby league champions, now found themselves relegated to the lower division and fell on hard times. Perplexed and angry at being 'left out in the cold', Manningham considered resigning its membership.

Association football was still trying to force its way into the sporting structure in the north and in March 1903 Manningham offered to share their Valley Parade ground with a professional football club by the name of Bradford City. Two months later, however, a hostile meeting called by Manningham's president Alfred Ayrton saw a vote of 75 votes to 34 in favour of football and not rugby being played at Valley Parade. Manningham disbanded and Bradford City was born.

The first Association Football League had been formed in 1888 by Aston Villa director William McGregor, whose club had been the most successful English club of the Victorian era and by the time of the death of the Queen had won five league titles and three FA Cups. With other prominent clubs of that era, such as Blackburn, Sunderland and Preston, the end of the 19th century saw Britain being swept by football mania attracting huge crowds of largely working-class men, but Leeds was the largest city in Britain not to have a major football team.

Joe was still thinking about the idea of football breaking through into West Yorkshire as he began to eat his supper – turtle soup. He loved the green jelly-like fat which was used to flavour the soup made from the long-boiled stringy flesh of the animal. When he had finished his soup he gulped the last few drops of his beer down and his gaze turned to a photograph on the nearby mantelpiece. It was of him and Myrtle and between them was their daughter Rose, who had died of diphtheria, aged 13, just three months earlier. In the photograph Rose sat up in bed looking straight at the camera, flanked by her solemn parents. Photography was still in its infancy, but it was quite common in those Victorian times when a loved one died to have a family photograph taken with the corpse in a pose. Often in those post-mortem photographs the subject's eyes were propped open, or even pupils painted on the eyes of the finished photographic print. Looking at this Adams family portrait, no one would guess that Rose in the middle of the photograph was in fact dead. For many Victorians, partly due to the expense, this would be the only time they would be photographed.

Interestingly, the nearby Crooked Billet, which Joe often frequented, had housed a mortuary until only recently. The Aire and Calder Navigation, a canalised section of the River Aire, ran behind the pub and bodies would often be fished out and taken to the morgue. A reward was given to anyone retrieving a body from the River Aire, but it was double if a body should be retrieved from the Aire and Calder Navigation. Often then, if a body was fished out of the River Aire, it would be taken to the Navigation and hopefully fished out in front of witnesses before being taken to the morgue for a double reward.

Joe Adams and John Bennett had been firm friends and work colleagues for many years. They had fought side by side in the infamous Leeds Gas Strike in 1890. Although the dispute didn't affect Joe or John directly, both men, being gas street lighters, felt compelled to stand shoulder to shoulder with their Leeds Gas colleagues. However, neither of them, nor anyone else, could have foreseen the large-scale disruption and riots that would unfold. Initially, in the dispute's infancy, Leeds Gas workers had been prevented from entering their respective gasworks across Leeds and replacements, blacklegs in effect, were brought in from other gasworks across London and Lancashire by train. These replacements would carry out the tasks of the stokers, the engineers, general labourers and any other roles that needed filling in the forcefully vacated gasworks. These replacements would become known only as 'Strangers' by Leeds Gas workers and things quickly escalated as the Strangers entered the different Leeds gasworks under police guard. Violence erupted at Meadow Lane and York Street and as a procession of Strangers surrounded by armed police made their way to New Wortley Gasworks, hundreds of Leeds Gas workers lay in wait on top of Wortley Bridge. The Strangers had come to realise by now that they had been brought to Leeds by the Gas Committee under false pretences but they were attacked from the bridge by a cascade of boulders, bricks, concrete slabs, iron pipes and anything that came to hand.

Hundreds of police reinforcements, including the mounted constabulary, were brought in, in an attempt to stabilise the situation and even the military was called in. Foot-soldiers from the Leeds barracks arrived armed with light, long gun firearms often used by high-mobility troops. Also ordered to the fray was a company of Carabineers from the 6th Dragoon Guard from the Strensall barracks at York.

Thousands upon thousands of Leeds Gas men stood firm and united and by the time the strike ended nine days after it had begun, hundreds had been injured or hospitalised – miraculously there had been no fatalities.

Joe and John also stood together on the touchline at Holbeck Recreation Ground on Elland Road as staunch supporters of Holbeck Rugby League Club, who had joined the Northern Union in 1896. They were actually founder members of the Leeds and District organisation after a meeting held at the Green Dragon, which John and Joe had attended, had decided to form a more local league with the other founder clubs being Bramley, Hunslet,

Kirkstall, Leeds Parish Church and the forerunner of Leeds Rhinos, Leeds St John's.

Known locally as the 'Reckry', Holbeck Recreation Ground was one of the best in Leeds. It was used for both codes of football and cricket. Pre-Headingley, Yorkshire County Cricket Club played there and among the records is a game in 1868 in which Yorkshire dismissed Lancashire for 30 and 34 in the second innings. The Holbeck Cricket Club used to play on Holbeck Moor, before moving to the Recreation Ground. The Reckry was well-appointed and extensive. It was situated on the top side of Holbeck Moor, where the streets known as 'the Recreations' now stand. It extended from the Waggon and Horses public house to Brown Lane, and from Top Moor Side, along Elland Road to the Neville Works, along Brown Lane to the vicarage. On one side of the ground was a grandstand – and it had a unique history. It once graced the old Leeds Racecourse at Pontefract Road. When this closed, it was dismantled and taken to Holbeck. While the Recreation Ground was occasionally used for soccer, it was in all intents and purposes a rugby ground, and so it came as a shock to the rugby public when in 1897, they were informed that their lease would not be renewed.

Later that same year, Holbeck purchased the Old Peacock Ground from Bentley's brewery. It had been located by the club's secretary, Mr Robert Walker, who had contacted the brewery, who in turn were no doubt influenced by the fact that there were two of their own licensed houses in the district and they would benefit further from the proposed scheme. The Old Peacock Ground was an open grass field at the foot of Beeston Hill and had taken its name from the nearby pub. Holbeck paid £1,100 on condition that it should remain first and foremost a football ground for at least seven years and Bentley's also insisted on retaining the catering rights. A new stand was erected by Holbeck as the ground gradually became known as Elland Road. The first ever soccer match to be played at Elland Road was the West Yorkshire Cup Final on 23 April 1898, Hunslet retaining the trophy by beating Harrogate 1-0.

Initially, however, Mr Walker's proposal met with strong opposition, many supporters contending that the ground was too far away, and at a crowded meeting in Holbeck schoolroom, there were some heated arguments between Mr Walker and local councillor J. Henry, one of the directors, who led the opposition. But in the end, when the vote was finally taken, the proposal to move to Elland Road received a large majority.

But, the making of the ground was soon beset with difficulties, chief of which was the shortage of labour. It so happened that the firms whose services were required were engaged upon a big scheme of demolition and building in the centre of Leeds – the scheme that swept away Wood Street, and established the Empire Theatre, County Arcade, Queen Victoria Street and King Edward Street. Work did proceed at Elland Road, however, but not without problems, one of which being the need to build a grandstand there. The provision of a new stand hadn't been in Mr Walker's original plans as he had intended buying one from the West Riding Ground, which had come to the end of its existence as a sports centre. But the stand at Meanwood Road was no ordinary structure. It had been designed to project over the beck that ran behind the ground, and its peculiar construction rendered it unsuitable for re-erection on another site, meaning that the deal was off and that a new stand would have to be built at Holbeck. The new ground, however, was not as pretentious as the present one. The pitch, for instance, was at right-angles to the direction it takes today, with the touchlines running parallel with Elland Road – it was a compact little ground.

At the end of the season 1902/03 Holbeck finished joint second with St Helens behind champions Wakefield Trinity. However, in the promotion play-off with St Helens on 14 May 1904, Holbeck were defeated 7-0, a result that put paid to Holbeck's ambition and indeed their future. The club decided, much as Mannigham had done the year before, that it would be financially unable to continue in the Second Division and folded. So, following the 7-0 defeat, Joe and John, along with another fan, John Brewer, trudged along to the Old Peacock to drown their sorrows. Even before the news had broken, everyone in the pub figured they had seen Holbeck's last game. And it certainly wasn't any compensation to them that professional football in the area was becoming a real possibility.

Chapter Two

'Socker' Finally Comes to Leeds

FOOTBALL in Leeds had been chipping away, relatively unnoticed, for a number of years and it was on this that James Spittle had based his hope. Spittle had done much research into this and had noted that several clubs in the Leeds area were trying to break through.

Football was indeed gathering pace from all corners of Yorkshire, and Sam Gilbert from Sheffield had been acting as what some called a football missionary to the West Riding. His enthusiasm as the cricket professional at Hunslet Cricket Club spanned to a desire to form a football club, which came to fruition when Gilbert founded Hunslet Association Football Club in 1878. Sadly though, a lack of interest meant that Hunslet AFC only lasted five years; but Gilbert's baton was picked up in 1889 when employees of Leeds Steelworks formed a football team which eventually became known as Hunslet FC, who after joining the West Yorkshire League in 1894, enjoyed considerable success, winning the West Yorkshire Cup four times and made a massive impact on the FA Amateur Cup, notching up an impressive win over the mighty Old Etonians. Hunslet, known as 'The Twinklers', fought back from two goals down to produce a dramatic 3-2 victory over the much-fancied Etonians, with future Leeds City player 'Tipper' Heffron grabbing one of the goals.

A club known simply as Leeds, was formed in Kirkstall in 1885, founded by Mr Leonard Cooper who resided at Abbey House, Kirkstall. Mr Cooper managed to attract players from Old Carthusians, Swifts and even Notts County. Leeds' first game was to be against Hull Town at Armley Cricket Ground on 3 October 1885, but the visitors failed to turn up. Leeds sometimes played their home games on a field adjoining the Star and Garter in Kirkstall, but didn't attract what could be described as a good attendance. It was these small attendances that led to the downfall of the club, as opponents were reluctant to play in front of a low number of spectators and they eventually bowed to the inevitable and the club sadly closed down. However, another club, also called Leeds, was formed in 1888 and they played on the same pitch at Kirkstall. Finding opponents continued to hamper progress and Leeds found themselves travelling far afield to places such as Gainsborough Trinity, Sheffield Wednesday and Darlington. The visit to Darlington emphasised another form of worry that frequently beset football clubs at this time. Two players missed the train and Leeds had to borrow two from Darlington. It's no small wonder that Leeds went down 7-0.

An opportunity came Leeds' way to play an 'A' team from Preston North End on 3 November 1888, the same day as Leeds were due to play Oliver's Mount School from Scarborough. The problem was solved by delegating the Oliver's Mount fixture to the reserve team, who fulfilled it at the Star and Garter ground, while the first team played at Cardigan Fields. The visit of Preston North End was attended by miserable weather and a small crowd of only about 2,000. Leeds won the game 4-0. As the season progressed, Leeds found it difficult to attract a crowd of any size, not only on account of people having little interest in soccer, but mostly because they did not understand it, and the players themselves had not acquired the knack of infusing personality into their play, ensuring dreary exhibitions. Still the club carried on, and despite low crowds, there was no shortage of players, or at any rate, men willing to learn. Many were called, but few were chosen – more than once.

A club called Leeds Albion played its first game, on 20 October 1888, at a rented ground on Brudenell Road against Harrogate, winning 3-1, their first ever goal coming from Walker. Albion had been formed at the company works of Messrs Wilsons and Mathiesons, and consisted of several Scotsmen. The man who formed Albion was called Mr Robert Mason. Albion's first home game at their own ground was a 1-1 draw with Bradford, with Murdoch scoring for Albion. Then came what is believed to be the first ever Leeds 'derby' day when, on Saturday, 10 November, Leeds Albion played Leeds at Brudenell Road. The Albion line-up that afternoon was: Harrison, Mason, Gamble, Scott, Murdoch, Lyons, Walker, N. Thompson, Brown, J. Thompson and Dunlop. Leeds, who triumphed 3-1, had C. W. Hurst in goal behind G. W. Hepper, A. Bagnall, J. R. Bickers, C. Gorham, E. W. Putman, J. Brunt, W. S. Hepper, Rev. C. W. Tyler, J. B. Wimbush and R. Storry-Deans.

Leeds played their home games at Kirkstall, but Albion moved to Armley in 1889. Football in these very early stages certainly struggled; most games were friendlies and consequently that meant small attendances and heavy expenses. As there was no local cup competition, Leeds entered the Scarborough and East Riding Cup, as they had done in the previous season. Leeds Albion did the same and both were drawn to play at home in the first round, Leeds being paired with Scarborough St Mary's and Albion drawn against Elmfield College of York. On 2 November 1889, both sides fulfilled their fixtures and both sides lost. But even cup ties failed to attract spectators, and the newspapers, too, showed such apathy that those two cup ties passed without any comment and even the results were not published. Trouble had been brewing at Kirkstall for quite some time and it became inevitable that Leeds were doomed and they went the way of the 'first' Leeds and went out of existence at the end of that season.

During that season a club was formed at Leeds Steelworks and their first game had been against Leeds on 26 October 1889, and although they played most of their games as a pastime, quite a number were semi-professional. Leeds Albion were left as the only flag bearer for association football in Leeds for the 1890/91 season and left Armley, moving into Cardigan Fields, which had been vacated by Leeds St John's who had transferred their headquarters to Headingley. During that season, Albion played several top sides, including Barnsley St Peter's, who would become Barnsley FC, but the fixtures were thin on the ground due to a shortage of teams.

Leeds Albion, however, were finding it an uphill battle; the local public's grip on the rugby code looked as tight as ever, and the end of the 1891/92 season saw an end to Albion's struggle. They had once again entered the FA Cup and met Rothwell in the qualifying round and after drawing away, they won the replay at Cardigan Fields 2-0. They were drawn away at Darlington in the next round, but the game, fixed for 14 November 1891, was never played. Albion, unable to make the journey, withdrew from the competition. It is unclear whether it was due to not having enough players, or a question of finance, but whatever the reason, the end was in sight. The public, wholly engrossed in the handling code, displayed such apathy to its rival that practically no club funds were derived from gate receipts so, as a consequence, Leeds Albion went out of existence. Once again Leeds was left without a soccer club of any standing.

And so, by 1891, soccer in Leeds was almost finished. If it was not dead, it was not far from it. Yet it received a chance to recover by a strange turn of events.

In the early 1890s several association clubs sprang up all across Leeds, but only playing soccer as a pastime. Whilst on their way to one of their games, the rugby public would pause to watch 'the other game' and usually assumed that 'it would never catch on'. But as the soccer game was heavily handicapped by the fact that friendly games didn't bring out the best in its players, the rugby folk never got to see soccer at its best. The soccer public became increasingly aware that competitive league and cup games must be introduced if they were to have any chance at all of breaking through the rugby stranglehold.

The forming of the West Yorkshire League in 1894 had given soccer a real boost and it is this turn of events that many regard as the real start of soccer – association football – in Leeds and surrounding areas. The clubs that formed the new league were: Leeds, Hunslet, Rothwell, Castleford, Altofts, Pontefract, Normanton, Oulton, Featherstone, Pontefract Garrison and Ferrybridge.

The new Leeds club were the third to be simply called Leeds, and their secretary was Mr Robert Mason, who had done so much pioneer work with Leeds Albion. Leeds played at a ground on Harehills Road. During the first season, 1894/95, the president of the West Yorkshire League, Mr M. Nicholson organised an exhibition match to be played between a team made up from the league teams and Preston North End, who sent a very strong team. Ellison of Leeds was picked to play in the game, which was played at the West Riding ground in Meanwood on 28 November and was attended by a healthy crowd of over 5,000, many attending their first ever soccer match.

The Football League were very impressed and had sent their president Mr J. J. Bentley to attend. The Preston side contained three internationals in the goalkeeper, Trainer, plus Holmes and Orr. There was also Becton, who was recognised as the one of the finest inside-lefts in the country, and became an England international shortly afterwards. Preston ran out worthy winners with five goals without reply, but the organisers were delighted at the success of the event and how it had ensured that the public of Leeds had finally witnessed some of the finer points of the game, in a truly professional manner. The Green Dragon was the venue for an after-match dinner which was attended by J. J. Bentley, Mr Nicholson, and Messrs Ord, Parker, Houghton and Charnley – officials of Preston North End.

In January 1895 Leeds held a meeting at the Lockharts Cocoa Rooms, Briggate, to decide on a new venue for the club. The choices on the table were to join Leeds Cricket, Football and Athletic Club, and play at Headingley; join the West Riding Athletic Club and play at Meanwood Road; or remain at Harehills Road. The meeting, presided over by Mr Soutar, decided to move to Headingley, in the hope that as a part of the Headingley set-up and the rugby team, they would be operating under a reputable body of sportsmen.

In an attempt to sustain the growing local interest in soccer, an ambitious arrangement was made to play Everton at home. A crowd of around 3,000 watched as Everton, with internationals in the side, produced an exhilarating display and beat Leeds 7-0. After the game, the players, officials and a few friends enjoyed tea together at the Wharton's Hotel, which was the headquarters of the Leeds club.

As with Leeds Albion previously, Leeds entered into the Scarborough and East Riding Cup, reaching the final on 30 March 1895 against Scarborough at the Scarborough Recreation Ground. The ground was not unfamiliar to Leeds, having beaten Oliver's Mount School there in the semi-final 8-1. But massive controversy engulfed the final.

The trouble arose over the question of playing extra time. Before the kick-off, both captains agreed that in the event of a drawn game, an extra ten minutes each way should be played. When, however, the extension became necessary owing to a 1-1 draw, Leeds declined to carry on. The referee, Mr F. Bye of Sheffield, gave them five minutes in which to make up their minds, but Leeds still refused to play. Accordingly, the referee awarded the match and the cup to Scarborough. But Leeds then lodged an appeal on the grounds that there was no rule that compelled them to play extra time. Scarborough then stated that they did not feel justified in accepting a trophy they had not won, and they agreed, subject to the acquiescence of the Association, to replay the match. Consent was given and a replay, played on 20 April, resulted in a 2-1 victory to Leeds after extra time. However, the clubs would cross swords again in a couple of years.

The week before this, Leeds had played in the semi-final of the Leeds Workpeople's Hospital Cup, which at the time was a much-prized trophy for the clubs of the West Riding, and once again the club courted controversy. Leeds and Hunslet came together for the semi-final at the West Riding Ground on 23 March, Leeds winning 2-1. But Hunslet appealed on the grounds that Leeds had played a professional in their side; the appeal was successful and in the resulting replay on 10 April, Leeds won 1-0. They then met Castleford (who had beaten Normanton in the other semi-final) in the final at Headingley on Easter Monday, 15 April, with Leeds winning 3-1. Leeds had recorded a good season by anybody's standard, winning two cups and the West Yorkshire League, finishing eight points clear of second-placed Castleford.

The following season Leeds retained the Scarborough and East Riding Cup, beating Pickering, but they were still receiving little support from the Leeds public, and more significantly, their hope that they would benefit from the surroundings of sports people at Headingley, was misplaced. They subsequently discovered that ardent rugby fans from north Leeds would not give soccer a second glance and after just one season, they left Headingley, moving to Meanwood Road. They did return to Headingley a year later, but without the support, they were clearly on borrowed time. Leeds' first game at Meanwood was a 4-2 win over Hunslet on 5 September and although Leeds fought for two cups other than the Scarborough Cup, they failed to lift the West Yorkshire Cup or the Leeds Hospital Cup, in which they lost the semi-final to Hunslet 3-2. Leeds were to spend only one year at Meanwood and after spending £367 on ground improvements, they were told by the owners that the lease would not be extended and they were given £200 back in compensation.

The meeting at the Green Dragon in 1896 had been influential in the formation of the Yorkshire League in 1897 and Hunslet were among the founder members. The others were Leeds, Bradford, Halifax, Huddersfield, Mexborough, Barnsley St Peter's and the reserve teams from Sheffield United, Sheffield Wednesday and Doncaster Rovers.

The 1897/98 season saw more controversy between Leeds and Scarborough as once again the two sides met in the final of the Scarborough and East Riding Cup at Pickering. The game was drawn and a replay was arranged for 9 April. Scarborough, however, asked for another date as on that day they had a match with Ossett, and had guaranteed that the visitors' share of the gate would not be less than £10. The new date was not convenient to Leeds so the cup committee ruled that the game should proceed as planned on 9 April. Scarborough were furious and refused to play. The outcome being that the cup was awarded to Leeds and, furthermore, Scarborough were 'suspended for the day', which meant that their game with Ossett could not take place. Scarborough were so angry that they withdrew from the Association, and for the next two years they refused to enter the cup competition. The trouble came to an end in 1900 following a split in the camp. Some of the players broke away and formed a club of their own, which they called Scarborough Utopians.

The new club entered the cup competition and won it at the first attempt.

For some time, the Leeds club had been running at a loss having received poor public support and sadly the club was forced to close at the end of the 1897/98 season. The club's last ever game was against Hunslet in the final of the Leeds Workpeople's Hospital Cup at Leeds Parish Ground at Crown Point, on 16 April. It ended in a 2-2 draw. The atmosphere had been electric, with both clubs jockeying for the honour of being the premier soccer club in Leeds, and the attendance of over 7,000 was the largest crowd that had ever assembled to see a soccer match in the city.

The replay took place two weeks later on the same ground. Previous to the replay, York Road and Bewerley Street had played the final of the Leeds Elementary Schools Cup with heavy rain falling continuously throughout. Therefore, by the time Leeds and Hunslet entered the field shortly afterwards, the pitch was an absolute quagmire. The teams battled gallantly on the sea of mud before Hunslet eventually triumphed 4-1.

Hunslet's victory, however, dealt a death blow to Leeds and after three seasons of soccer, Headingley had to face the fact that there was no future for the game of football there. Although the club had not managed to repeat their success of Harehills Road, they had been amongst the best in the West Riding. But unfortunately, north Leeds was not soccer-minded, and so the club passed out.

The 1895/96 season had been good for Hunslet. Having entered the FA Amateur Cup, they disposed of West Hartlepool, Loftus in Cleveland, Buxton and Old

Etonians, before putting out Darlington. At the end of the season, they tied with Bradford at the top of the West Yorkshire League. The cup victory over Old Etonians had undoubtedly been the highlight of the season. Nobody expected to beat such a prestigious side, especially after having been two goals down after just seven minutes of play. The heroes of the hour, Collinson, Heffron and Callaghan, grabbed three goals between them to bring about a historic victory.

But unfortunately, once again, the support from the public was lacking. At the Annual General Meeting held in the summer of 1896, the balance sheet was revealed. At the start of the season, Hunslet started with a deficit of £37. The total receipts for the season were £177, and expenditure was £176. Debts amounting to £36 remained unpaid, so the deficit for the season was £35. Hunslet did, however, remain focussed, continuing to play in the Yorkshire League.

Around 1896, several church teams were formed around Leeds. The Leeds Malvern Club was an off-shoot of the Beeston Hill Parish Church Club. Membership of a church club meant that players must attend church but a large number of boys disagreed with this condition and formed another club, which was the original Leeds Malvern, the name of the club coming from the road on which Beeston Hill Parish Church stands. For the 1897/98 season Malvern joined the West Yorkshire Junior Competition, playing their games on a ground behind the Tommy Wass pub, which still stands on the corner of Dewsbury Road and Old Road.

Leeds Malvern would go on to have considerable success after the war, becoming one of the best amateur clubs in the country. Winning several local trophies, they also competed well in the FA Amateur Cup, including a third-round trip to Portsmouth, where they lost narrowly, 2-1, to the Royal Marine Artillery. By this time, Malvern played close to the Wheatsheaf pub on Gelderd Road. Sadly, in 1925, the club suffered financially and they went out of existence.

In 1898/99, a new league was formed for Leeds church teams. The Leeds Association League consisted of: Salem Church, Stourton United, St Silas, Beeston Hill Congregational, Woodville, Burley, Holbeck Unitarians, St Jude's Mission, St Patrick's, Leeds Acme and Hunslet Parish Church. Leeds Woodville, incidentally, became the strongest club in the Leeds League, and actually shared the Elland Road ground with Holbeck during the 1902/03 season. In their first game there, they beat Hunslet Wesleyan Mission 3-0. Another prominent church club of this period was Armley Christ Church, enjoying considerable support from the people of west Leeds. They played their games at a new ground called Pasture Hills, before moving the following year to Park View.

After beating Leeds in the final of the Leeds Workpeople's Hospital Cup, Hunslet continued their success by winning the West Yorkshire Cup with a 1-0 win over Harrogate watched by a crowd of around 3,500. Hunslet continued as a major force and in 1900 they won the West Yorkshire Cup for the fourth consecutive time and the Leeds Workpeople's Hospital Cup for a fourth consecutive season, beating Altofts 5-2 at Elland Road on 7 April. Hunslet completely dominated football in the West Riding and in fact the only serious opposition they encountered came in the form of Huddersfield, who they met in the final of the West Yorkshirel Cup on 31 March 1900 at Fartown rugby ground.

The first game was drawn 1-1 and the replay at Parkside Rugby Club, two weeks later, resulted in no goals whatsoever. In a second replay at Crown Point on 28 April, Hunslet finally came through 2-1, winning this trophy also for the fourth time.

On Easter Tuesday 1900, Hunslet got the opportunity to pit their wits against Bolton Wanderers at Leeds Parish Church ground at Crown Point. Bolton were a Second Division side at this time and sent a very strong team which included J. W. Sutcliffe, the famous goalkeeper, who also was an international at both soccer and rugby. There were only two other players who held this distinction, R. H. Birkett of Clapham Rovers and C. P. Wilson of Cambridge University. Once again, the Leeds public did not give this game their full support, but the 3,000 that did attend witnessed a thrilling 1-1 draw, with both goalkeepers sharing the limelight. Lemoine in the Hunslet goal went on to become one of the best goalkeepers in amateur football, gaining international honours in 1908/09 against Ireland and Belgium and in 1909/10 against Denmark.

On a regular basis, Hunslet still competed in the FA Amateur Cup with varying degrees of success, but they never managed to emulate their famous victory of 1895/96.

In the 1901/02 season Hunslet once again met Altofts in the Leeds Workpeople's Hospital Cup final. Played at Armley Christ Church's ground, Hunslet won the game 2-1. However, Altofts protested that two of Hunslet's players, Scobie and Riley, were ineligible. The appeal was upheld and the game was replayed at Parkside Ground. The game ended 0-0 and the cup committee decided, because it was too late in the season, that the second replay should be played the following season. Unfortunately, this replay never took place, as by the time the following season arrived, Hunslet had ceased to be.

The major disadvantage with Hunslet, had always been the fact that they didn't own their own ground. Sometimes playing at the Laburnum Ground at Parkside, where they had a short lease, they had to constantly shift to different grounds, such as the Wellington Ground on Low Road, Hunslet. During the close season officials from Hunslet scoured south Leeds for a ground they could call home. It was to no avail and the frustration of not having a permanent home overshadowed their previous on-field success. They had been playing their recent home games at Nelson Ground, also on Low Road, but just as they were all set to join the reformed West Yorkshire League, they lost the lease on their ground and, unable to find an alternative home, their opening match away against Dewsbury Celtic, on 13 September 1902, was cancelled and the club sadly disbanded.

So there went out of existence a club that could be included among the pioneers of association football in Leeds. Under their former name, Leeds Steelworks, Hunslet had played the game long before there was organised soccer in the city. The club had formed in 1889 and played their first game on 26 October against the second Leeds club. When they joined the West Yorkshire League in 1894, the name had been changed to Hunslet.

Despite the fact that these pioneering teams of association football in Leeds eventually fell by the wayside, there is absolutely no doubt whatsoever that the game would not have prospered without them. And out of the ashes of Hunslet arose a new football club in Leeds.

Chapter Three

The Birth of
Leeds City AFC

A S the Victorian era came to a close and Prince
Edward came to the throne in 1901, an
exuberant opulence ensued. Fashion had
become much smarter and, in many cases, glamorous,
and Leeds was finally making positive strides towards
bringing a professional football club to the city, still
the largest city in Britain not to have a major football
club. Edward's mother, Queen Victoria, had been on
the throne since 20 June 1837 and when she died at
the age of 82 in January 1901, all football was banned
for two weeks and the FA Cup was postponed for a
month in order to express the grief felt by the FA and its
members on the death of Her Majesty. It is said that local
footballers up and down the country stood in doorways
and met over fires to discuss future prospects and the

new king. And as the Edwardian era took a hold, a new era was dawning with massive changes ahead for most walks of life, including football.

The Griffin Hotel has stood on the corner of Boar Lane and New Station Street in Leeds since 1872. Rebuilt on the site of a 17th century coaching inn of the same name, it had been reconstructed as a railway hotel owned by the joint railway companies of the North, North West and the North East to serve the new train station just around the corner.

On 30 August 1904 the Griffin Hotel was the setting for a group of football enthusiasts and businessmen to gather with the hope of forming a new football club. There hadn't been this much excitement in the city since the appearance of the world-famous Houdini at the equally famous City Varieties Theatre just a couple of hundred yards up from the Griffin two years earlier. It was a historic visit by one of the world's most renowned escape artists, who reputedly received the equivalent of £7,400 for his performance at the City Varieties, a performance, incidentally, where it is said at some stage Houdini failed to escape from a Tetley beer barrel; he blamed it on the barrel not having been washed out properly and the beer left inside had left him overpowered and confused.

Meanwhile, and just as historic for many, hundreds of football enthusiasts, including many members of the disbanded Hunslet Football Club, crammed into the Griffin meeting room on the first floor where they emptied several tankards of ale amid thick plumes of smoke from pipes and cigarettes. The large gathering sat with their backs to the windows that looked out on to Boar Lane as they were told that the time was ripe for a professional football club in Leeds and just under two hours later it was unanimously agreed that the new club would be called Leeds City Association Football Club. Norris Hepworth, the major shareholder, was elected as the club's first ever chairman and A. W. Pullin, the *Yorkshire Evening Post* journalist known as 'Old Ebor', was elected deputy chairman.

It was also agreed that the club move to Elland Road, paying £75 for the year, with an option to buy the ground for the sum of £4,500 the following year. Now the job of building the football club could begin. Leeds Woodville FC had been using Elland Road but were unable to compete financially and made way for the new club.

John Bennett was at the Griffin meeting, but his friend and colleague Joe couldn't attend; he had been ill for quite some time with tuberculosis and his condition was worsening with each passing day. Both men had to come to the conclusion, however, that although rugby would always be in their hearts, they were beginning to become more receptive to the idea of association football being played in Leeds.

John shook Joe's hand at his bedside with a promise that he would return with the latest news regarding the formation of City. Very sadly, this would be the last meeting between the two life-long friends and Joe died in his sleep that very evening. He is buried in the grounds of St Mary and the Virgin church in Hunslet.

John's companion at that meeting in the Griffin Hotel was a collie pup called Roy. It is believed that John had acquired the dog from a friend he often drank with when he frequented his local pub at Holbeck, the Bull and Butcher on Copley Court, and John decided to take Roy along to the Griffin for a walk. Roy became the first mascot of Leeds City Football Club, later becoming known as Roy the City Dog and living to a good old age of 16.

The start of Leeds City's first season of 1904/05, spent in the newly formed West Yorkshire League, was without a recognised manager, and their first ever game was away at Scratcherd Lane, Morley, with Leeds grinding out a 2-2 draw. Three members of the former Hunslet club played for Leeds at Morley: inside-right Trearney, left-back T. Tennant and outside-left J. Eggington. Initially the first of City's home games were played at the Wellington Ground in Hunslet. During this first season, on 17 September, City played away at Rockingham Colliery in the First Preliminary Round of the FA Cup. Things didn't start well for Leeds, who arrived half an hour late, and the team lined up thus: W. H. Mallinson, who had signed from The Wednesday, Skelton, H. Dixon, R. Morris, J. Morris, T. Tennant, P. Heffron, who had also arrived from the defunct Hunslet club, Page, coming in from Liverpool Reserves, Musgrave, Cummings from Nottingham Forest Reserves, and Simpson. City were soundly beaten 3-1, and had it not been for a superb performance by Mallinson in Leeds' goal, it could have been much worse. Leeds' centre-forward, Musgrave, got City's consolation goal.

City's opening league games were played mainly away, with the exception of two, and City's first ever win was away at Huddersfield Town, 3-1 on 24 September 1904. But as well as competing in the West Yorkshire League, City played a number of friendlies against Football League sides such as Sheffield United, Preston North End and Derby County. When these games clashed with West Yorkshire League games, City would field a weakened side for the league game. City saw it as a way of gaining attention from the Football League. Guest players were invited to turn out for City; Frank Spiksley, an FA Cup winner with Sheffield Wednesday, being one of the more notable ones. Tom Morren of Sheffield United also played a major role. Spiksley had arrived at Hillsborough from Gainsborough Trinity where he had scored a remarkable 131 goals in 126 games. He later turned out for Watford before taking up several coaching positions, including a spell with the Swedish national team. Morren, an amateur, was a competent centre-half and made 160 appearances for Sheffield United.

One such friendly came on 15 October 1904, when City finally moved into Elland Road, taking on Hull City in their first game in their new home, but Leeds lost the game 2-0 in front of 3,000. Interestingly, on the very same day, City were due to play Dewsbury and Saville, but because of an outbreak of smallpox in Dewsbury, City refused to play them at Leeds. In November, City recorded a fine 7-2 victory over Burton, with inside forward Gordon Howard smashing in four goals. Then on 10 December, whilst one Leeds City team lost 5-1 to

Bradford City, the other Leeds City team were beaten in a friendly at Grimsby 8-0. Christmas Eve was no kinder, as one City team lost away to Hull City in a friendly 3-2, and the other lost 4-0 away to Morley in the West Yorkshire League. New Year's Eve saw a disastrous 4-2 defeat at Altofts and on 11 March, City lost their league game at Elland Ramdonians 4-0.

On Monday, 13 February 1905, an advert in the *Leeds Mercury* appeared under the heading: 'Leeds City Association Football Club – Wanted, energetic and efficient Manager. Application, stating age, qualifications, salary expected and accompanied by copies of two testimonials should be forwarded and marked to "Manager" to J. Wilson, Solicitor to the Club, Trinity Chambers, 71, Boar-lane, Leeds.' Having been made aware of this advert by a close friend, Gilbert Gillies duly applied along with over 100 other hopeful applicants. When this list was reduced to just five, the City sub-committee decided that Gillies, a tough Scotsman with a no-nonsense attitude, who had taken Chesterfield FC into the Football League, was their man. He was given a three-year contract worth £156 a year. Gillies had a great ability to organise and was not afraid to change a side if things weren't working according to plan.

He took up his new post on 16 March 1905 and two days later he oversaw his first game, a West Yorkshire League game at Beeston Hill Parish Church, less than a mile from Elland Road. Leeds turned in a comprehensive display, winning 5-1, but later that day they lost to Heckmondwike at Elland Road, 3-1. The club didn't fare well at all during the month of March, losing all three friendlies at home to Hull City 3-1, Lincoln City 3-1 and Derby County 2-0.

And City ended their first ever season with a West Yorkshire League win at Armley Christ Church. Dixon, Mackay, F. Howard and a penalty from Clay ensured a 4-1 win; gaining a bit of revenge for a 2-1 defeat in February by Armley in the Leeds Hospital Cup. Earlier on the same day as the 4-1 win at Armley, a goal from Simpson saw Leeds beat Huddersfield Town 1-0 at Elland Road. Leeds also finished off their programme of friendlies on 29 April with a win; a thrilling 4-3 victory over Barnsley.

Because of the number of friendlies, City fell behind with their league programme and in an attempt to catch up they would often play two league games on the same day. Owing to the friendlies, City's league performance inevitably suffered and they finished 11th, winning only seven of their 24 games, missing three games, and gaining 21 points.

Despite the disappointment, however, City officials had confidence in the club's ability and with the increasing attendances of over 2,000, a meeting was held on Monday, 10 April 1905, at the Griffin Hotel, less than a year since Leeds City had been formed there, and it was here that they decided to float Leeds City as a limited company. There were 15 directors with a capital of 10,000 £1 shares, the main shareholders being Norris Hepworth, a well-respected wholesale clothier and the club's first ever chairman; Ralph Younger, who was the landlord of the Old Peacock pub on Elland Road; and A. W. Pullin, who was a sports journalist with the *Yorkshire Evening Post* under the pen-name 'Old Ebor'. Frank Jarvis was elected honorary secretary while John Furness became honorary treasurer. Other directors included: Oliver Tordoff, who, with the vice-chairman, formed the management committee of the club; R. S. Kirk; Joseph Henry, prominent businessman of the well-known Holbeck Engineering firm, and who would later become Lord Mayor of Leeds; D. Whittaker; W. Robinson; F. G. Dimery; W. Preston; W. G. Child; John Oliver, formerly of Tottenham Hotspur; and R. M. Dow, former treasurer at Woolwich Arsenal.

With the crowds ever increasing and City now on a creditable financial footing, Leeds City applied and were accepted into the Football League on 29 May 1905. City, with 25 votes, were voted into the league alongside Chelsea, Hull City, Clapton Orient and Stockport County. Leeds City were at long last a league club, but the challenge was just beginning. In 1906, this is how 'Old Ebor' of the *Yorkshire Evening Post* described City's eventual induction into the Football League:

'In the season 1904/5, Leeds City ran experimental teams with the view of feeling the public pulse. The results were so satisfactory that not the least doubt was left as to the future success of the club in the event of admission to the Second League being secured. Preparatory to this a limited company was formed with a nominal capital of £10,000 though there was no intention of asking anything like that sum of money from the public. As

THE BIRTH OF LEEDS CITY AFC

a matter of fact, up to the time of writing, only about £2,000 in shares has been issued, but it is known that this amount can be increased at any time the club may require it. By accepting the chairmanship of the board of directors and contracting to purchase the ground for the club if required, Mr Norris R. Hepworth, one of the oldest and best-known sportsmen in Leeds enabled the whole scheme to take practical shape. But for his timely assistance it is doubtful if the club would have been in a position to apply for admission to the Second League in May last (1905). As it was, Mr Hepworth, on behalf of the club, was able to put so good a case before the league delegates that Leeds City secured election to the second division by a clear majority of votes over all applicants. The directors were fortunate in securing the services as secretary-manager of Mr Gilbert Gillies, who was formerly the manager of the Chesterfield club. Mr Gillies brought to bear upon the fortunes of the club all the loyal services of which he is capable and his football experience like that of his able directors has proved invaluable in enabling Leeds City to thus early reach a high standard among Second League clubs. Since last August (1905), the ground has been almost entirely reconstructed and a fine covered stand capable of accommodating 5,000 spectators erected. How the public of the city and district appreciate the improvements as well as the football fare provided is forcibly shown in the fact that the gate receipts at the end of December, that is after only four months operations as a Second League Club, amounted to over £3,500. On the occasion of the match with Bristol City, £430, while when Bradford City appeared at Elland Road on the last Saturday in December, over 20,000 persons were present and the receipts amounted to £487. In building up their league team, the management committee of the club were careful to select players who would in every sense of the word, do credit to professional football. As captain an excellent appointment was made in Richard Ray, full-back who has had experience with Manchester City, Stockport and Chesterfield. The responsibility of steering a new team seemed to sit heavily on him, to the detriment of his play, but latterly he has thrown off this and proved himself alike a skilful leader and a full-back of courage and class. His fellow full-back, John Macdonald, formerly of Ayr and Blackburn Rovers, was the first player to engaged for the league eleven, and he too has given full satisfaction. Latterly, D. B. Murray, who came from a Scottish junior club (find out who) to England and has played with Everton and Liverpool, was secured from the Liverpool club, and as a partner to either Ray or Macdonald he has played exceptionally well. Prior to joining Leeds City, Harry Bromage did most of his goalkeeping for Derby County and Burton. He has done splendid work with his new club, indeed, there are few, if any, better custodians in the League than the Leeds City representative.

'His understudy is Dixon, formerly of Aston Villa. The halves are Charles Morgan (Liverpool and Tottenham), Harry Stringfellow (Everton and Portsmouth), and James Henderson (Bradford City), with Fred Walker, late captain of Barrow, reserve. The forward rank is

composed of Fred Parnell (Derby County), Robert
Watson (Woolwich Arsenal), Fred Hargraves (Burton
United and Aston Villa), Dickie Morris (Liverpool and
Welsh International), Harry Singleton (QPR), Thomas
Drain (Bradford) and David Wilson (Hull City), the last
named having seen added to the club's strength late in
December. The team are under the care of George Swift,
who has proved himself to be in every way well qualified
for the office of trainer.

'Just by way of injecting further team information,
the average weight of the team is 11st 4lb. Meanwhile the
shareholders consortium had successfully floated Leeds
City Football Club as a limited company and the League
were suitably impressed.'

The Annual General Meeting of the English Football
League was held on the Monday morning of 29 May
1905, at the Tavistock Hotel in central London, Mr
J. J. Bentley presiding. There were eight applicants for
the three places in the Second Division – Burslem Port
Vale, Burton United, Doncaster Rovers, Chelsea, Clapton
Orient, Hull City, Leeds City and Stockport County.
Leeds, Burslem and Chelsea were elected.

The proposition before the meeting that the league
should be extended to 40 clubs, 20 for the First and 20
for the Second Division, was carried with a three fourths
majority. Four more clubs were thus eligible for election
and the successful applicants were Burton United, Hull
City, Clapton Orient and Stockport County. Doncaster
Rovers were not elected. Applications for entry into the
First Division were made by Notts County, Bury, Bristol

City and West Bromwich Albion. Bury and Notts County were elected. The proposal by Bradford City that in the event of an extension to 40 clubs being granted, the three highest in Division Two shall take the place of the three lowest in Division One and the three lowest in Division One shall go into the Second Division – essentially a promotion/relegation system – was defeated.

It had been 25 years since the first rumblings of 'socker' in Leeds, with varying degrees of success, had begun. Now at last, there was to be a local professional association football club in national league football – in Leeds. But the *Leeds Mercury* was still troubled by the slow progress being made in the area:

'In one striking particular, Leeds holds a unique position in the world of football. It is the only city in Great Britain with a population of over a quarter of a million which does not possess a first-class association team, and indeed, prior to the dribbling code being taken up with such tact and foresight at Bradford, the latter place, together with Leeds and Hull, were for many years the only cities in the British Isles with over 150,000 inhabitants where association football of the highest class was not firmly established. The fact that the three great Yorkshire cities mentioned have lagged behind other large cities in the kingdom has to be attributed, of course, to their connection with the Northern Union code. But the Bradford City Association Club, with average attendances approaching 10,000 and gate receipts of nearly £200 per match, have shown what may be attained in one season with a surrounding population of 280,000.

What, therefore, may be expected of a club conducted with the same amount of tact and foresight in the area of Leeds, with its 440,000 inhabitants?

'Leeds can and ought to have a status in this pastime. It is the fifth largest city in the country, but as a football centre, compared with Birmingham, Sheffield, London and other cities, it is a nonentity. The association game is proving itself week by week to be a sport, which in its appeal to human interest has no rival except cricket, and it is a pastime in which the amateur can and does play side by side with the professional without losing caste. The strides it is making suggest that sooner or later Socker will capture the whole of Yorkshire, and Leeds, as the geographical centre of the county, will have to play its part in the movement.'

By the time the 1905/06 season arrived, Leeds had retained only two players from the previous season, the *Leeds Mercury* noted: 'The managers of the Leeds club have been very energetic, and their work in securing an eleven which will meet all demands is in a very forward state. In this connection Mr Gillies and Mr Jarvis, the manager and secretary respectively, are to be congratulated on the result of their labours. Though the team that has already been got together is fairly satisfactory, it is probable, now that a place in the competition has been obtained, that it will be strengthened. One can well understand that the managers wish to walk before they can run, as it were, and the developments which are made will in a large degree depend upon a measure of support they receive.'

But Leeds City were well under way with their preparations for their first ever Football League season, 1905/06, and as mentioned by 'Old Ebor', quite a few potential stars had arrived at Elland Road. Dickie Morris, an inside-forward, joined from Liverpool and would become Leeds' first international. Leeds born centre-half John Morris was drafted in by Gillies. Goalkeeper Harry Bromage was an amazing signing, who very quickly became a fans' favourite with over 150 consistent performances between the sticks. Dick Ray had been persuaded to join Leeds. Ray, aged 29, had played under Gillies at Chesterfield as his captain, and would assume the same role at Elland Road, as well as fulfilling the roles of committee man and secretary of the club; he would eventually manage the newly formed Leeds United. Several other key players had come to Leeds City and Gillies, along with his trainer George Swift, had completely reassembled a playing squad in a very short time, and they would have to gel together pretty quickly if they were to be a success in league football.

It was now time to put things to the test for the season's opener.

Leeds' club colours were taken from the City of Leeds traditional colours of blue and gold, and they lined up for their first ever league game at Bradford City on 2 September 1905 wearing dark blue shirts with gold trim, white shorts and blue socks. They adopted the name of the Peacocks, in reference to the pub close to the Elland Road ground, although they would also be referred to as the Citizens for a number of years.

The historic Leeds team that day was, in a 2-3-5 formation: Harry Bromage (brought from Burton United), Jock McDonald (Blackburn Rovers), Dick Ray (Chesterfield) captain, Charlie Morgan (Tottenham Hotspur), Harry Stringfellow (Swindon Town), James Henderson (Bradford City), Fred Parnell (Derby County), Bob Watson (Woolwich Arsenal), Fred Hargraves (Burton United), Dickie Morris (Liverpool), Harry Singleton (Queens Park Rangers).

Archive material on www.mightyleeds.co.uk says: 'Ray had played under manager Gilbert Gillies at Chesterfield and he was Gillies' choice as the first ever captain of Leeds City. He was to play a major part in the formation of Leeds United in the future and would manage them on two occasions before moving to Bradford City in 1935.'

The *Leeds Mercury* wrote: 'Several of the men who have been engaged to fill the positions in the front rank are excellent exponents. Inside-left, Morris, formerly of Liverpool, is a Welsh international. Watson comes from Woolwich Arsenal with the reputation of being one of the fastest forwards in the south, playing either at inside-right or centre. Derby County have lost a good man in Parnell, who lost his place alongside Bloomer through the brilliant form shown by the young amateur, Hounsfield. Another man to be engaged from Burton United is a very capable player, Fred Hargraves, the centre-forward, is a good shot, and feeds the wings well, and should prove a very useful man for the very important position he is to fill. Amongst the other players who have entered into agreement are Drain of Bradford City and Howard, a youth who operated with such marked success with City last season.'

Leeds City felt ready and willing for the challenge ahead and it wasn't just on-field matters that were being improved at the club as Dave Tomlinson explains in *Leeds United. A History*: 'Ground improvements were in hand at Elland Road, increasing the overall capacity to 22,000. The new West Stand, 75 yards long and 35 feet deep, cost £1,050 and could house 5,000 spectators, while the playing area was increased to 115 yards by 72 yards. Season tickets were priced at 10s and a guinea, and shareholders will be entitled to the higher priced tickets for the sum of 15s. The lesser priced tickets will admit holders to the ground only, while the others will pass to the ground and stand. In all offering attendance at all 36 Second Division matches, and all reserve team games.'

The archives of www.mightyleeds.co.uk say: 'It has been decided to erect a new covered stand. On it 4,000 or 5,000 persons will be, if necessary, accommodated. In the centre a commodious press box will be constructed. In addition, the old stand at the north side of the ground has been pulled down, and it is proposed to erect a wind shelter right along the west end. The present stand is in a dilapidated condition, and its demolition is already in progress. On the terraces new 'treads' will be constructed, and each terrace will be faced with creosoted battens. There will, when the work is finished, be about 30 terraces extending right round the ground, and accommodation for spectators will be largely increased. It is also proposed to place posts inside the railings for a short length down each side, but the rails at each end will be brought back a few feet, and this will lengthen the playing area considerably, with 10 to 11 feet between the touchlines and the rails. The ground will then be quite large enough for the playing of any matches governed by the rules of the Football Association.'

The *Yorkshire Evening Post* set the scene for the Bradford City opener: 'These two pioneering clubs of West Yorkshire never imagined that after over a decade of uphill work, two professional clubs representative of the cities of Leeds and Bradford would be meeting in first class football on grounds formerly occupied by rugby clubs of note. Only a few of the founders of the game are at present entirely identified with the sport, but the fruit of their labour is apparent.

'In the years to come today's game at Valley Parade, Mannigham, will be looked upon as historic, but the enthusiastic Bradfordian responsible for the wording of the bill announcing the match, was evidently anxious to make history prematurely, "A historic encounter" being writ large across its face. Keen rivalry in encounters such as what will take place this afternoon is bound to exist but there is no reason why, anytime, it should get beyond the bounds of sportsmanship, and what the future has in store for the cities cannot be foretold. But it is to be hoped that in the near future the clubs may be found contending in the final of the English Cup, thus emulating the performances of Aston Villa and West Bromwich Albion etc. The Bradford team was considered the best that has ever represented the club, and the ultra-enthusiastic supporter of the Valley Parade team had no doubt as to the result of the game before the commencement of hostilities. On the other hand, a quiet confidence pervaded the ranks of the officials of Leeds City, although they recognised the magnitude of the task set their men at such an early stage of the campaign. As regards to today's programme, the absence of any reliable data upon which to form an opinion as to the relative strengths of the competing teams renders it obviously too speculative a matter to venture prophesies. All that need be done, therefore, is to take a general survey of the afternoon's programme. Long before the time appointed for the kick off the popular parts of the ground were filled and the turf looked in good condition capable of withstanding a season's wear and tear. When the teams appeared, quite 15,000 spectators, including many thousands from Leeds, were present, and both teams received a characteristic Yorkshire reception.

'The game throughout was interesting although both sides missed chances, but both sides showed good promise of things to come in the future. Leeds' display was especially creditable, considering the players were practically strangers to each other. City hit the crossbar. Bromage was excellent – at one point he was charged at by Smith, but Bromage stood firm. The second half continued much as the first, but Smith scored after 75 minutes after a scramble in Leeds' goalmouth. Leeds pressed hard for an equaliser but the home side held out. There is no denying, however, that Leeds had made an impression on League football and looked more than capable of holding their own.'

The *Yorkshire Post* said: 'Leeds City have no reason to feel disappointed with the first performance of their men. Their greatest fault was in front of goal. Had they taken advantage of the chances that came their way, a very different story would have to be told. Bromage more than once proved himself a capable defender of goal.'

The *Leeds Mercury* said under the headline of 'Leeds Men's surprising performance':

'Leeds City have undergone their baptism with flying colours. It is true they did not succeed in gaining their first competitive victory over Bradford City but their performance was so entirely satisfactory, considering the whole of the circumstances, that their "trial trip" must be regarded as such – a meritorious performance. To be candid, even those in the best position to appraise the capabilities of the 11 men who have been drawn from the corners of the country to constitute the side, did not go so far as to anticipate victory – the advantages of Bradford City were so very pronounced, but if the game at Valley Parade may be taken as any guide as to the merits of the Leeds players, it is evident that they are going to take up a very strong position amongst the Second League clubs. When it is remembered that Bradford City have already experienced two years of strenuous league football and that they were able to place in the field the strongest team they have yet possessed, with the additional advantage of playing on their own ground, the difficulties which confronted the Leeds men will be fully appreciated.

As was only natural, they suffered much through their comparatively brief acquaintance of each other's methods. It was not that their combination was particularly at fault, but that they delayed the moment of thrusting home an attack in front of goal.'

Leeds City's first ever Football League game at Elland Road was against West Bromwich Albion. City lost 2-0 but, although it was two defeats in two games, there was hope. The *Yorkshire Post* acknowledged: 'Although Leeds City lost the match, they certainly carried off the honours in the game, except in the manner of the league points. For quite three fourths of the time they monopolised the attack, and ought to have scored, but the forwards showed a lamentable want of dash when at close quarters.'

Leeds City's first ever league point was won with a 2-2 draw at home to Lincoln City on 11 September 1905. A poor crowd of just over 3,000 attended. Reserve centre-forward Tommy Drain had been brought in from Bradford City two years previously, but despite making an appearance against West Bromwich Albion, had yet to break into the first team properly. Centre-forward Fred Hargraves had been injured during the opening game, his debut, at Bradford giving Drain an opportunity and he didn't seem to hinder his chances any when he got both City goals. But the *Leeds Mercury* wasn't too impressed: 'Whilst Leeds are undoubtedly a strong team, one weakness has characterised their work, namely, their inability to find the net. In midfield their combination has been excellent, but when the time arrived for the pace to be forced, and extra pressure put on the opposition, they failed to carry out their mission. Though an improvement in this respect was noticeable yesterday, the inside men still dallied with the ball too long, and, but for this defect, there can be little doubt that they would have won by a considerable margin. They had innumerable opportunities in the first half to open their account, and instead of being on level terms they ought certainly to have possessed a lead of three clear goals – a lead which would have removed all danger.'

The *Yorkshire Evening Post* remarked: 'City looked nervous throughout the whole side. However, there were signs that, with a little more confidence, they could make good strides.'

Leeds City only had to wait five more days to record their first ever win. Fred Hargraves returned for the visit to Leicester Fosse and Gilbert Gillies could play the side that opened the season. Outside-left Harry Singleton had made his debut on that opening day after joining City from Queens Park Rangers. Against Leicester he opened his scoring account, although – and Singleton would be the first to admit it – the goal was very fortunate. The *Yorkshire Evening Post* on 18 September 1905 described the whole affair, in great detail:

'A genial summer sun smiled upon the meeting of Leeds City and Leicester Fosse on the "Fossils" ground this afternoon. Football under such conditions, naturally enough, proved very attractive to spectators, though the players, no doubt, found such warm conditions very tiring. Leicester Fosse do not, as a rule, operate before very big crowds of spectators, and it speaks well for the attractiveness of the fixture that the attendance at the beginning of this afternoon's match numbered about 6,000 spectators. This was considered very good, especially in view of the fact that Leicester Rugby Club, in their spacious ground across the way, had an attractive match with West Hartlepool. There was a big crowd there, according to all accounts, and it is very significant that, despite the competition of the "socker" code, the old amateur rugby club in Leicester continues to hold its head proudly aloft. Leeds entered upon this afternoon's match with a team that inspired a good deal of confidence.

'It was the same as that which played a drawn game with Lincoln on Monday, with the exception that Hargraves displaced Drain at centre-forward. The ex-Burton man had, it appeared, been suffering from an injury to his hip, but his play in the reserves match on Tuesday showed that he had recovered sufficiently to be given another trial with first team.

'Leeds City started the game, and right at the outset some good combination was shown by Stringfellow and Hargraves, but the latter lost the ball just when he had got into a good position for attacking. The "Fossils" forwards rushed play to the Leeds goal, where Ray cleared a long kick. Play had fluctuated considerably from the start, and it wasn't long before Leeds were back again at their opponent's goal, a strong bit of play by Hargraves putting them in that aggressive position. The Leeds centre passed to Watson, who in turn transferred to Singleton at outside-left. The latter sent in a long swinging shot at goal. Strong play by the Leicester forwards caused the game to take a fast and furious turn and Leeds were compelled to act on the defensive. They met the attack of the "Fossils" very well. Leicester, continuing to attack, forced Leeds to concede a corner, and in the ensuing effort in front of the net, Morgan headed, only to send the ball over the bar for a corner kick. Bromage and his co-defenders continued to have a lively five minutes. Durrant, the home right-wing forward, put in some useful sprints and on one occasion he was loudly applauded on taking the ball half the length of the field, eluding Singleton. He had a long shot at goal, but it was an "approach" and nothing happened to trouble the goalkeeper. Rallying, the Leeds forwards set up an attack on the opposing goal. They were worried a good deal by the Leicester backs, but in spite of Hargraves, Morris and Co managed to give the home supporters some anxious moments.

'Singleton on one occasion headed from a cluster in front of goal, but Smith had no difficulty in clearing. Parnell had a long-range attempt at goal, but he also failed to get past the custodian. The best bit of work was seen when Morris, the nippy inside-left, beat Cox and Moody and went away with a fast dribble. The opposing backs, fast as they were, could not touch him, and when Morris became associated with the movement by Hargraves a score looked almost inevitable. The latter, with a brilliant dribble, reached the goalmouth, and it was only an equally brilliant save by Smith, who ran forward and took the ball from Hargraves' toes that prevented a score. Leeds continued to attack, though it was notable that a combination of the visiting forwards was a good deal upset by the Leicester backs, who were successful in breaking up many of the visitors' movements. None the less, the "Citizens" were always pressing, and showed if anything, better passing than that of the home lot, one fine effort was initiated by Morgan, who fed Hargraves in a good position. The centre man transferred to Parnell, who showed his cleverness by circumventing Hodgkinson and Gould before centring to Watson. There was nothing in the latter's shot at goal, and Smith easily cleared. Leeds had another spell of defensive play, but towards the end of the first half the visiting forwards again splendidly rallied, and they had the satisfaction of taking the lead, though the goal which they scored was a very lucky affair. Play was being contested near the "Fossils" goal, and then Morris getting possession kicked as if intending a pass to Hargraves. The home custodian came out of goal to intercept the ball, but he miscalculated its direction, and before he could do anything to prevent it, the ball had screwed round the upright and into the net. Half-time was called soon after with the score: Leeds City 1 Leicester Fosse 0.

'Leicester resumed the game amid considerable excitement and at once forced a corner pressuring all the Leeds team. Durrant, the home outside-right, who had all along been playing a magnificent game, put in a very good centre, which Tinuld vainly endeavoured to head the ball into the net. Then Watson was conspicuous with a tricky run, and concluding it with a shot at goal which gave Smith some difficulty in clearing. Leeds were very closely pressed after this and Bromage twice had to negotiate the most stinging of shots from the Leicester centre. Still the "Fossils" continued to swarm round the Leeds defence and three corners were forced in rapid succession but failed to find anything tangible. Parnell transferred play to the City with a quick run, but in attempting to convert his centre, Watson shot high over the net. The spectators saw a good deal of mid-field play after this and in general tactics the "Citizens" showed the trickier and faster. Morris in particular exciting at inside-left. As play progressed it was seen that Henderson watched Durrant very closely, and seldom did the latter get the ball. Parnell made another run up the right wing, but his centre was not quite enough to be put to any advantage. Result: Leeds City 1 Leicester Fosse 0.'

A crowd of 13,654 arrived at Elland Road the following week for the encounter with Hull City and undoubtedly Leeds' most impressive performance so far. The *Yorkshire Post* remarked on the continuing growth of 'socker' in the area, writing: 'The struggle to establish the dribbling code on a sound and attractive footing in Leeds has been an uphill one, but there were many smiling faces around the pioneers at the old Holbeck rugby enclosure. The game itself was full of incident and excitement. Leeds were clever and spirited throughout the game.'

City had found themselves languishing in the lower department of the division in recent weeks, but this win over Hull saw them beginning to climb up the table to eighth. Morris had got two of the goals while Hargraves added a third. The Hull goal was scored by David 'Soldier' Wilson, who Leeds City were known to have a very keen interest in signing. The *Leeds Mercury* reporting on the game, said: 'Hull, indeed, received a rude shock. In all departments except at the back they were completely outplayed, the weakness of the forwards and half-backs being very conspicuous, compared with the corresponding lines of the opposition. With regard to the Leeds forwards, they were thoroughly alive, taking possession of the ball very smartly, and the readiness with which they embraced their opportunities was very gratifying. In contrast to some of their previous exhibitions, one felt they had capabilities of scoring, they had shot with more vigour, and altogether played with much more devil.'

The following week, City travelled to Lincoln and once again Hargraves got on the scoresheet. He added to an earlier penalty kick, scored by Parnell. He was fouled as he rounded the Lincoln goalkeeper and dusted himself down to convert the spot kick himself.

Lincoln registered a late goal, but City went back to Leeds with a 2-1 victory.

Leeds were on FA Cup duty on 7 October and quite an amazing 11-0 victory over close neighbours Morley put Leeds into their own record books. For the record, the goals came from Hargraves 4, Morris 4, Watson 2 and Parnell recorded a single.

Back in the league, a 2-0 defeat at Port Vale temporarily halted City's surge up the table but the week after, in front of around 12,500 at Elland Road, Leeds beat Barnsley 3-2. Hargraves once again scored, so too did Dickie Morris and the winner came from an unlikely source: a contribution from a Barnsley defender, who inadvertently steered the ball into his own goal with ten minutes remaining. A second successive home game saw another victory: this time Grimsby were on the wrong end of a 3-0 scoreline. Hargraves grabbed another two goals and a fine solo effort by Stringfellow, beating three Grimsby defenders, saw Leeds closer to the summit. The following week Fred Parnell got City's goal in a 1-1 draw at Burton United.

Threaded in between these last few league games was an epic, three-game FA Cup saga with Mexborough. Two 1-1 draws and finally a third game resulting in a 3-1 win, saw City through to the next round. Hargraves, Morris, Parnell and Watson all found the net.

The next round of the FA Cup brought them back in the ring with Hull City. Leeds took a full-strength team across to the East Riding. Lining up for Hull was David 'Soldier' Wilson, who Leeds were apparently still keeping tabs on. Hargraves put Leeds ahead early in the game, but Hull fought back and, although he didn't score himself, Soldier Wilson orchestrated the Hull attack and they soon equalised to earn a replay at Elland Road.

But first up was a league encounter against Chelsea, and once again a crowd of over 20,000 packed into Elland Road, but despite a fairly lively performance from both sides, the game ended 0-0.

Chapter Four

Soldier Wilson

HULL City arrived at Elland Road for the FA Cup replay on 29 November 1905. Once again Leeds took the lead; a clever move down the right saw Fred Parnell cut inside and unleash an unstoppable shot into the top corner of Hull's net. But still Hull City would not lie down, and again came at Leeds, led by Wilson. Hull progressed into the next round of the cup with a 2-1 win, but in less than three weeks David 'Soldier' Wilson would be a Leeds City player.

A 4-1 defeat at Gainsborough in front of a paltry 2,000 crowd was best forgotten, Watson getting Leeds' goal. Leeds responded, in a fashion, the week after, by grinding out a 1-1 draw with Bristol City in front of an eager 15,000 crowd. Glossop were the next visitors on 23 December 1905, David 'Soldier' Wilson making his long-awaited debut for Leeds City, having cost the club £120.

Leeds City could have cashed in with Wilson, receiving several offers in excess of £500, but Gilbert Gillies and his directors, seeing his great potential, refused all offers.

The *Athletic News*, 25 December 1905 said: 'There was a Christmas air about the play in the match between Leeds City and Glossop North End at Elland Road. Leeds won the match all right, but their display was erratic, and gave one the impression that they rather underrated the calibre of their opponents. Owing to some disciplinary trouble, the Glossop committee had felt compelled to suspend three of its players, and they had to rely upon a reorganised team. But it was to the credit of the substitutes that they played well, and together made a good fight. Wilson, the recruit from Hull City, made a first appearance for Leeds, but he had to play out of his accustomed position owing to the absence of Morris, the inside-left, who had been out of town during the week owing to a family bereavement. It had been decided to play Watson at right-half, but the absence of Morris compelled Leeds to keep Watson in his usual place and play Wilson at inside-left. Another trial was given to youngster, outside-right, Gordon Howard. There was a satisfactory gate of around 8,000 present and the takings amounted to £167. Leeds played in somewhat lackadaisical fashion in the first half. Twenty minutes passed before the first and only score of the match. Glossop had been penalised for off-side, and Watson, securing the ball from Murray's kick, passed it in front of the goal to Hargraves who gave the goalkeeper, Davies, no chance. Play was inconclusive and scratchy in character up to the interval. Little need be said of the second half. Glossop held their own fairly well, but they never looked like a winning team and with least bit of luck, Wilson would have scored twice for Leeds, who won by a goal to none. Their combination was not quite as good as usual, but individually Howard, Singleton and Hargraves all played well in the front rank. Henderson was the best of the half-backs and Ray did much useful work at full-back, while what little goalkeeper Bromage had to do, it was excellently accomplished. Davies was well tested in the Glossop goal, but he came through the ordeal splendidly. Considering that the constitution of Glossop's team had been so upset they came out of the match with considerable credit.'

The *Racing Post* said, 'Glossop were weakly represented at Leeds on Saturday, but did well in only losing by one goal. The home team had their latest capture playing – Wilson of Hull City – and earlier attacked the visitors' lines. Hargraves getting through to score. Glossop played up well, but did not test Bromage to any extent, while at the other end Watson missed an open goal. On resuming in the second half, Wilson had hard lines with a shot that hit the post, and Cameron, for Glossop, was but a few inches with a capital effort.'

Two defeats followed, at Stockport 2-1 and a disappointing 2-0 reverse at home to Bradford City. Leeds ended 1905 with defeat but began 1906 with a resounding New Year's Day victory at Blackpool by three goals to none. Injuries sustained in the Bradford City defeat forced several changes in the Peacocks' line-up. Bob Watson was replaced by David Wilson at centre-forward, who recorded his first goal for his new club. Hargraves had to be replaced by John Morris in defence, while McDonald went in at right-back in place of Ray. Dickie Morris and Harry Singleton added to David Wilson's goal.

Wilson scored again for City five days later in a 2-1 defeat at West Bromwich Albion. It was City's first visit to the Hawthorns and incessant rain for 24 hours had left the pitch in a dreadful state. Heavy rain continued to fall during the game and the players of both sides had trouble even staying on their feet, let alone playing football. Albion took the lead on half an hour but Dickie Morris levelled before half-time. In the second period, Leeds, led from the front superbly by David Wilson, attacked the West Bromwich goal relentlessly, but Albion fans breathed a huge sigh of relief when they went back in front and held on for a victory which kept their promotion hopes on track.

City bounced back with a fine 3-0 win nine days later at Bank Street Ground over a team formerly called Newton Heath, who later moved to Old Trafford under another name. The *Yorkshire Evening Post* commented: 'This was the second attempt at fulfilling this fixture; the first attempt being thwarted by fog. Although City defended very well for most of the game, their attack line was excellent, gaining a brilliant, if unexpected, victory.

Bob Watson, returning from injury, David Wilson and Harry singleton all scoring without reply.'

City followed that up with a 4-1 win at Elland Road to complete a league double over Leicester Fosse. Leeds then went on to extend their run to six matches unbeaten, before going down 3-0 at Barnsley on 24 February. Leeds came back with a 3-0 win over Chesterfield on 27 February with Wilson grabbing a brace and Parnell getting the third from the penalty spot.

Wilson was on fire and excelled even further four days later when City trounced Clapton Orient 6-1. The wintry conditions were horrendous and inevitably the playing surface suffered, but Leeds coped much better than their London rivals.

The *Leeds Mercury* said: 'The ground was again in a wretched condition, and this was undoubtedly a severe handicap; but no matter what the state of the turf, or mud, had been, on the day's form it is difficult to conceive that the home men could possibly have lost even a single point. Though City are naturally a fair-weather team – the short passing they indulge in requires a good surface to be successful – they have, by force of circumstances, become very skilful in the mud. Wilson again showed what a dangerous man he is when within range of the opponents' net. His assumed indifference seemed to have a disconcerting effect on the opposition; and then, suddenly, without jostling for a position, he drives the ball clean and hard. The number of times he deceives the opposition this way is really remarkable. It was not only as a marksman that the City centre was seen to advantage. He led the front rank splendidly. He has a fine knack of drawing his opponents, and then passing out to the wings, and in this way the opposition were frequently beaten.'

Leeds moved up to sixth. Hargraves and Parnell got one apiece, and Wilson hit four; he had a fifth disallowed and rattled the bar with a thunderbolt. He had now scored 13 goals from 15 games and he registered two more the following week in a 4-3 defeat at Burnley. But after a very bruising encounter at Grimsby seven days later he was ruled out for eight games.

The *Leeds Mercury* commented: 'Grimsby Town were determined to avenge the defeat sustained at Leeds City last November. They had to recourse to methods which, to say the least, were of a decidedly vigorous character, so much so indeed that half a dozen members of the Leeds City eleven who appeared at Blundell Park were more or less seriously injured. In the very first minute the Elland Road men discovered that the fates were unkind to them, for Wilson, their crack centre-forward, was brought down heavily by McConnell as he was making tracks for the Grimsby goal. The Leeds man rolled on the ground in agony, and after being attended to on the touchline for a few minutes, he had to be chaired off suffering from a torn ligament in the leg.'

Dickie Morris, Walker, Hargraves, Morgan and Ray also suffered injuries at the hands of the very aggressive Grimsby eleven, but still managed to come away with a 1-1 draw thanks to a goal by former Glasgow Rangers full-back David Murray, signed from Liverpool in

December for £150. But the ordeal at Grimsby left Leeds ill equipped to sustain their late promotion push.

The *Leeds Mercury* said: 'It was a strange sight to see the team of cripples arrive back in Leeds on Saturday night. They were met at the train station by a sympathetic crowd of supporters, many of who had witnessed the bloodbath first hand, and when the men got out of the train – Morris and Wilson had practically to be lifted out – they had become quite stiff owing to the long ride. Both Wilson and Morris were placed on a luggage waggon, and were trundled to the cab rank, where they were placed in a cab and thence conveyed home.'

Leslie Gibson from Whitkirk, Leeds was on that train back from Grimsby. He had been supporting Leeds City from the start of the club and his great grandson, Michael, who still lives in the family home close to the Woodman pub, has grown up with Leslie's exploits: 'My great grandad was a big Leeds City fan and I still have newspaper cuttings from those City days. He came back on a train from Grimsby when the City team had been kicked black and blue by a vicious Grimsby Town team. My great grandad, who I think was about 20 years old, was with a few other City supporters and when they got back to Leeds, they helped the players off the train. He said a man in a black coat and a hat gave him some coppers, but he didn't know who he was.'

The following week, City's team was depleted, Dave Tomlinson's *Leeds United. A History* says: 'Centre-half John George was signed from Tottenham Hotspur and inside-left Jack Lavery from Denaby United to reinforce the side, but there were only nine players fit enough to travel to Chelsea at the end of March. Bob Watson's car broke down in Burnley, and the City party sent a telegram to Elland Road summoning reserves. Unfortunately, the second eleven had already set off for a fixture in the north east and only Harry Stringfellow was available to join the squad, Desperate times call for desperate measures, and the only option was to draft in trainer George Swift, still registered as a player, to fill in on the left wing; it was three years since he had played any first team football and he did little to suggest there would be a comeback.

'With Singleton playing for the first time at centre-forward, matters became desperate when Ray sprained his knee after 20 minutes and had to be withdrawn, with Swift reverting to his accustomed full-back role. City kept Chelsea at bay until Ray suffered his injury, but the Londoners then ran riot, winning 4-0. And all hopes of promotion vanished.'

However, Leeds' season did finish on somewhat of a high. David Wilson returned to the side after his injury and scored the winner in a 2-1 win over Glossop; Parnell scored City's first. Rain and wind swept through the ground from end to end and Bromage had to be on top form in goal to preserve City's win. As the last ball of the 1905/06 season was kicked and a promotion challenge ended in tatters, the club could reflect, however, on one or two shining lights. David Wilson had been outstanding and he had led the attack admirably. Harry Bromage had proven that he was still one of the finest goalkeepers around with faultless displays week after week. Fred

Parnell on the right wing and Bob Watson inside of him, had created many a threat for the opposition defences and John George, the new recruit from Tottenham Hotspur, had been solid at centre-half in the closing weeks of the season. And Jack Lavery, operating alongside Wilson, had provided an alternative threat up front.

The 1905/06 season had seen Leeds Rugby League Club's average gate slump from 9,022 to 5,632 as the Leeds public flocked to see Leeds City, whose average home attendance exceeded 9,000. They had got 22,000 for the visit of Bradford City and 20,000 against Chelsea, generating a season profit of £122. But Wilson's winner against Glossop in the final game would be his last ever goal as tragedy struck the club in season 1906/07.

Extensive drainage work was laid under the Elland Road turf to deal with the problems that had been experienced with the mud and the waterlogged pitch all through the previous season. The City players needed dry and firm conditions, wherever possible, to make the best of their passing game and had been forced many a time to ply their trade in conditions resembling a swamp.

And it appeared to reap dividends as Leeds City began the new season with yet another opener against Bradford City at Elland Road. Although Bradford had won the first fixture of last season, and done the double over Leeds, they had finished below them in the league, but Bradford had strengthened their side considerably. One of their biggest signings, in every sense of the word, was goalkeeper William 'Fatty' Foulke, one of the most famous players of his day. He had won FA Cup medals with Sheffield United in 1899 and 1902, and had joined Bradford from Chelsea. Foulke was the tallest player to have played for England so far, standing at a whopping 6ft 6in, and weighing in at an incredible 26 stones. During his day, a goalkeeper didn't have to stay on his line for a penalty kick, and he would race out and put the fear of God into the taker with his massive physique, earning himself a reputation as an expert penalty stopper. Leeds meanwhile had a few new faces of their own. Two Scots had joined the ranks: Andy Clark from Plymouth Argyle and Jimmy Kennedy coming in from Brighton after formerly being at Celtic. Henderson, Morgan and Jefferson were all unavailable so Leeds lined up thus: Harry Bromage, David Murray, Andy Clark, Jack Morris, John George, Jimmy Kennedy, Fred Parnell, Bob Watson, David Wilson, Jack Lavery and Harry Singleton.

Bradford, however, looked the fitter of the two sides from the outset and the day was a scorcher. The *Leeds Mercury* said: 'It was not a fit day for football, with the thermometer 92 in the shade, and no player should have been asked to play in such a temperature. As a test of endurance, the encounter must rank really high. The perspiration simply rolled off down these well-trained athletes, while the straw hatted, flannel-suited spectators almost groaned in misery under the hot sun. Wallace Smith, a constant threat down the Bantams' right wing, opened the scoring for Bradford in the first quarter of an hour after a beautiful move. The goal only confirmed the home team's dominance, they held a vice like grip on the game and knew it, as did Leeds City. Harry

Bromage denied Bradford time and time again, stopping everything that was thrown at him. Bradford slackened off as full time approached, convinced they had done enough to secure the points, but their complacency was their undoing. With just five minutes to go, George, Morris and Wilson combined well to contrive an opening for Lavery, who equalised with a low shot that goalkeeper Foulke never got near to stopping.'

'Flaneur' of the *Leeds Mercury* observed, 'I heard two remarkable diverse opinions on the result as the huge crowd of over 20,000 emptied itself from the remodelled and now excellently appointed Elland Road ground. One enthusiast asserted that on the run of play the draw was a fitting result. But he was, no doubt, a red-hot Leeds partisan, and I imagine he had his tongue in his cheek. The other pointed out that Bradford City ought to have won by six goals. I am convinced he was a Bradfordian. The impartial man would strike a balance between these two rather wild party opinions. He would tell you, if he understood the game, that Bradford should have won on the play by two or three goals, and he would be right. With the exception of Bromage in goal, and Murray at right back, the Leeds men were behind their opponents in all departments. Andrew Clark seemed unable to cover the deficiencies of his half-backs as well as Murray, who was always good. Both backs, were however, too hard worked. The half-back line was the worst department. Morris and George changed places in the second half, but neither this couple nor Kennedy showed such form as characterised the opposition. There was an entire lack of combination between them and their forwards, of whom Wilson was the chief disappointment. Parnell and Watson did fairly well, but Singleton lacked dash and enterprise, and Lavery was no match for the tall Bradford captain Robinson. It will not surprise me to find a few changes, especially in the half-back line, in the Leeds City team for the next match.'

The performance was a bitter disappointment for everyone connected with the club, and Gilbert Gillies and his staff reacted anxiously with a number of changes for the following Saturday's visit to West Bromwich Albion. Right-half Morris was injured in the first half against Bradford City, and was replaced by John George, whose position at centre-half was in turn taken by Fred Walker. Lavery and Singleton were summarily dropped, and Stan Cubberley and Willie Murray were installed as the new left flank pairing. But the changes made no difference, in fact it was worse, and City were soundly and comprehensively beaten 5-0 at The Hawthorns. The greatest weakness was again in the half-back line-up, as the fast West Bromwich forwards ran the show. Albion were two up after a quarter of an hour and four up at half-time. They made it five in the closing minutes through Pheasant. Gillies needed a rethink in his strategy.

But this severe run of poor form prompted a bout of soul searching and derision from supposedly loyal supporters. The *Leeds Mercury* ran a series of angry denunciations in the opening weeks of the season, so pointed that they provoked retaliatory correspondence and remarks from Gilbert Gillies.

'True Peacock' wrote: 'It is quite obvious that some changes must be made. The passing of the forwards has been very weak, in fact, shocking to a team like Leeds City. There has been an entire lack of fire and dash in their play, and even when they get to the goalmouth they seem as if they don't know where the net is.'

'Pitchfork' said, 'Now that we have seen the practice matches and the opening match against Bradford City, and have been mercifully spared the blight at West Bromwich, and carefully marked and digested the efforts of the club's players, such as they are, it raises the above question in our minds. We take, for instance, Bradford City, who have as manager a tried and approved player, who has this season put in the field a team that is a credit to him and his club – a team that can practically do as it likes with the Leeds team and who have sold a player for £1,000. We dare not allude to the eight goals' smashing the Reserves gave the Leeds Second Team at Bradford. The majority of his players are smart young athletic fellows gathered from various smaller clubs, and so on.

'We take Hull City with its manager, Ambrose Langley, the old Sheffield Wednesday player, a man who can spot young talent when he sees it, and is capable of selling at a fancy price to the Leeds City club David Wilson, a man who has had his day, and Ambrose Langley knew it, if the Leeds City management did not. Hull City club's players are like Bradford City, for the greater part, rising young players secured from smaller clubs, at small prices.

'Candidly, leaving out these two capable and class men, Bromage and David Murray, the composition of the

Leeds City team can best be described as old crocks and League Club cast offs. Why not have secured as manager a man like Fred Spiksley, the old Sheffield Wednesday internationalist. Leeds City had him here in Leeds two seasons ago. What Fred Spiksley does not understand about football and young talent, surely, should not be worth knowing.

'In conclusion, I am not picking out imaginary faults, and what is more I have no axe to grind. What I like is to see a good football match, but I am honestly convinced that under present conditions I shall be disappointed at Elland Road.'

Gilbert Gillies was incensed over the attacks and responded furiously on 12 September with a letter of his own to the *Leeds Mercury*: 'I am rather surprised that the columns of your valuable paper should be open to letters such as the one written under the nom de plume of "Pitchfork". When consideration is given to the short period which Leeds City has been in existence, I think the success it has attained is sufficient reply to the scurrilous attack. Comparisons are drawn between myself and other managers, but Pitchfork seems to have forgotten that two of those named had teams and grounds when they were engaged. The City ground was covered with Pitchforks and weeds when the club was formed into a company, and the team was not even a skeleton of a West Yorkshire as reference to your files will show. In reply to "Pitchfork's" attack on the players and myself, if he will only have the courage to sign his own name and address, he will receive a reply to that address which should remove his accumulation of bile and spleen since he found himself on the wrong end of the fork.

'As far as the players and myself know, and we have the best grounds for saying so, we have only one enemy in Leeds. That enemy adopted several nom de plumes last season, and spent his Sundays in writing letters to the Press when we had struck a bad patch, and "Pitchfork's" letter was in the same old strain. Perhaps he is a disappointed man, as his letters are all very much alike. Inquiries were made at one place last season, but no one knew the name of the writer, who had given a certain address. Having had some experience of Press work, and having on many occasions read the postscripts, "Whatever you do, you must not publish my name" etc, I may say that I have the greatest contempt for the man, if such he can be called, who attempts to injure others through the medium of the Press under a nom de plume.

'Considering the difficulties under which the season has been started, I think the team ought to be at least given a chance until they are fully represented, as it is early yet to pass, or to be a party to passing, any such sweeping condemnations as used by "Pitchfork". For "True Peacock's" information I beg to state that at the time of writing, Henderson, Morgan, Walker, Morris, Wilson and Bromage are on the injured list, and to add to these misfortunes, Jefferson's services have not been available up to the present.'

Gillies, however, was not without his proponents and 'True Supporter' offered an ironic comment regarding the views of 'Pitchfork': 'On reading "Pitchfork's" letter, it makes one wonder how it was that the City officials missed such a chance. His letter showed him to be a rare man with rare qualities. Look at his reasonableness. Look at the unbounded confidence which he has arrived at. I should like to suggest to the City officials that they make every endeavour to get to know who he is and engage him. He would use such good judgement that they would not need any committee meetings. He would always do the right thing. He would never make a mistake, and before long we should have a team that would be able to hold its own with any First Division club.'

The friction between the club and its supporters continued for a while, but the depth of the feeling of disappointment within the fans and the Leeds public as a whole grew stronger with each passing game.

The next two home games saw City draw 1-1, with Lincoln City and Leicester Fosse respectively, Bob Jefferson scoring on his debut against Leicester. Next Nottingham Forest welcomed City to the City Ground on 27 September and beat their visitors with ease, 3-0. City picked up a point at Sincil Bank a week later with Jefferson scoring again in a 1-1 draw with Lincoln City. And Leeds finally won a game at the seventh attempt, with a fine 2-0 win at Burton United; Lavery and Watson on the mark for City. Leeds continued their winning ways with a satisfying 4-3 victory at Grimsby Town, exacting a slice of revenge for the vicious beating that City were given during the corresponding fixture the previous season. Watson's two goals, a penalty from Murray and a winner from Lavery gained the honours for City.

Leeds' three match winning streak came to an abrupt halt, in ways unimaginable, when Burnley were the visitors to Elland Road on 27 October 1906. David 'Soldier' Wilson had become a firm favourite with City supporters, but so far that season he had been frustrated in front of goal, and was yet to score, so was determined to put that right.

Wilson had been born in 1883 and had served in the Boer War, hence his nickname of Soldier. Stationed in Gibraltar with Cameron Highlanders – The Queens Own Highlanders – he played a lot of association football before being transferred to the 1st Battalion Black Watch, which was an infantry battalion of the Royal Regiment of Scotland, and subsequently to South Africa and the Boer War. Dundee Football Club bought Wilson out of the army and he later moved on to Heart of Midlothian FC before moving south to Hull City and subsequently to Elland Road.

Against Burnley in what would be a game in which no quarter was given by either side, he was being watched by his wife, who attended every game her husband played. At around 1.15pm Mr and Mrs Wilson had left their home at 8 Catherine Grove and walked the half mile or so down Beeston Hill to Elland Road, together with their ten-month-old son in the arms of Soldier. During the match Wilson felt unwell and after about an hour of play he left the pitch complaining of chest pain and looking very pale. He had been winded in a first-half clash with two Burnley defenders and collapsed in the second half after the heading the ball goalward.

Underneath the main stand Dr Taylor of New Wortley tended to Soldier Wilson and amid concerns for his health he strongly advised that Wilson not return to the fray and a cab was called to take him back to his home. But Wilson, upon learning that Harry Singleton and John Lavery were playing with injuries sustained in the continuing on-field battle, ignored the doctor's advice and returned to the field of play to the sound of loud cheering by the 14,000 crowd. Wilson had even told the doctor that he was not in good form and should have scored two goals in the first half and he aimed to put things right. However, after only a few minutes on the field he returned to the dressing room in great discomfort and he fell to the floor. He had been accompanied from the pitch by Police Constable John Byrom, who with the aid of club trainer George Swift, lifted him up and helped him undress before submerging him into a hot bath. But almost immediately Wilson collapsed. He was lifted out of the bath and placed on top of a table but despite the frantic attention of Dr Taylor he died within a few seconds. Officer Byrom said, 'I assisted him to the dressing room, and helped him to undress. He said he would have a hot bath, but all at once after getting into the bath he laid down and started kicking his legs violently. I took hold of him and held his head out of the water, but he seemed to lose consciousness, and never spoke again.' His demise coincided with the return of the players after the final whistle. One can only imagine the distress that shrouded the dressing room in those initial few moments. David Wilson was just 23.

On 29 October *Leeds and Yorkshire Mercury* wrote: 'Both sides were evenly matched in the first half, with both City's John Lavery and Harry Singleton causing problems for the Burnley defence. It was on one of these raids that Lavery was tripped from behind by a Burnley defender and fell heavily on his head; it was several minutes before he was brought round. The incident called for the referee to take strict action with the offending Burnley player, but he received nothing more than a telling off. Even the Burnley officials had said, "that the culprit should have been sent off".

'Lavery never fully recovered, and although he remained on the pitch, City were in effect playing with ten men. It was soon after this, that David Wilson was seen to leave the field of play, and the hope of a Leeds victory had all but vanished when Ingelton, City's outside-left, was brought down and he too was disabled, leaving City now with practically nine men, and with virtually no attack line. It was seen that Wilson returned to the pitch, but he appeared to be still unwell, and although he was loudly cheered, he left the field again after a few minutes. It was too much for Leeds to hold out, and Burnley scored the only goal of the game, scoring a short range free-kick, and City suffered an unlucky defeat. When the players returned to the dressing room they learned that David Wilson was dead. The news was a terrible shock and cast a deep gloom over all, none being more sincere in their sorrow than the Burnley players and officials.'

The Scottish newspaper the *Courier* reported: 'David Wilson the Leeds centre-forward and old Dundee and Raith Rovers player, was seen to leave the field suddenly suffering from severe pain. No one saw that he had been injured and apparently, he had strained himself in heading the ball. He suffered considerably when attended to in the directors' room, but gradually appeared to recover and against the advice of the officials and doctor present he decided to regain his place in the team. In just two or three minutes, Wilson had to leave the field again, and this time he was escorted to the dressing room, where he died practically before any real assistance could be rendered to him. When his colleagues reached their quarters after play had ceased, they were distraught to discover their teammate had died. Apparently, his death was due to heart weakness but this is a matter which will be cleared up at the coroner's inquest. His tragic death has cast a gloom over City's supporters' in Leeds.'

On the final whistle Mrs Wilson had left the ground with her young child and made her way back up Beeston Hill – unaware of the tragedy. Mr Gillies raced up Beeston Hill and intercepted Mrs Wilson at the top to give her the distressing news before escorting her and her son to their home. David 'Soldier' Wilson's body was returned home a few hours later by the police ambulance and the rest of the Wilson family, who all lived in Leith, Scotland, were informed by telegraph.

On the day of the funeral a short service was held in the family's home on Catherine Grove attended by Leeds City and some Burnley players, before a contingent of Leeds City staff, including Gilbert Gillies and George

Swift and other mourners from Leeds, boarded an early train from North Eastern station to Leith for the service.

A few weeks later at the coroner's inquest held at the Imperial Hotel in Beeston, a police report concluded that the deceased had not complained of being hit or injured, although it was stated that on his return to the field he had headed the ball towards goal and this was deemed a fatal action. The verdict was a suspected heart strain, adding that he had 'died from heart failure, from over exertion in a football match'.

Mrs Wilson was said to be overwhelmed at the national outpouring of grief by other clubs, fans and football's governing bodies and a benefit match at Elland Road against Hull City on 19 November saw all proceeds given to Wilson's widow. Over 3,000 spectators gathered to watch the 3-3 draw.

The Leeds City club were in a complete state of shock over the loss of Soldier Wilson, and not surprisingly it transferred to the pitch. City suffered four consecutive defeats immediately following his sad demise; the club slumped to the edge of the re-election zone.

The week after the Burnley game, they were still visibly affected as they travelled to Chesterfield and lost 1-0. The *Yorkshire Post* said: 'There was only a moderate attendance on the Chesterfield ground for the match with Leeds City, the weather conditions being about as bad as they could be. For the first 20 minutes the game was very interesting, both sides making some well-directed attacks. Once Watson and Page got right through the Chesterfield defence, and in the final effort

Page, who had received from Watson, had an open goal, and shot wide. The same player, a minute later shot over the bar. For the rest of the first half, Chesterfield had advantage, Marples kicked and tackled faultlessly, and Baker at centre-half was continuously feeding the forwards. However, at half-time the Leeds defence had not been broken down, and neither side had scored. At the beginning of the second half, Lavery, who had been taking the outside-left position, with Cubberley inside him, changed places and the Leeds attack seemed to improve greatly in quality and sting. Leeds were proving to be dangerous, and kept the Chesterfield goalkeeper, Cope, very busy. Chesterfield, however had a bit more in the tank than their opponents, and after some good work down the left, they scored what proved to be the winner, from Willows, with two minutes of the game remaining. In the final seconds of the game, Leeds goalkeeper Bromage and Chesterfield's Munday were going for the same ball, as the referee blew for full time. Hearing the whistle, Bromage kicked the ball to Munday, but he continued to go around the keeper and tapped the ball into Leeds' net. The referee wagged his finger at Munday and disallowed the goal. 1-0 to Chesterfield.'

Leeds were still clearly feeling the effect of the demise of Wilson, and their form continued to suffer. Down at Barnsley the following week City endured their third successive defeat. On a heavy pitch City began using the wings well, but Barnsley always had the edge, although it was still goalless at half-time. All was to change in the second half, however, and a penalty for handball by

Murray was put away by Barnsley, quickly followed by a second goal minutes later. Murray had the chance to pull one back for City, when referee Mr Horrocks awarded Leeds a penalty, also for handball, but Murray missed his kick. A miserable afternoon for City was complete when Barnsley added a third near the end of the match. A collection by the crowd had raised £10 for the fund set up for the widow and family of David Wilson.

Chelsea were the visitors to Elland Road on 17 November and they were flying high.

National newspaper *Athletic News* wrote: 'Saturday was a big day at Leeds, for not only were Chelsea on view, but the new covered stand received an official opening by the Lord Mayor of Leeds, Joseph Hepworth, the father of the Leeds City chairman. The occasion, however, was propitious on two accounts; rain fell heavily almost throughout the entire match and worse still the home team lost 1-0. The rain notwithstanding there was an attendance of just short of 9,000 and under the circumstances, they saw a fair game. The pitch, despite the inclement weather, was in capital order, and the City played some clever tricks and some pretty movements, but Chelsea were undoubtedly the better of the two teams. I unhesitatingly place Chelsea's prospects before those of West Bromwich Albion. Leeds' goalkeeper made one or two uncharacteristic errors – he made two bad clearances; the first, he mishandled the slippery ball giving it to Kirwan instead of lifting it down the field. Kirwan centred the ball correctly and Bromage was again at fault, and Hilsdon took full advantage of the opportunity offered to him. Hilsdon made two other good attempts to find the net and once Bromage only cleared by coming out of his goal, well it was hardly a clearance, as the ball rebounded from him, but had he not run out the probability is that another goal would have been scored. Because of the muddy conditions, City appeared in red and white striped jersey's after the interval, but a change of colours did not bring about a change of luck, for the score remained unaltered. By adopting rush methods City certainly created more damage than in the first half, but the forwards were not good enough to out-manoeuvre the Chelsea defence, though in the last five minutes Laverley might easily have equalised, but Whiting threw up his hands to a rising ball, and Henderson cleared. Bromage overall kept a good goal and it was a pity that he should have practically given the victory to his opponents. His backs had not full command of the slippery ball. Had I been captain I should have played Hargraves at centre-forward in the second half (he had been dropped in at centre-half) for Page was anything but an ideal leader, and Johnson who made his debut on the outside-left, was no better than Page. Most dangerous player for City was Parnell, who was well served by Watson.'

The following week, Leeds completed a miserable sequence of five defeats in a row with a 3-2 loss at Wolverhampton Wanderers. It had marked the debut of Leeds new boy Billy McLeod, signed the day after the Chelsea defeat. Leeds handed over £350 cash, plus receipts from one game, to Lincoln City for the marksman with a growing reputation for scoring many goals. On his debut, however, he seemed slightly subdued and although he struggled to get into the game, he did show glimpses of his undoubtable ability. 'Nimrod' of the *Leeds Mercury* reported: 'To be candid, he was not altogether brilliant, but at the same time he must be said to have been decidedly useful. I believe that he is a dangerous man, and the manner in which he worked his way past the backs on the occasion when Lavery missed the goal was brilliant and striking. He is a hard worker, speedy, and passes nicely.' The *Yorkshire Post* added, 'McLeod played with a dash and confidence that seemed to inspire the whole team.'

Wolves took the lead after David Murray brought down Roberts in the box and Wooldridge converted the resultant penalty. However, Leeds City led at half-time with a goal by Jack Lavery and then David Murray made amends by scoring a penalty of his own after he himself was tripped in the Wolves penalty area. But within minutes of the restart, Wolves equalised and eventually sealed a win with a third goal 20 minutes later.

Billy McLeod would go on to become one of the most lethal and prolific goalscorers in the game and would build a glittering reputation at Elland Road, as well as becoming a firm favourite with the Elland Road faithful. But by the end of November, City sat precariously two points above a re-election place; only Barnsley, Glossop North End, Blackpool and Burton United lay beneath them and only two points separated the five teams.

Billy McLeod's scoring boots were introduced to 10,786 spectators the week after, when he grabbed one of City's goals in a 3-2 home win over Clapton Orient with the other two coming from Watson and Parnell. But two successive defeats followed to knock Leeds off track again, losing at Blackpool and at Gainsborough, both by 1-0.

McLeod netted again for City a week later at Elland Road against Stockport County. John Lavery registered a hat-trick and Bob Watson added a brace in an emphatic 6-1 victory. Lavery was on target a week later, three days before Christmas 1906, but Leeds City were beaten at Hull City 2-1. On 29 December goals by McLeod and Tom Wilson earned City a 2-2 draw away at Bradford City. Wilson, an outside-left of small stature, had signed from Bolton Wanderers and only made his Leeds debut in the 6-1 win over Stockport. He was an expert at providing accurate centres and was prominent in a relentless Leeds attack that for most of the match pinned down a Stockport side who were one of the division's promotion hopefuls. The evening before the game, thieves had broken into the Elland Road ground and stolen whisky and cigars from the Leeds directors' room – Stockport County could be forgiven for feeling that they were being blamed.

New Year's Day heralded a 2-0 defeat at Glossop and on 5 January 1907 they lined up at home against title favourites West Bromwich Albion. Referee Whittaker of London got this competition under way and Albion, who were expected to win easily, took immediate control, leading 2-0 at half-time. Leeds, however, fought valiantly in the second half with McLeod and Bob Jefferson levelling the score. When McLeod scored the winner for City in the dying seconds, the 14,400 Elland Road crowd erupted. The victory was even more remarkable given the fact that two of City's top forwards didn't play after being suspended by a club disciplinary sanction.

A 4-1 FA Cup defeat at First Division Bristol City followed a week later, but City's priority was focussed on moving away from the lower regions of the Second Division. Leeds stuttered along and, after a heavy 4-1 defeat at home to Nottingham Forest, they massively improved, losing only once in their next five matches. And after McLeod scored eight goals in 12 games, City managed to climb the table and eventually finished tenth; but on the whole the supporters weren't satisfied. After a sterling debut season, this season had failed to live up to expectations; only the shining light of newcomer Billy McLeod had offered a glimmer of hope for the Elland Road faithful. There were other players worthy of note, such as Bromage, in goal, Hargraves and Parnell, but there was clearly still much work to be done by the club.

The directors had poured money into the club from the start, but with the 1907/08 season upon them, they were demanding that Gillies delivered this time around in their bid for promotion. The directors did continue to support the manager, however, and City installed two more new recruits during the close season in 1907: Fred Croot and Tommy Hynds. Croot, a speedy left-winger, came from Sheffield United and as well as being drafted in as a provider for Billy McLeod, Croot could also cut in and shoot himself, becoming one of the country's top-scoring wide men. Hynds was a reliable centre-half but had been involved in an illegal payments scandal whilst at Woolwich Arsenal, and was suspended from football between June and December 1906.

City's season started brightly at home to Glossop North End, but a fairly low crowd of barely over 4,000 showed the Leeds fans were still to be convinced of the club's ambitions. Leeds had still to win their opening game of a new season, but they managed to achieve that with a somewhat scrappy 2-1 win over Glossop after the visitors had gone ahead. New recruit Fred Croot excited the crowd and afterwards, the *Leeds Mercury* noted: 'In Croot, the club have obtained a really good man for the outside-left position. He pleased the crowd with his splendid turn of speed and the accuracy of his centres. He knows how to play to his inside man.' No other City player, however, really merited a mention. After a 2-2 draw at Leicester Fosse the following week, where a rare mistake from Bromage allowed Leicester to escape with a point, City returned to Elland Road with a convincing 5-2 win over Clapton Orient in front of a slightly improved crowd of 6,147. Croot scored his debut goal, with Bob Watson and John Lavery getting two apiece. The win was historic for City as they climbed to the summit of the Second Division, a point ahead of Hull City, for the first time in their brief existence. They held that position a week later in a pulsating contest at Blackpool, Lavery, Watson and Parnell getting the honours for City in a 3-2 victory. Parnell scored again the following week, but City went down 2-1 at Stoke.

McLeod was on target as Leeds returned to winning ways seven days later with a narrow 1-0 victory over West Bromwich Albion, whose sudden loss of form at the end of the previous season had seen them finish fourth and miss out on promotion, 13 points behind champions Nottingham Forest. An encouraging crowd of over 24,000 crammed into Elland Road for the win over Albion. City's form then became somewhat erratic; a five-goal thrashing at Valley Parade was followed by a thrilling 3-2 home victory coming from behind with two goals from Billy McLeod and another from Bob Watson, all wonderfully supplied by Fred Croot. But then a catastrophic 6-1 thumping at Derby County brought City back down to earth. A week later a 2-1 home victory over Lincoln City offered some respite to City, but there had been a major change in defence. Harry Bromage bore the brunt of the blame for the slump and was subsequently dropped and replaced in goal by Tom Naisby who signed from Sunderland. Reporting on the shock absence of Bromage for the home game against Lincoln City a week later, 'Nimrod' of the *Leeds Mercury* said: 'The critics certainly looked forward to the appearance of Naisby in goal with some curiosity, and there were those who would have said bitter things at the expense of the management for having the temerity to displace Bromage had Naisby failed to make a satisfactory debut. Bromage's ability is well known; he still has the skill, and one must sympathise with him on having so many goals scored against him of late. But he is not primarily to blame, for it must be borne in mind that the defence has not been above reproach, particularly in the wing half-back positions, though the backs have not been too steady. Naisby was fortunate in this respect on Saturday; he was well supported by those in front of him.'

By 27 October, the win, despite the previous loss of form, had seen City in second place, three points behind Hull City and only a point in front of all five teams behind them: Bradford City, Oldham Athletic, West Bromwich Albion, Leicester Fosse and Fulham.

But inconsistency was hampering any chances of promotion and Leeds failed to win any of their next five games. On 14 December City beat Grimsby Town 4-1 at home thanks to a goal by McLeod, two from Croot and one which David Murray converted from the penalty spot.

However, Leeds failed to win a game over the Christmas period; after a 2-0 defeat at Wolves on 21 December, 'Wanderer' wrote in the *Leeds Mercury*, 'Leeds City seem determined not to secure another victory away from home. The only time they have notched two points on "foreign soil" this season was 14 September at Blackpool, and since then they have not brought a single point back to Leeds. And it is all the more aggravating when one takes into account the form shown by the team on the Elland Road ground.'

City did manage to win away, a New Year's Day victory, 2-0 at Glossop. Considering that the home team were unbeaten on their ground all season, City's away victory was even more baffling. Two in-form players, McLeod and Croot, shared the goals. But then, once again, City failed to win in their next five league games, drawing 1-1 at home on 4 January to a strong Leicester Fosse side in front of 10,000. City then lost in the FA Cup away against a strong Oldham Athletic side, 2-1. It was Oldham's first season in league football and at the time of the cup tie they were sitting joint top alongside Derby County, Bradford City and Hull City. City then lost all their next four games. One of those defeats came on 1 February against Bradford City by a goal to nil, but the crowd of over 35,000 was a record attendance, bringing gate receipts of £682. The last of those four defeats came against Hull City at Anlaby Road and a 4-1 defeat left City hanging by a thread above the re-election zone. The downward spiral was halted briefly with a 5-1 thumping of Derby County who were top of the league and hadn't been beaten since just before Christmas. 'Flaneur' in the *Leeds Mercury* was suitably impressed: 'It can no longer be said that the City forwards cannot shoot, or that McLeod lacks the essentials of a centre. Whether recent criticisms have had their effect on the ex-Lincoln City man I do not know, but I do know that on this occasion he played like an artiste. Instead of hanging about on the off chance of getting an opportunity to shoot, he really led his forwards, and the manner in which he kept the whole line moving was very effective. One hardly knew which to admire more, his increase of energy or his deft touches to the wings. It was McLeod transformed, and the centre forward will no longer be fearful of losing his place to Jefferson or anyone else for that matter. Whether McLeod's remarkable improvement made all the difference it would be difficult to say, but there is no doubt the forwards played their game of the season.'

Less than a week after this game, however, news broke that secretary-manager Gilbert Gillies had quit the club. It had been rumoured that all was not well, and for a number of weeks, City had been operating a kind of team selection committee system, which wasn't exactly to the liking of Gillies. He was said not to be happy at all with the current situation at Elland Road.

The *Leeds Mercury* said: 'Our announcement yesterday that Mr G. Gillies had resigned his position as secretary and manager of the Leeds City club will no doubt have caused considerable surprise to the general public, though some of us have been quite prepared for the step for a few weeks past. It was hinted to us some little time ago by a gentleman who has considerable knowledge of the inner workings of the club that Mr Gillies would probably retire from his position at the end of the season, and the name of a probable successor was mentioned. Mr Gillies has not been altogether comfortable this season, and he has at length felt he has no alternative but to resign his position.'

Gillies had been Leeds' first manager and he was responsible for successfully guiding Leeds City Football Club into the Football League. The first season had gone beyond all expectations and the club had finished sixth in the table; quite a phenomenal achievement. But City didn't continue the momentum, for whatever reason, and a gradual fall in performance, with inconsistency undoubtedly the cause, hampered City for the next few seasons. It was widely accepted that Gillies hadn't been in sole charge of matters at the club. Many reports suggested that team selection was taken away from Gillies; the team selection committee had seemingly left Gillies in charge more in stadium matters rather than team matters. Supporters had of course vented their anger at Gillies' supposed inability to motivate the team, and of course, as reported, Gillies responded angrily to fans' criticism. Whatever had gone on, the fact was that Gillies' three-year contract was coming to an end and it became increasingly obvious that it would not be renewed. There was no doubt that Gilbert Gillies had failed to stamp his authority on the team, but he had brought in top name players, Harry Bromage in goal, prolific goalscorer Billy McLeod (to replace Soldier Wilson) and Fred Croot, a very fast and strong outside-left, and numerous others.

Gillies always maintained that he was made a scapegoat and he wasn't short of support from some fans. Mr W. Simpson told the *Yorkshire Post* readers: 'One man is not to blame for the sorry state of affairs at Elland Road. Mr Gillies came with a strong reputation and gave the club's directors the benefit of his vast knowledge of the association sport. Had he been given more help in his task then I firmly believe he would have got City promoted.'

A 'Thorough Peacock' wrote to the *Leeds Mercury*: 'I have been a member of Leeds City FC ever since it started, and now I am about disgusted with the club I support. I noticed that the gate on Saturday (against Bradford City) realised £682. I think the committee would be economising if they put another £318 to that and bought three good inside men. I say let them speculate and get a good team like Bradford City, and what they spend will soon come back again. If they only look round, they will see the gates gradually falling off week after week. I should like to ask if there is any way or means of doing like our friends at Headingley – that is getting an open meeting of all members. I am an old association player, and I should like to see a team in Leeds that would hold a good position in the First Division. I know very well "Rome wasn't built in a day", but the directors have had time to put a better team in the field. Good men are to be got if they will only speculate.'

Gillies' decision to resign, although understandable given the circumstances, must have hurt the man inside. And although he went on to lead Bradford Park Avenue for around three seasons with some degree of success, his pride had clearly been dented and he dropped out of football altogether and returned to the Derbyshire area, where he ran a hotel in Matlock.

A couple of days after Mr Gillies' departure, City travelled, as yet without a new manager, to Lincoln City. Sincil Bank was rocked by one of the most violent storms ever experienced on a football field, a storm which wrecked the members' stand and caused serious injury to several of its occupants. A gale was sweeping the ground when the players began the match, and there were streaks of lightning and thunder rumbling in the distance. In a few minutes the storm burst all over the ground with great fury. Large hailstones pelted down; the lightning, thunder and cyclonic wind made the game one not to be forgotten. The roof was ripped off the stand, injuring five spectators, with play impossible for some 40 minutes. The match should have been abandoned, but referee Mr Horrocks decided to play on in atrocious conditions, with players struggling to keep their feet in the teeth of a horrific gale, and the half-time break dispensed with to get things over more quickly.

The City players were dispirited and thoroughly dejected. They seemed unable to raise any kind of resistance and slumped to a miserable 5-0 defeat. It was symbolic of their entire season.

Meanwhile the directors at Elland Road had appointed a sub-committee to select a replacement for Mr Gillies. One had been already been earmarked, but a few details needed to be ironed out before they finally got their man. On 25 March 1908, he was announced.

Frank Scott-Walford was typical of the Edwardian era. Dressed impeccably with a prominent, somewhat flamboyant waxed moustache (he had arrived at Elland Road as a potential candidate for the vacant managers job, coincidentally, on the same day as Gilbert Gillies' contract expired – 16 March 1908). He was suitably attired in a smart bowler, black calf-length coat worn open to reveal a grey waistcoat, and plus fours. High length socks and shiny two-tone shoes completed his appearance. It is said that almost 30 journalists and photographers were there for his arrival.

Scott-Walford's credentials were not overly appealing; he had flaws. His playing career, as a goalkeeper, had been average at best. Switching periodically from amateur status to professional. He had kept goal for Tottenham Hotspur and Lincoln City, amongst others. Born in Birmingham in 1865, he had played for both Birmingham clubs, Aston Villa and Small Heath (later known as Birmingham City), before venturing into managership with Brighton and Hove Albion in 1905. He had been among 88 applicants for the job at Leeds City, but because he still had two years of his contract left at Brighton, they refused to release him. However, once Brighton pinpointed a replacement, they let him go to Leeds City.

In April 1906 Scott-Walford had been suspended for four months by the FA. The reason being was that after finding himself with just three players, he made a desperate attempt to recruit more players at Brighton but he was found guilty of making approaches to other clubs' players before their contracts had expired. The Leeds directors, however, were undeterred by this.

First on the agenda of Scott-Walford was to ensure that Leeds retained their Second Division status. He observed Leeds City struggle through another five consecutive games without a win. On 28 March a 2-1 defeat at home to Oldham Athletic left Leeds 15th in the table and just six points clear of the re-election places. Scott-Walford now had the reins in his hands.

'Flaneur' in the *Leeds Mercury* said: 'If the Leeds City team were as satisfactory as the ground and arrangements at Elland Road, the directors of the club would have no misgivings on the score of ways and means. There is a large and enthusiastic public for soccer in Leeds; there would be a larger and more enthusiastic public if the City club were making a fight, like other young Second Division organisations, for a place at the top of the table instead of languishing among the bottom half dozen. Leeds City have accomplished one performance this year, their victory over Derby County, that has given them a claim to be regarded as a team of somewhat greater ability than the three or four clubs that are fighting to escape the attendant upon an application for re-election, yet they can still attract as many as 15,000 people. It will be for the new secretary-manager, Mr Scott-Walford, to so remodel the team that next season the City record shall be more worthy of the support the club already receives. Mr Gillies showed, when he was appointed the position, that it was possible for an association manager of experience to build up a good side. Perhaps if the purchase of players had throughout been left entirely to him Leeds City would have had an equally good side today. Mr Scott-Walford may be given more freedom in the matter of team building than Mr Gillies was permitted, and, if so, Leeds City should rise out of the ruck at the bottom of the table next season. It is too much to suggest that the club will this year attain even the moderate position held 12 months ago, when, though they were seen below their three Yorkshire rivals, they occupied tenth place in the league table. Since January 1st Leeds City have captured six points by beating Derby County and Barnsley and drawing with Leicester Fosse and Chesterfield. They have been beaten by Stoke, West

Bromwich Albion, Bradford City, Hull City, Lincoln City, Fulham, Burnley and Oldham Athletic (twice). And four of those defeats have been sustained at home. Indeed, they have only taken four points from the seven matches played this year. This is not a record of which either the team or the directors can be proud, yet the club can still demand a gate of 15,000.'

The poor form of the teams around them had given City some breathing space, and on 17 April Leeds finally gave their new manager a victory. A 3-0 home win over Stockport County watched by just short of 13,000, followed the week after by another home victory over Wolverhampton Wanderers ensured City safety and a 12th position in the table.

Despite City struggling financially, they sanctioned an exodus from Brighton, with Scott-Walford bringing in six of his former players: Davie Dougal, Jimmy Burnett, Dickie Joynes, Tom Rodger, Willie McDonald and Tom Morris, widely recognised as the best defender in the Second Division. But crowd favourites Fred Parnell and Bob Watson left the club. Lavery, Kay, Hynds and Jefferson also passed through the Elland Road exit door. Interestingly, Scott-Walford was given a position of sole selector.

The fixture list for 1908/09 produced Tottenham Hotspur as Leeds City's first opponents, at Elland Road. Tottenham had won the FA Cup in 1901 to become the only non-league side to win it. Having just been elected, this was their first ever season in league football. A crowd of over 24,000 arrived at Elland Road, once again filled with optimism. Leeds were sporting a brand-new kit, dark blue shirts with a distinctive old gold pinstripe. It was an almost new line-up for City with seven new starters, but the crowd were puzzled, if not angry, that Billy McLeod was not included. He had been replaced by Adam Bowman, a centre-forward from Brentford, who had scored a hat-trick in a pre-season game against the club's own reserves.

City beat Tottenham 1-0 thanks to a goal by Tom Rodger, one of the Brighton recruits. Leeds were undefeated when McLeod was brought back into the side, three games in, and he fired home a brace without reply at home to Barnsley, and Leeds were sitting second in the table.

Leeds had started well, but three consecutive defeats shook the club and despite regaining their momentum with just one defeat in nine games, they went down 6-0 at Oldham on 19 December 1908; this was the first of seven consecutive defeats. City never really recovered from this severe string of defeats, and although they did gain some stability in the second half of the season, suffering six defeats in 15 games, the club had to be content with a final position of 12th for the second year running. There were signs that Scott-Walford could turn the club around, however. He had instigated a special training and bonding exercise at Ben Rhydding near Ilkley prior to a third round FA Cup replay against Oldham at Elland Road. And on 20 January 1909, just short of 20,000 watched an invigorated City team triumph 2-0 against a very good Oldham side. But, all in all, there was much more work to be done.

As the club prepared for the 1909/10 season, the directors, clearly showing frustration at a record £1,200 loss, put Scott-Walford on notice that improvement was essential rather than an optional extra. With funds so tight, the manager, after spending a considerable sum the previous season, was forced into the low budget option. A couple of 21-year-old Irishmen – Tom 'Steve' Mullholland, an inside-right, and Billy Halligan who could play centre-forward or inside-left – were recruited from across the Irish Sea and a handful of other new faces was drafted in at relatively low cost.

In April 1901 a new maximum wage of £4 had been introduced, but in 1907, following the formation of the Players' Union, players began to recognise their worth and began to express dissatisfaction. The Football League and the Football Association were worried about players becoming organised, possibly even affiliating to the Trades Union movement. They threatened to impose a ban on players who took up union membership. Some players fell into line but many revolted and eventually a deal was struck between the governing bodies and the players and wages were increased to £5 a week.

Leeds had an indifferent start to the season, opening with a 5-0 trouncing of Lincoln City at Elland Road, but then falling to a 3-1 defeat at Hull City three days later. October saw four consecutive losses including a 7-0 humiliation at home to Barnsley. Halligan was proving worthwhile, however, and by October he was the club's leading scorer with nine goals; McLeod meanwhile was still being overlooked by Scott-Walford, featuring just twice in the opening couple of months of the season.

Leeds failed to find anything resembling a run of form and a 2-1 home win over Clapton Orient was only their fifth success of the season. They beat Blackpool 3-2 two days later, but did not win again until a 2-1 home victory over Birmingham City in mid-February. A 2-0 victory at Orient was their next win at the end of March, and they only recorded two more wins all season, finishing a disappointing 17th in the table. When McLeod was finally given a consistent run in the side at the end of December, he finished the season with a tally of 13 goals, but problems were clearly afoot at Elland Road.

During the summer of 1910, with money as tight as ever, Scott-Walford made a massive gamble on more Irish players, untested and inexperienced. Leeds were to forge a bond with Shelbourne FC from Dublin over many years and two of these Irish players came from that club – Joe Enright and Joe Moran – who both went on to win international honours while at Leeds, for Ireland against Scotland in 1911. Billy Gillespie was brought in from Derry City along with around half a dozen Irishmen in total. To make the Irish contingency feel at home in their strange and new surroundings, Scott-Walford bizarrely changed the club's colours. Research by Leeds fan and author Dave Tomlinson in 2010 revealed that in the 1910/11 season Scott-Walford attired the team in green jerseys and the club even placed green touch flags down pitch-side. On 5 September 1910 the manager told the *Leeds Mercury*, 'It must be remembered that these Irishmen are very young men, who have been brought into a higher class of football than that to which they have been accustomed, and that they were playing their first match amid unfamiliar surroundings.'

In his programme notes for the first game of the new season, 3 September, against Blackpool, Scott-Walford addressed his new players and wrote, 'Should your efforts deserve success, and it is denied you, we shall extend our sympathy, when you do badly we shall still think you have done your best.' Joe Enright scored that day – a 2-1 loss. Enright also scored in the next game – a 2-1 loss at Glossop. City had to wait until 15 October for their first win, 1-0 at home to Hull City, Billy Gillespie scoring the winner. Gillespie and Enright continued to score around 20 goals between them, but even with a 14-goal tally from City's reliable and prolific marksman, Billy McLeod, City only finished 11th in the table and over the next couple of seasons they slid away again.

The Irish acquisitions hadn't quite made the grade and even a doctor was installed in goal. Dr Cecil G. Reinhardt was the son of the renowned Leeds chemist Johann Christian Reinhardt, who founded Johann's I' Briggate, a physic emporium. Dr Cecil Reinhardt was spotted playing in goal for Leeds University and made his City debut in a 5-0 defeat at Wolverhampton Wanderers, on 16 December 1911, where he was man of the match. But he left the club after just 12 appearances. Veteran keeper Harry Bromage had left the club to join Doncaster Rovers in 1911, leaving Dr Reinhardt and Tony Hogg as the only goalkeepers at Leeds, and Irish keeper Leslie Murphy was signed from Belfast Celtic and installed as the club's number one goalkeeper.

Leeds continued to struggle with very little money to back the manager, and were forced to sell Gillespie to Sheffield United for £400, a move which angered Scott-Walford and supporters alike. Leeds nosedived the following season and, despite a further 14 goals from McLeod, finished 19th and had to make arrangements to seek re-election.

Meanwhile, stress was building up for Scott-Walford and his health was deteriorating rapidly, and then early in 1912 he threw in the towel. He had written to the club's vice-chairman, Joe Henry, in February, 'At the last board meeting I was instructed to prepare a scheme to continue the club, forming a minimum financial outlay to agree with the income from all sources derived in the present year's working, and to call a special meeting of the board to present the scheme and discuss my agreement with the company, which expires on the 31st March next. I have prepared a scheme, and should like to discuss the same with you and Mr Hepworth any day this week.'

The club never did consider the scheme, and as the end of Scott-Walford's contract neared, he wrote another letter, this time to the directors, which was published in several local papers in March: 'Gentlemen, – Re my agreement. After very serious consideration, and recognising the unsatisfactory financial position of the club, in fairness to myself, I think it is my duty to inform you that I find it impossible for me to conduct the affairs of the club any longer under present existing circumstances. As you know, I have had to meet expenses, players wages, etc, times without number, also to advance transfer fees, signing on fees, and summer wages during the past three years, which has been reported at directors' meetings, and has been duly notified in the minutes. The strain of these worries has caused a breakdown in my health, for, as you know, I have been ill for some considerable time. I should, therefore, feel grateful if the directors will endeavour to relieve me of the financial obligations that are due to me from the club on or before March 31st, 1912. I sincerely hope that you will not consider this letter in any way disrespectful to any of you. I recognise the kind courtesy and consideration I have always received from the present directors, but I feel it is a duty that I owe to my wife and family, and you will agree it is not fair that a servant of the company should be continually called upon to meet the club's liabilities. I must, therefore, kindly ask you to make proper financial arrangements or relieve me of my duties as secretary and general manager of the club on 31st March next.'

www.mightywhites.co.uk says: 'If the letter was intended to get the board to pay the manager his due, it backfired. The directors took the letter as Scott-Walford's resignation, which they accepted. Without deigning to reply, they quickly placed an advertisement for a replacement.'

The *Leeds Mercury* reported: 'Mr Scott-Walford has resigned his position as manager and secretary of the Leeds City Football Club, and the directors have accepted the resignation, and are advertising for a new manager. Mr Scott-Walford came to Leeds from the Brighton and Hove Albion Club in 1908 as successor to Mr G. Gillies. The club had not been doing so well as the directors hoped, and they looked to the new manager to pull it round, but after four years' work Mr Scott-Walford has found the task too much for him. For some time, the club has been in a most unsatisfactory position, both from a financial and playing point of view. The attendances at Elland Road have been very disappointing, and the best players have been sold to pay current expenses.'

Despite the financial restraints on the club, Scott-Walford had strived to find a way forward and in 1910 he even paid the players' wages out of his own pocket as he continued his uphill struggle to make City successful.

The club bore no malice towards Scott-Walford, and at a dinner in his honour at the Cyprus Cafe in Leeds, he was given several mementos. The Leeds club captain, Tom Morris, presented him with a large silver boat-shaped flower bowl, with the inscription, 'Presented to Mr F. Scott-Walford by the players and staff at Leeds City Football Club, April 17th 1912.' He was also given an inscribed gold medal and his wife was given a silver mounted oak biscuit box.

Scott-Walford went on to become manager of Coventry City, but unfortunately the financial situation was worse than at Leeds City. With World War One looming, it was a huge struggle to field a team of 11 men, finances became worse and when the business was wound up, Scott-Walford was still owed £100 in wages.

During Scott-Walford's time at Elland Road, the directors and shareholders had tried tirelessly to correct the financial strain on the club. In September 1910 shareholders were asked to take up debentures worth £4,000 and this, together with £8,000 pledged by some directors, would provide essential working capital. The shareholders formed a committee to work with the directors on all financial affairs. But then the club's bank announced that it was going to call in the club's £7,000 overdraft, which had kept the club afloat, and therefore threatened the very existence of Leeds City Football Club.

Norris Hepworth put in more cash and appointed Tom Coombs as Receiver, who ran City's affairs for the next three years as the financial crisis continued to blight the progress. But the full extent of the financial aid and overwhelming generosity that Hepworth had given the club became apparent at a public meeting held at the Grand Central Hotel, Leeds on Thursday, 11 April 1912. The hotel, as the name suggests, was a grand affair; originally a coaching inn from the 1800s called the Bull and Mouth, the largest and by far the busiest in Yorkshire, housing 30 horses. Situated on Briggate, just up from Duncan Street, it became the Grand Central Hotel in 1903. On the day of the meeting, several prominent people arrived, well dressed and sporting a variety of flat caps, trilbies and bowler hats.

Alf Masser had been appointed by the shareholders as a director and it was duly announced to the gathering that the club's major benefactor, Mr Hepworth, had spent £15,000 on trying to keep Leeds City afloat. At an extraordinary general meeting held just days later at the nearby Salem Church in Hunslet, the full extent of the financial crisis at Leeds City Football Club was revealed. Total liabilities were £15,782, total losses, since 1904, were £11,321 and assets stood at just £7,084. There was no alternative to the company being wound up and thereafter it was agreed that Coombs be installed to run the football club.

Several offers came from outside the club to take over Leeds City, Leeds Cricket Club being one of them, but the club at Elland Road stood firm, hoping. And that hope was rewarded when, in May 1912, an audacious attempt to lure Northampton Town manager Herbert Chapman as their new manager succeeded – but only after great confusion surrounding the Elland Road club. At the end of April, City had been forced to issue strenuous denials over a number of recent announcements, none more so than the claims that Leeds City had appointed George Morrell of Woolwich Arsenal as a replacement for Frank Scott-Walford. It was also denied that two local businessmen, Ed Wood and Samuel Samuel, had offered to invest the £7,000 required to get the club back on a sound financial footing. Alf Masser had held positive talks with Wood and Samuel but so far nothing has been agreed. Also, it was reported in the *Yorkshire Evening Post*, 'most of the City players are up in arms regarding an announcement in several local and national papers that only eight of them were to be signed for another season'.

The Receiver, Mr Coombs, declared that a list of players to be retained had not yet been drawn up and would be done so later in the week. Mr Coombs was also angry about misleading statements that seemed to be circulating everywhere, claiming that they did nothing but harm at a difficult time for the club. He told the *Yorkshire Evening Post*, 'Association football in Leeds ought to be successful, can be successful and will be successful. If only the public of Leeds will stand by the club and have a little patience and confidence, we shall yet have a club at Elland Road capable of taking its place in the front rank of association football club.'

Mr Hepworth confirmed that he had held discussions with George Morrell in London and that it was, '1,000 to 1 that Mr Morrell will get the appointment as manager. But I have practically only settled with him this morning, so that no one in Leeds had any authority for stating last night that Mr Morrell had been appointed.'

Meanwhile the *Yorkshire Evening Post* said of Mr Morrell, 'He has been looked upon as almost a permanent fixture at Woolwich, and during the four and half years in which he has been associated with the club he has seen many exiting periods. He had to take charge of the club when it was in a bad financial position. Messrs Norris and Hall of Fulham came along with money and assistance, once this was done the way was paved for Mr Morrell to build up a team. He went in mainly for young players, and was never keen on paying large transfer fees. A native of Glasgow, he was, prior to taking up the reins at Woolwich, manager for Greenock Morton, a famous Scottish club, for three and a half years. His first experience in football management, however, was as assistant to William Wilton, secretary of Glasgow Rangers.'

Within a week, however, it was announced that Morrell had turned down the post at Leeds City after originally indicating that he would accept it. A number of friends and acquaintances had persuaded him to remain at Arsenal.

Chapter Five

Herbert Chapman

ON 6 May 1912, the *Leeds Mercury* reported that an appointment had finally been made. 'The Leeds City club appear to have made a distinct capture in their new football manager, Mr Herbert Chapman. It was about a decade ago when he first made the acquaintance of the Cobblers. He left there to play for Spurs in 1904, but came back as player/manager in 1907. The Cobblers were at the time in terrible straits. They were the wooden spoonists of the Southern League, and only A. J. Darnell's persistent pleading saved them from relegation. Mr Chapman was the physician called in, and he succeeded in healing their wounds. In his first year the Cobblers climbed into sixth position in the Southern League ladder. The next year they actually won championship honours. The balance sheet showed splendid gate receipts and members subscriptions totalled £1,855 in April 1907; in the return published for 1910/11 they aggregated £5,309, and when the complete return is issued for the past season further progress will be seen. Both the ground and the stand have been materially improved. Northampton folk will be sorry indeed to lose Mr Chapman, but there is not one of them who will not wish him the best of luck.'

Having finished 19th in the 1911/12 table, Leeds City had to seek re-election for the following season and Herbert Chapman immediately campaigned to keep City in the league, writing to clubs and going round personally to some, canvassing for votes. Thanks to his tireless efforts, on 4 June 1912, Leeds City were re-elected with 33 votes and Gainsborough Trinity dropped out of the league at the expense of Lincoln City. 'I will take Leeds into Division One,' proclaimed Chapman.

Herbert Chapman was an affable, yet firm man. He had been born in the South Yorkshire mining town of Kiveton Park on 19 January 1878 to John and Emma and had one sister and six brothers, two of which, Harry and Thomas, became professional footballers and Mathew a director at Grimsby Town.

The Education Act of 1870 made school attendance compulsory up to the age of 12 and at the age of five Herbert was learning to read and write; something that millions before him, including his parents, had never had the privilege of. Of course, sport was very important to most boys and the young Chapman became captain and secretary of his school football eleven.

It was usual for a boy to eventually follow his father down the pit, but Herbert had opted instead to use his education to take a course in mining engineering as well as studying for a certificate in colliery management. Already a pattern was emerging as to which way Chapman's future would unfold.

Alongside his technical studies, he played for many amateur clubs in and around his area of Sheffield. By the time he was 19, Chapman had carved out an amateur career as an inside-forward. He would be the first to admit, however, that it was an undistinguished playing career, and he would never reach the level of talent that his two brothers achieved at The Wednesday and Grimsby Town, although he had played alongside them both in his local junior team. Over a 13-year playing career, he remained mainly a committed amateur, allowing him to continue with his studies or find employment close to the club that he played for at that time. Chapman did, however, play as a professional in 1901 when he was 23. He still harboured the intention of going into mining engineering once his playing days were over, but on signing professional terms with Northampton Town, he came to realise the importance of other players making arrangements for when they too retired. Chapman played for Northampton Town in 1901/1902 and again in 1904/1905 on loan, and he returned to the County Ground on 9 April 1907 as player-manager – but he wished it to be only temporary as he still wanted to be a mining engineer. Almost two years later Herbert Chapman played his last game as a professional but over the next three years would show his true potential as of one of the country's leading managers. He had turned a less than average team of cannon fodder into a more than adequate team of championship and cup contenders. His astute tactical awareness came very much to the fore as well as his growing reputation as a gentleman of the sport. Chapman once said, 'Never do anything on the field to an opponent that will later prevent your meeting him in the street or in the church later and shaking hands with him.' He was the first to make himself responsible for team selection and buying and selling players. He was the first to fly his teams to games abroad. He was the first to suggest floodlights for evening games. He was in the sights of Leeds City Football Club.

Everything that Chapman had achieved at Northampton he had achieved on a shoestring. But aside from that he had done it in a predominantly rugby stronghold. The president of Northampton Town, Pat Durnell, was himself a rugby man; but it is said that he once inadvertently wandered into Leicester's football ground by mistake – and was instantly converted. The ability of Herbert Chapman to both operate on a stringent budget and sway people from the oval ball game to the round ball persuasion would appeal to the directors of Leeds City. Chapman had abandoned his ambitions of becoming a mining engineer and had decided fully to involve himself into the world of association football. Leeds on the other hand had abandoned their present regime and its ambitions were higher than ever. Chapman's return to Yorkshire and his announcement to the Leeds public that 'I am here to get Leeds City into the First Division' had the whole city and its supporters buzzing. The *Yorkshire Post* heralded his 'shrewd judgment and tactful management' as Chapman added, regarding promotion, 'It is, of course, a matter of time, but if it is humanly possible, it shall be attained.'

Chapman's first game in charge was on 7 September 1912 at Fulham's Craven Cottage in front of 21,300 spectators, including almost 900 from Leeds. Leeds never looked like winning at any stage of the game after Fulham had scored within a minute, and worse still, it was 4-0 at half-time. Luckily for City, the home side relaxed more in the second half, but City couldn't make a breakthrough and the score was unchanged at full time. Despite the defeat, Hugh Roberts, on the right wing, gave a good account of himself, so too did Fred Croot on the other flank. Andy Gibson, making his debut, showed some promise at inside-forward, and the other inside-forward, also making his debut, Jimmy Robertson looked comfortable on the ball; Evelyn Lintott, a new signing from Bradford City and yet another debutant, showed that he still had much to offer. Lintott was an accomplished centre-half and considered to be a great acquisition for the club, but he inadvertently became embroiled in an administration error at his new club. He and two other new recruits, goalkeeper, Billy Scott, from Everton and George Law, a prolific full-back from Rangers, were each offered a full year's wage of £208 by Chapman.

However, as two months of their previous contracts had already elapsed, the three players were, in effect, getting more than the permitted wage of £4 per week.

The City directors, realising they had breached the rules, reported themselves to the Football League immediately. The club was fined £125 and the three players concerned were ordered to pay back the excess payments given to them.

The following week, over 15,000 filed into Elland Road and witnessed an impressive 2-0 victory over FA Cup holders Barnsley; Croot and Robertson getting a goal apiece.

The *Yorkshire Post* had noticed that there hadn't been a great deal of changes from the team defeated at Fulham: 'Changes in two or three departments may be found necessary before a thoroughly balanced and capable combination can be evolved. The left full-back (Ferguson) was slow and rather weak in kicking. Neither outside-half distinguished himself. Cubberley was not exactly a failure at inside-left, but he lacked speed and incisiveness, and Croot cannot hope to give his abilities full play until he decides to meet resolute backs with equally resolute aggression. In other respects, the team played like a good, sound side. Scott was as fine in goal as ever he was for Everton, and really made victory possible by the masterly way in which he dealt with the Barnsley attacks in the first 20 minutes of play. George Law, too, was like the full back that won the highest honour that Scotland can bestow; and Lintott, save possibly in the matter of speed, reached more to his international level than he has done since making his home in Yorkshire. McLeod got little help from his left-wing, but was well served by Roberts and Robertson. The latter pair promise to be more effective on the attack than any of their recent predecessors in the City team.'

Chapman stuck by the same eleven a week later at Bradford Park Avenue, and was rewarded when his team returned home with a 1-0 win, courtesy of Cubberley. For the following two matches, however, City could only manage two draws, the first 2-2 at home to Wolverhampton Wanderers in front of 20,000, McLeod getting his first goal under Chapman and Croot scoring the second from the penalty spot. The following week saw the second draw away at Leicester 1-1, Robertson scoring Leeds' goal. Then, McLeod netted twice in a 2-1 home victory over Stockport County, and things were beginning to take shape for Chapman. An unlucky defeat followed a week later at Preston North End. Leeds equalised twice before conceding what turned out to be the winner, although City players contested vigorously that it had definitely been offside.

On 26 October 1912, Leeds City played host to Burnley and gave them a good thumping by four goals to one, but City again slipped up on their travels the week after when they suffered a heavy 6-2 defeat at Hull City. But Leeds, again, bounced back with a win – a convincing 4-1 victory over Glossop NE, McLeod grabbing his first hat-trick under Herbert Chapman. But again, frustratingly, defeat followed victory and on 16 November City were beaten 2-0 at Clapton Orient. A disappointing 2-2 draw a week later at home to Lincoln was scrutinised by the *Leeds Mercury*: 'I heard it said that the changes made in the home team had proved successful. I do not think so.

Affleck did not play as well with Copeland in the rear division as was anticipated, and Cubberley at inside-left was by no means as good as he is at half-back. Allan, too, was not a success in Cubberley's original position. The display given by Leeds City was not what it should or could have been. Their combination of a fortnight ago was absent, and the shooting of the forwards should have been improved upon. With all their faults, City played with determination in the initial half of the game, and for the major portion of the game did the attacking. But what opportunities they missed! In turn each forward was presented with a chance of scoring, but either erratic shooting or hesitation spoilt their attacks. Roberts, at outside-right, was chief offender in this respect.

'Leeds were triers, and deserved the goal they secured through Robertson just before the interval. It was in the getting of their goal that Cubberley did his best piece of work during the afternoon. He headed the ball against the crossbar in a very clever manner, the result being that from the rebound Robertson had only the goalkeeper to beat to score. Lincoln scored in the first minute of each half and on both occasions, Billy Scott should have prevented the goal. On the second occasion, in particular, he seemed to make no serious attempt to save the effort, simply watching transfixed as it entered the net.'

The *Yorkshire Evening Post* was also fairly critical: 'Leeds City need to put this game behind them as a matter of great urgency. Too many players were off-form and improvements are required when City travel to Nottingham in a week's time.'

It was clear to all concerned that Herbert Chapman had work to do if he wished to build a side that was capable of challenging for promotion. The *Yorkshire Post* said: 'The present players will never blend, as their styles are so dissimilar. Individualism is by no means to be deprecated, but cohesiveness should be the first aim of an attacking line.' The Leeds City fans too, were growing agitated. Stephen Studd in *Herbert Chapman, Football Emperor* wrote: 'Disappointed supporters demanded to know why Chapman had not signed any new players since the summer. It was not, he answered, through want of trying: clubs were either unwilling to sell so early in the season or were asking too high a fee. Even junior clubs were holding on to their players. It would not, he admitted, be hard to find players who were 'fairly good', but they would not strengthen the team; nothing but the best would do. Then in November came a golden opportunity. Northampton Town, languishing since Chapman's departure and losing money at the rate of £30 a week, were open to offers for Fanny Walden. Chapman jumped at the chance, but the Cobblers supporters were determined that Walden should stay at the County Ground, and a 'shilling fund' was set up to thwart the designs of their former manager. It worked, and by the end of the month the deal was off.'

Chapman confessed, 'In no instance have I personally suffered so great a disappointment.' He remained hopeful of securing Walden in the future, for he 'would be the making of the Leeds City team if only I could get him to Elland Road'. Chapman would secure Walden's services at a later time, but under entirely different circumstances.

City travelled to Nottingham Forest and pulled off a much-needed 2-1 victory. The *Yorkshire Post* described it as City's 'best performance of the season' but there were obvious problems in certain departments. Hugh Roberts had notched up over 112 appearances, scoring 15 goals, since joining City in 1909, but the right-winger had suffered a loss of form of late, as noticed by, amongst others, the *Leeds Mercury*: 'He has yet to show that he is the Roberts of old, despite scoring in the game. His notable loss of form could affect the team if not addressed accordingly.'

Chapman acted swiftly on team matters and by the time Bristol City arrived at Elland Road a week later, 7 December 1912, a young outside-right, Simpson Bainbridge, had been brought in on trial and went straight into the starting line-up in place of Roberts.

In front of an expectant 10,357 Elland Road crowd, Robertson scored in a 1-1 draw. But despite only managing a point, the performance had been above average due in no small part to the inclusion of Bainbridge which was reported by the *Yorkshire Post*: 'Much local interest centred round Bainbridge. It was quite a relief to see a player in that position with skill sufficiently pronounced to justify a lengthy trial, as Bainbridge undoubtedly possesses merit beyond the ordinary. He played with judgement, kept his place and shot accurately. His appearance upon the scene may save the club hundreds of pounds.'

Bainbridge was also the catalyst for McLeod scoring City's two goals the following week in a 2-2 draw at Birmingham City. The first goal by McLeod was admirably his 100th for the club.

As Christmas approached, City found themselves lying eighth in the table, six points off the leaders and about to face Huddersfield Town at Elland Road, where City had remained undefeated since the March of the previous season. Unfortunately, a disappointing City team totally capitulated against their close neighbours and found themselves on the losing end of a 3-0 scoreline. Worse was to come, as this was just the start of four consecutive defeats over Christmas – unbelievably, all at Elland Road!

A Christmas Day 2-1 defeat by Grimsby Town was followed, on Boxing Day, by a 2-0 reverse against Blackpool, but despite losing 3-2 to Fulham on 28 December, a new player had made his City debut that day and had impressed greatly. Inside-forward Arthur Price had been brought in from Worksop Town and would go on to score 25 goals in 78 Leeds City appearances. But Chapman had also secured a real gem from Bradford City. Leeds paid a club record of £1,400 for Bradford's captain, Jimmy Speirs. Inside-left Speirs had scored Bradford's winning goal to lift the 1911 FA Cup. Speirs, who won a Scottish cap whilst at Rangers, had been having difficulty with the Bradford regime and had numerous fall outs with the club – this hadn't gone unnoticed ten miles away by Herbert Chapman, who swooped and took the disgruntled player to Elland Road.

The *Yorkshire Evening Post* was full of admiration: 'The enterprise of the Leeds City management in securing Speirs would have staggered those in charge of the club a few years ago.'

Speirs and Price had made their debuts against Fulham, as well as their mark. Bainbridge continued with flair down the right wing, and both Price and Bainbridge were on the scoresheet. The *Leeds Mercury* reported: 'Speirs made a great impression, being responsible for many fine passes and shots, but he was inclined to wander out of position. Price delighted the spectators and, together with Bainbridge, made a capital right-wing.'

City had been leading Fulham 2-1 at one stage, but late errors by both full-backs, Charlie Copeland and John Ferguson allowed the London club to take, and hold on to, a 3-2 lead.

On his arrival in May 1912 Herbert Chapman had announced that he would get Leeds City into the First Division within two seasons. The poor results at Christmas, however, had seen City plummet to 15th in the table. But with the acquisition of Jimmy Speirs, Chapman remained confident that his side could soon be challenging for promotion come the new year.

On New Year's Day 1913, City travelled across to Blackpool, on the back of six games without a win. Another Leeds debutant came in at right-half – Tom Broughton, a signing from Grangetown. George Law replaced Charlie Copeland at right-back and George Affleck started just his second game of the season at left-back. A very strong forward line of Bainbridge, Price,

McLeod, Speirs and Croot immediately put the Blackpool defence on the back foot, as City cruised to much needed 3-0 victory. The *Leeds Mercury* was gushing with praise: 'Leeds exhibited much superior tactics. The attack was characterised by plenty of vim, the whole of the forwards showing plenty of dash and a perfect understanding, which made them well nigh of irresistible. Robertson, McLeod and Speirs were frequently in the picture, and the wing men, Bainbridge and Croot, showed a rare turn of speed, which was very useful at times.' Leeds' goals had been supplied by Croot after 11 minutes, Bainbridge made it two in the second half and McLeod finished the 'Seasiders' off with a third ten minutes from time. However, Leeds' mini revival was derailed three days later at Barnsley. Gales and heavy rain favoured the home team more as they swept City aside 2-0.

Eleven days later, an FA Cup tie at home to Burnley provided some brief respite from the league; it was the second attempt at playing the tie, the first one being abandoned four days earlier because of heavy snowfall. It was a thrilling match for the crowd of over 13,000, despite the melting snow having turned the pitch into a mudbath. Some brilliant team play enabled McLeod to beat two Burnley defenders before scoring a tremendous goal past the oncoming Burnley goalkeeper, Jerry Dawson. With Leeds missing several chances to increase their lead, they then conceded a silly penalty which Burnley captain Tom Boyle converted to make it 1-1. With the score still level as the game entered the last 15 minutes, Burnley went ahead with a free kick on the edge of City's box. Burnley then went 3-1 up with just eight minutes left. But to their credit City kept plugging away and were rewarded with a goal just two minutes later from Foley. They continued to press the Burnley defence and were extremely unlucky not to draw level on a couple of occasions, but Burnley held on to their lead.

However, the *Leeds Mercury* was full of praise for the home side: 'Though beaten, Leeds enhanced their reputation, and had fortune been a little more kind, they would now be in the second round of the FA Cup. They played quite as good football as Burnley, and in fact were the better team up to those last 20 minutes. The men on the side who distinguished themselves most were Lintott and Foley. These two half-backs fairly excelled themselves all through the piece, their tackling and playing being excellent. Allan also did a lot of good work at right-half, till he went lame in the second half. Of the forwards, Speirs, McLeod and Bainbridge were in fine form, but Robertson and Croot were both below par. Affleck was a sound defender all the way through. Law played well in the first half, but fell away towards the finish. Hogg made several capital saves, and was in no way to blame for any of the three goals scored against him.'

The *Burnley News* also praised Leeds City: 'With Burnley leading 3-1 and with less than ten minutes to go, the game looked finished. But the Leeds City club would not give in. After Foley made it 3-2, Burnley came under intense fire and in the end they were a tad fortunate to escape with a victory.'

Leeds got back on track in the league on 18 January with a tidy 2-0 win over Bradford Park Avenue at Elland Road, on a pitch that hadn't improved from the terrible conditions of the cup-tie with Burnley; in fact, it had got worse. That said, City coped much better than their opponents and in the second half Mick Foley opened the scoring and just a minute later Jimmy Speirs added a second – his first goal for the club.

The following week, Wolves forced a draw at Molineux, but the *Leeds Mercury* reported: 'Nothing but sheer hard luck prevented Leeds City from emerging triumphant from a good, if not brilliant game. In the first place, there was a clear case of a penalty when McLeod was brought down just before the interval – but the referee declined to allow it – and in the second place, when Foley had the misfortune to put through his own goal while endeavouring to stop the ball preparatory to clearing. On the day's play there was little to choose between the teams, but the City thoroughly deserved their lead at the interval. Their display, both in defence and attack, was better than that of the Wanderers, and the goal scored by Bainbridge was a merited reward to one of the many attacks made by the City.'

On 1 February 1913 Leeds City fans got a surprise look at someone who they had thought was on his way to Elland Road just over two months previous. Now, Fanny Walden had arrived at Elland Road, but as an opponent. Because of Leeds' exit from the FA Cup they filled their blank Saturday with a friendly against Northampton Town. City had one new signing in their side, having acquired left-winger George Fenwick from Shildon, in County Durham. Leeds won the game easily, and gave Fanny Walden a rousing send-off, unaware that he would return one day, in a Leeds shirt, albeit under different circumstances.

Fenwick, who had scored a couple against Northampton, kept his place for the following league match at home to Leicester Fosse. City were on fire and defeated Leicester 5-1, but as the *Leeds Mercury* noted: 'Leeds City are slowly rising back up the table and this victory over the Fosse takes them to ninth. City were accomplished throughout proceedings and triumphed with ease. Worthy of note is the young chap Fenwick from the non-leaguers Shildon, he looks indeed to be a very worthy addition to Herbert Chapman's plans.' Leeds scored after 20 minutes when Price was put through so superbly by Speirs that he simply couldn't miss. Speirs himself then added a second and three more goals came in the second half through Fenwick, Price and McLeod. Leicester did record a consolation but City won this easily.

The *Yorkshire Post* noted: 'Changes in the City team have been numerous throughout this season, and Mr Chapman, the manager, is slowly but surely evolving a set of players from whom much may be expected in the future. His latest acquisition is a youth named Fenwick, from Shildon, and although his methods are rather crude at present, he evidently possesses talent capable of being turned to good account under skilful training. Speirs' display was the outstanding feature of the match, as in addition to scoring a goal direct, his work paved the way for two other successful efforts. McLeod's goal was the culmination of a fine piece of individualism, which elicited generous acknowledgment from the crowd.'

But once again, a defeat was always lurking and it came seven days later when Leeds travelled to Stockport County and were well and truly spanked 6-0. After 60 minutes it was 1-0, then in half an hour, City were absolutely blitzed by a rampant County side, the final four goals coming in the last ten minutes.

Leeds, still licking their wounds, will certainly not have relished the visit of Preston North End one week later and must have been, quite frankly, fearing the worst. But once again, in the face of adversity, Leeds City rallied and produced quite possibly their best performance of the season.

The *Leeds Mercury* said: 'There was never a doubt as to the ultimate destination of the points, Leeds City being complete masters of the proceedings throughout. Right from the commencement of the game to the finish did the home team display wonderful form. Seldom have the team, as a whole, played better, and individually the players did some very clever things, especially Scott (returning to the side after missing the four previous games), the custodian, who gave some of his international form; while the headwork of Lintott was another feature of the game, as also was the goal headed into the net by Bainbridge.'

Leeds City had attacked from the very start; the Preston keeper was lucky when he fumbled an early effort from McLeod and it bounced harmlessly away. A deflection off Preston defender McCall resulted in a corner, which City wasted with a high header from Robertson, and McLeod had a goal disallowed for offside, a decision which the City players thought was a very close call that could have been given either way. Then after just 12 minutes, Fenwick was fouled in the box and Affleck coolly converted the penalty. Preston tried to make a way forward but Leeds' defence, particularly the backs, Copeland and Affleck, held firm. City then established a three-goal cushion (Foley and Bainbridge) before Preston pulled one back just before half-time, but any signs of a comeback were extinguished when, in the second period, Fenwick scored two goals to round it off at 5-1. And, just for good measure, Leeds' goalkeeper, Scott, saved a penalty from Halliwell.

City then had the chance to exact some revenge on Burnley, for their FA Cup exit in January, but upon arriving at Turf Moor, City quickly found that Burnley weren't about to grant them that privilege. Leeds soon found themselves two down and once again staring defeat in the face. Leeds, however, weren't about to take it lying down and mounted a comeback. With just over two minutes left, the intrepid City duo McLeod and Speirs scored a goal apiece to gain a priceless point. The *Mercury* summed up proceedings: 'The first goal was a beauty for Law, who was some considerable distance from goal, dropped the ball out to Fenwick, the winger headed in to McLeod, and that player popped the leather into the net with his head. McLeod had a big share in the scoring of the second goal, for which it seemed almost certain that the ball would go over the dead line. He nipped in, turned it into the centre, and Speirs put on the finishing touch.'

The *Yorkshire Post* said: 'In Billy McLeod and Jimmy Speirs, Leeds City surely have, by a country mile, the two brightest jewels in the division.'

The *Yorkshire Evening Post* added: 'An utterly outstanding performance throughout the entire side.'

City carried the momentum with them into the next game, beating Hull City 1-0, thanks to Billy McLeod, and 20,117 home fans. McLeod netted just before half-time as huge gales and hailstones swirled around Elland Road. Goalkeeper Billy Scott had been placed, at his own request, on the transfer list prior to this fixture, but nonetheless he put in a faultless performance; the rest of the team did likewise. With Scott expressing his desire to leave, Tony Hogg was recalled as goalkeeper for the trip to Glossop on 15 March, but City were defeated 2-1, McLeod scoring City's goal. McLeod also scored twice in the next game, a Good Friday clash at Grimsby Town, but once again City finished on the losing side, 3-2. City needed to correct things fast if they were to achieve their goal of promotion.

The following week at home to Clapton Orient, they set about doing just that: McLeod was on the scoresheet yet again, and two from Jimmy Speirs ensured a 3-1 win. McLeod was on the mark again three days later at Bury, snatching a goal in the last minute to cancel out Bury's early goal. The following day, Bury had to travel to Elland Road, and Leeds were in the mood to finish the job. Billy McLeod simply could not stop scoring and he was on the mark again in giving City a 1-0 half-time lead. McLeod was being watched by England selectors, as too was Evelyn Lintott, and both gave a good account of themselves. The forwards in particular were in blistering form and it wasn't long in the second half until McLeod got his hat-trick. Jimmy Speirs made it four, but it has to be said that the 4-2 scoreline flattered Bury. Affleck missed a penalty, McLeod missed a close-range attempt, Speirs hit the post and Bainbridge came very close on at least three occasions.

Leeds were pegged back at Lincoln, four days later, in an entertaining 3-3 draw, Speirs, McLeod and Croot all finding the net. The week after, McLeod was again on target in a 1-0 win over Nottingham Forest. This was the ninth consecutive game in which Billy McLeod had scored and so it was fitting that the Forest match also doubled up as a benefit game for him. Another bumper Elland Road crowd ensured that McLeod received £500 in gate receipts, and in addition he received another £100 in subscriptions and collections. Never has such a reward been so well deserved for a player who had been phenomenal in seven years at the Leeds City.

On 12 April Leeds travelled to Bristol City. Promotion had long been impossible, but City were still determined to achieve their highest position since their first league season in 1906. A 1-1 draw at Bristol, Speirs getting the goal, kept City on track. Only an upright denied Billy McLeod from scoring in ten consecutive games. Leeds played their final home game against Birmingham on 19 April. They were determined to send the Elland Road crowd home happy, and they did just that. Jimmy Speirs opened the scoring after great service from Bainbridge, returning after missing the Bristol City game, and shortly afterwards, Speirs got his second. McLeod found the net again to make it three before Foley added the finishing touch with a fourth near the end of the game.

Leeds lost their final game, at Huddersfield 1-0, but finished in sixth position, their highest so far. But for their poor away form, things could certainly have been better. They had been very strong at Elland Road, with the exception of the inexplicable four consecutive defeats over Christmas; the only league defeats at Elland Road all season. All the top four teams were put to the sword at Elland Road: Preston North End – 5-1; Burnley – 4-1; Birmingham City – 4-0; and Barnsley – 2-0. The average home attendance had risen from just over 8,000 the previous season to 13,356. And the crucial signings of Jimmy Speirs, Evelyn Lintott and Simpson Bainbridge were sure to put the club in good stead for next season.

Joe Enright, who had played in all but four of the games in the 1911/12 season, only played half a dozen games under Chapman the following season and was sold to Newport County in October 1913. Other casualties as Chapman continued to sweep the decks were Dubliner Joe Moran and Stan Cubberley, who had played almost 190 times for City. By the summer of 1913, a dozen players had passed through the Elland Road exit door and had been replaced by a dozen more.

City's new recruits included Tom Lamph, who would also become a future Leeds United player, and 24-year-old Ivan Sharpe, who chose the path of an amateur. He was a former gold medal winning Olympian and he became a left-wing sensation with City. He combined his playing career with that of a sports journalist and he too would go on to play for Leeds United. Chapman was moulding a side together which mixed new players with existing players such as the goalscoring phenomenon Billy McLeod, who had been at the club since signing from Lincoln City in 1906. Goalkeeper Tony Hogg, who had made his debut for City at Blackpool in 1910, was also retained by Chapman. Wing-half Mick Foley and full-back George Affleck were both asked by Chapman to remain at Elland Road as he brought in his former captain from Northampton Town, John Hampson, and 19-year-old full-back Albert Urwin, who was in great demand. Chapman persuaded him to join the Elland Road bandwagon, amidst tempting offers from Sheffield United, Middlesbrough, Bristol City and Tottenham Hotspur. Chapman's revolution was gathering pace, but more important it was attracting attention nationwide. John Dunn, Manus Divers, John McDonald, Webb Richardson, James Johnson and Neil Turner all arrived from junior clubs and Third Lanark centre-forward David Davidson resisted the invitation of Celtic and Dundee to join Leeds City. Chapman arranged regular players' meetings where they were encouraged to speak their mind and discuss any problems out in the open. There were golf sessions and team days out where the players built a strong comradeship. And not only were players flocking to Elland Road, fans' interest in the club had soared so much that before a ball was kicked in the 1913/14 season, £2,000 in season ticket sales was registered.

For the opening game of the season, on 6 September, over 8,000 arrived at Elland Road to watch City against Glossop NE. It proved an encouraging start for City, who went ahead through a headed effort from Jimmy Speirs, after a clever cross from Ivan Sharpe. Glossop, however, proved worthy opponents and threatened the City defence on a couple of occasions. It took two goals within five minutes from Billy McLeod to settle the game in City's favour, 3-0. After a disappointing 2-1 defeat at Stockport the week after, City bounced back with a resounding 5-1 victory over undefeated Bradford Park Avenue in front of a home crowd that had almost trebled from the 8,000 who saw the opening game of the season. But City's form continued to be somewhat erratic and they were thumped by Notts County 4-0 the following week. However, several newspaper reports concluded that the scoreline flattered County and if it hadn't been for a below par performance from referee Mr J. Pearson, of Dudley, the score could have been much different.

The *Leeds Mercury* stated: 'It must not be imagined that they had a runaway victory. They scored twice in each half of the game, but it was only in the last 15 minutes of each half that they got their goals, and there is not the least doubt that it was the manner in which they got their first goal that paved the way to their success.

There was nothing to choose between the teams till the fateful goal came after half an hour's play. Bassett, the County outside-right, was in possession of the ball when he was bowled over by Hampson just inches inside the penalty area. It was a perfectly fair charge, but the referee thought otherwise, and, to the consternation of the Leeds players and their coterie of followers, he awarded a penalty, and Richards scored with a shot which hit the crossbar before entering the net. It is no exaggeration to say that not one in 20 referees would have taken the view of this referee. All the pressmen were astonished at the decision of the referee in awarding a penalty. Apart from this instance, Mr Pearson did not please by his handling of the game as several of his callings were rather curious. The Leeds City players also strongly appealed against the third goal scored by Flint 12 minutes from the end of the game, on the grounds that the County inside right was offside, and the referee consulted first one linesman then the other before confirming his decision.'

The *Yorkshire Evening Post*, regarding the penalty incident, commented, 'A dark coloured flat cap was deposited close to the feet of the referee, presumably from a Leeds section of the crowd.'

Chapman worked hard on the training field to put together some consistency in results and two consecutive victories, over Leicester Fosse at home, 2-1, and away at Wolves, 3-1, seemed to bear fruit; but once again City suffered a 2-1 defeat at home to Hull City a week later in front of 20,000, followed seven days later, on 25 October, by a convincing 4-1 win at Barnsley. The

Yorkshire Evening Post reported: 'No result was so totally unexpected as that in which Leeds City inflicted upon Barnsley their first defeat of the season ... what a baffling business is the form of the Leeds City team. One week they win at Wolverhampton Wanderers, the next week they slipped up at home before a very weak Hull City team, only to recover themselves again and startle the football world by running away with Barnsley to the extent of 4-1. Speirs, the City captain, was the best man on the field, and at a time when there is an agitation for the reinstatement of Lintott at centre-half, it is singular to report that the next best contributor to Leeds City's success was Hampson, who seldom went for the ball without securing it. A change of tactics, organised by Speirs, enabled Leeds City to win hands down. The winners played two distinct styles of football in the course of the game. They played Barnsley at their own game in the first half, and scored their first goal by means of long swinging passes from wing to wing, but it was in the deftness with which Speirs, McLeod and Price practised the short passing game that they excelled. Speirs was the best on the field. It is no more than his due to say that it was his individual cleverness and genuine leadership that brought triumph to his side.'

By the beginning of November, City were sitting fifth in the table. A 2-1 win on 1 November consolidated that position in front of another 20,000 Elland Road crowd. A 1-0 home win over Lincoln, thanks to a late Billy McLeod header, was sandwiched between two draws at Huddersfield and Blackpool respectively; however, the game at Blackpool once again provided a controversial penalty decision. The *Leeds Mercury* was beside itself: 'Why on earth was the penalty kick given against Leeds City? Everyone was asking the question ... The referee's explanation is, I believe, that Affleck butted, or attempted to a butt a man in the back, but what grounds he had for coming to his decision appears to be known only to himself. Of course, the referee is in a better position to see things than the spectators, but not one solitary supporter of the Blackpool team did I hear express the opinion that there had been any infringement.' The *Yorkshire Post* seemed to be in agreement: 'It will remain a mystery for some time to come how a penalty kick was awarded to Blackpool.'

As 14,000 filed in through the Elland Road turnstiles the following week on 29 November, they could have had no idea what feast was to be served up before them. A tactical plan by Herbert Chapman meant that the inside-forwards, Jimmy Speirs and Arthur Price, switched positions. Ivan Sharpe, who had played on the right wing at Blackpool the previous week, reverted to his favoured left wing, and Simpson Bainbridge returned to the right wing. A five-match unbeaten run had seen City move up to second in the table, just three points behind leaders Notts County, but with three games in hand. Nottingham Forest, on the other hand, sat at the foot of the table.

Leeds City got off to a blistering start. The *Leeds Mercury* reported: 'City were in devastating form, Price was clever on the ball, and played with considerable directness of purpose. Whenever he saw an opportunity he dashed straight away for goal, but he saw his way barred to his objective, he passed with promptness and decision. The play of the other forwards was characterised by the same methods, but Price was the most conspicuous man in this respect. It was the first half that the home team laid the foundations for their excellent victory. In just over half an hour they were three goals to the good, and the match, to all intents and purposes, was all over bar the shouting. They played against the wind, and even with this handicap they always did well. When the forwards had the ball, they attacked with headlong impetuosity, and with no mean skill.'

A brace from Price and one from McLeod gave City a 3-0 half-time lead and there was to be no let up for Forest in the second half either, as Hampson headed a fourth from a Sharpe corner and that was followed by a goal from Billy McLeod to make it 5-0. Mick Foley fluffed a penalty opportunity before Jimmy Speirs got in on the action with a sixth for City. And two more late goals from McLeod, making it four goals for him, completed the rout and a miserable afternoon for Nottingham Forest.

The *Leeds Mercury* added: 'The City forwards were a brilliant lot, who displayed fire and resolution in their attack. They were supported by a trio of halves who did their work excellently, while Copeland and Affleck were a puissant pair of backs.'

The *Yorkshire Evening Post* said, 'The hopes of their numerous supporters will naturally dwell all the more lovingly upon promotion prospects.' The emphatic 8-0 victory was recorded as a club record, but strictly speaking, this wasn't entirely true as City had beaten Morley in a rousing 11-0 victory on 7 October 1905 in a preliminary round of the FA Cup at Elland Road; courtesy of four goals each from Fred Hargraves and Dickie Morris, two from Bob Watson and one from Fred Parnell.

The 8-0 victory was good psychologically for their next fixture against Woolwich Arsenal, who had been relegated to the Second Division the previous season, but were still regarded as a formidable outfit, and lay just two places beneath City. The game, at Highbury, where Arsenal had just relocated to, was watched by 20,000 and because of inclement weather conditions had been given a 2.30 kick-off.

Herbert Chapman, who would become a future Arsenal manager, understandably stuck with the same eleven from the 8-0 victory over Forest. City made a strong start and were awarded four corners in the first ten minutes, but to no avail. City were, however, fortunate not to concede shortly after 20 minutes, when referee J. E. Hall of Birmingham ruled out an Arsenal goal because he claimed he had given a free kick against City earlier in the movement for a foul on an Arsenal forward, and play was brought back. The home crowd were incensed and even more so when Harding wasted the free kick, sending the ball high over Tony Hogg's crossbar. With honours pretty much even, the referee awarded a penalty to the home side, after deciding that full-back Charlie Copeland had deliberately tripped Arsenal winger Lewis. From the resulting spot kick, Hogg got his hand to Benson's effort but the ball spilled over the line to make it 1-0 to Arsenal, a scoreline that remained until full time.

On 8 December 1913, the *Leeds Mercury* carried this report: 'On the general run of play City had been quite the equal of their opponents in points of skill, and a goalless draw would have much better represented the teams. It was a hard-fought game from beginning to end, and one of the best features of play was the remarkable pace that was maintained. The forwards, it is true, failed to make the most of many fine opportunities that were given them in front of goal. That was their only fault, however, and it is seldom that such fine, open attacking is so successful. There was no great attempt to combine by either line of forwards ... Nothing tangible happened simply because the play of the full-backs was one of vigorous character that an incoming forward was bundled off the ball without ceremony, and what they failed to accomplish, the goalkeepers, Lievsley and Hogg, did in a convincing matter. One of the best efforts in the first half came from the visitors, and it was Bainbridge who made the running. He directed his centre admirably, and Price fired in a powerful shot that was magnificently saved by Lievsley. That was the nearest approach to scoring accomplished by the City, although they made many other fine attempts. City showed better form than Arsenal, but the play of the home inside-forwards was certainly more convincing than the Leeds trio, of which Speirs was the best. McLeod was always a great worker, but he was closely shadowed by Sands, who was none too particular in which way he stopped the City's pivot.

If we were to judge the teams by the form which they showed on Saturday, it is easy to fancy either for a high place in the league table, and the promotion prospects seem decidedly promising.'

Leeds City quickly got over the disappointment of their defeat at Highbury, and embarked on a four-win sequence beginning with a 4-1 home victory over Grimsby Town, but the crowd of just over 10,000 had been hampered by an early kick-off and a strike by Leeds municipal workers which resulted in a tram strike. Before the Birmingham game on 20 December, City were still suffering financial difficulties, but with healthy takings continuing to come through the Elland Road turnstiles, Chapman persuaded the Receiver, Tom Coombs, to free up some funds, and with the resulting £1,000, Chapman was able to bring in 23-year-old Scottish inside-forward, John Jackson, from Clyde, in whom several English First Division sides had shown considerable interest. He would later play for both Celtic and Rangers during World War One. Jackson went straight into the side against Birmingham, but failed to make an immediate impact. The *Leeds Mercury* explained: 'Jackson was not an overpowering success, but that was largely due to the fact that he suffered from being sufficiently fed. Very few openings were made for him, in fact, and he did not get many chances to shine. Neither did he show conspicuous ability in making his own openings; but then he was new to the side, and too much cannot be expected from a man in a strange environment. Jackson did some smart things towards the close, and he showed that he can manipulate the ball; he must be at least have a good trial before one's mind can be made up as to whether he is going to be a striking success or not.'

The *Yorkshire Evening Post* agreed: 'Jackson could not be expected to settle down to the robustness of English League football all in a moment, and possibly he suffered on Saturday from a want of understanding on the part of Price, who was to some extent all at sea in the unaccustomed position as winger. Presuming that Jackson and Price will be played together for a time as the right-wing pair, there is promise of good results in their association, and that is the most that one is justified in saying at this juncture. The other wing, upheld by Jimmy Speirs and Ivan Sharpe, was undoubtedly the more effective, and whilst speaking of Speirs as the most of successful schemer of the match, it will be pleasing to Sharpe's friends that the goal he scored was the crowning point of an excellent afternoon's work.' McLeod and Sharpe, both from crosses from Price, secured a 2-0 win for City.

The Christmas schedule would see three games played in three days. On Christmas Day a bumper 30,000 crowd watched as City played host to Fulham. Some reports put the attendance as higher; there was just no way of knowing. In every part of the stadium, people were wedged in and at one point the railings gave way down the touchline of the pitch, but no one was injured and play was not disrupted. Meanwhile, Ivan Sharpe was on top form, and it was his cross that led to the first goal by Billy McLeod on 22 minutes. Five minutes before half-time John Hampson scored City's second and despite

Sharpe having a penalty kick saved Leeds won the points with a 2-1 win.

The following day, Boxing Day, saw City travel down to London for the return match with Fulham at Craven Cottage in front of 25,000 spectators. The game was extremely close, but when Sharpe's cross found the head of Billy McLeod in the six-yard box, it was 1-0 to Leeds with less than 20 minutes to go. That's how it remained, but the result of this game would be overshadowed by controversy.

Apparently, City had not been able to immediately pay Fulham their cut from the Christmas Day game, so Fulham retaliated by withholding Leeds' share for the game at Craven Cottage. Both clubs reported each other and so a Football League management committee had to pass judgement. City reported that there had been a tram strike on Christmas Day and as a consequence many supporters had been delayed. There were no police to stop them rushing into the ground and as a result the club had to take admission money on account. The committee were satisfied that City had acted in good faith and the club were let off with a verbal warning for not taking money at the gate. Fulham were ordered to pay the £20 4s 10d (approx. £20.30) to City from the Boxing Day gate, plus three guineas (approx. £3.15).

According to the minutes of the meeting, 'The committee desire it to be known that while approving the course adopted by Leeds City Football Club, under the exceptional circumstances, they do not approve of money being taken except through the regular and usual turnstiles and in the usual manner. Any departure from this course must be regarded with suspicion whether the gate is being pooled or not, and clubs in their own interests as well as evidence of honesty ought not to be parties thereto.'

The day after the Boxing Day game Leeds lined up away at Glossop, who proved to be much more difficult opponents, as they had been on the opening day of the season at Elland Road. City had to come from behind to salvage a point thanks to a goal by Bainbridge. The dropping of that point meant that City slipped to fourth in the table, but only a point behind Hull City who were top, Notts County and Arsenal, who were all on 28 points, but City had games in hand on all three teams. As the year drew to a close, it was clear to them and their supporters that securing promotion was definitely a possibility.

And City began the New Year with a 5-1 demolition of Stockport County at Elland Road. Three goals up after just a quarter of an hour, City went in at half-time five goals to the good. John Jackson had bagged his first goal for the club, and then a second; Jimmy Speirs found the net, as did Billy McLeod and Ivan Sharpe. City conceded a goal to Stockport in the second half, but the *Leeds Mercury* noted: 'The forwards did not exert themselves too much in the second half as they were evidently satisfied with the formidable lead they had gained in the first half.'

In the FA Cup the following week, City swept aside Gainsborough Trinity 4-2, with Jackson getting another brace, in a fine, hard-fought, 4-2 win. The game had been scheduled to be played at Gainsborough, who had agreed to waive their right to stage the game at home after City guaranteed them a payment of £500, assuming there would be a decent crowd in Yorkshire. But an eventual crowd of 14,000 provided receipts of just £520.

The next round of the FA Cup gave City a chance to pit their wits against one of the finest clubs in the country, West Bromwich Albion, winners of the cup twice in the 1890s. West Brom's captain was England left-back Jesse Pennington, who earlier in the season had helped detectives in a match-fixing controversy. A man called into Pennington's shop in Smethwick in November, and introduced himself as Sam Johnson. He immediately asked Pennington if it would be possible to fix the outcome of Albion's upcoming match with Everton, for a fee of £55: £5 per man. Johnson wanted a draw or an Albion defeat, and agreed to pay Pennington after the game, and signed a memorandum to that effect.

Pennington then told his chairman and the police and showed them the evidence. After a 1-1 draw between Everton and Albion, which was not planned as the rest of Albion's players were unaware of the arrangement, Johnson, whose real name was divulged as Pascoe Bioletti, arrived at the shop to pay Pennington. He was greeted by detectives who also found him in possession of a book of betting slips for a £1,500 bet he had placed on the game. Bioletti was arrested, charged and received a five-month prison sentence on top of a six-month sentence for trying to bribe Birmingham full-back Frank Womack in a similar incident. It transpired that Bioletti was the father of William Alfred Bioletti, who operated a similar scheme in Geneva under the guise of White Fisher, issuing thousands of circulars, inviting ordinary gullible people to back certain teams, offering very good odds.

Meanwhile, Pennington shook hands with City's Jimmy Speirs and the cup tie at Elland Road got under way. A crowd of just under 30,000 watched a very tight game between two evenly matched sides, which finally went the way of the visitors with two late goals from Albion's Bentley and Jepcott. More worrying for City, however, was their loss of form in league games. Nestled around the West Brom cup game, City lost three consecutive league games, the heaviest being the last one, a 5-1 thumping at Leicester Fosse. It was a surprising result, as the *Yorkshire Evening Post* noted on 9 February: 'Soccer is in a bad way at Leicester at present. Fosse have been doing badly, and in six league games since Christmas they had lost five and drawn one, losing at home to Blackpool and Woolwich Arsenal. As the club needed funds, they recently sold Clay and Sparrow to Woolwich Arsenal, and this incensed the majority of Fosse fans.

'The visit of Leeds City attracted no more than 4,000 spectators. Fosse were expected to get another licking, but to the great delight of the crowd, the players gave one of their best displays of the season and won with ridiculous ease. It was a remarkable game in many respects, and the scoring was curious. Leeds City appeared to derive a great advantage by winning the toss, for there was a very strong wind blowing almost from goal to goal. The Fosse, however, took the lead eight minutes after the start, and 20 minutes later they got two more in rapid succession, and thus made the issue practically certain. Leeds City never looked like saving the match. They reduced the lead of the Fosse with 15 minutes to go, through Jimmy Speirs, but Fosse fully held their own for the remainder of the game and scored two more goals in the last five minutes. The result flatters Fosse considerably, for they are not a strong side. They are mostly young players and under ordinary circumstances Leeds City should have beaten them comfortably. But Leeds City are demoralised at present. They touched zero on Saturday and gave a very poor account of themselves. There was not one man on the side who played up to form with the possible exception of Croot, who filled the outside-left position through Ivan Sharpe being engaged in the amateur international at Plymouth. Croot played with plenty of dash, but all the other members of the team appeared to be demoralised and could do little right. It certainly seemed a risky experiment by Chapman in playing Jackson on the right wing. He was never comfortable in that position and before half-time he returned to his old place at inside-right, Price going out on the wing. The forward line was disjointed all through the piece.'

Despite losing, City still retained fifth place, but were now six points off the promotion spots.

Their Jekyll and Hyde like scenario continued, however, as City put their season back on track a week later, with a 5-0 thrashing of Wolverhampton Wanderers at Elland Road, Billy McLeod recording a hat-trick, Jimmy Speirs and Ivan Sharpe chipping in with the other two goals. Other results, apart from leaders Notts County, who won at Glossop, went in City's favour: Woolwich Arsenal, Bradford Park Avenue, Hull City and Bury all lost and Fulham could only draw at Blackpool.

In an attempt to further strengthen, their team and their league position, Chapman paid Huddersfield Town in the region of £1,000 for Fred Blackman, who the local press had described as 'one of the best full-backs in the Second Division' and 'possibly the most stylish and polished back in the Second Division'. However, tragic news hit the Elland Road club.

After a short illness, chairman Norris Hepworth died. He had been chief benefactor at the club since its formation and his generosity was legendary. It was said that at the time of Mr Norris's death, the club's debt to him was around £18,000. The funeral was held at Lawnswood Cemetery on 20 February and was attended by many representatives of the club. Directors J. W. Bromley, J. C. Whiteman and A. W. Pullin were joined by manager Herbert Chapman. Among the players present were, Billy McLeod, Fred Croot, Jimmy Speirs and George Law. Tom Coombs and his wife were also present, as were representatives of J. Norris and Son clothing firm.

The following day, City travelled to Hull and suffered a 1-0 defeat. Charlie Copeland had been replaced by new recruit Fred Blackman at right-back, and despite the defeat he was seen as a good addition to the team. On 23 February, the *Leeds Mercury* said this of him: 'He was the outstanding man on the Leeds City side, he showed us on Saturday that he never gets flurried no matter how tight the corner he gets into. There is no force about him, and no hurry. He is one of the coolest backs in the country at the present time ... It may have been Blackman's influence, and it is a fact that Affleck played a fine game on Saturday. City were desperately unlucky to lose, Affleck and Hampson got in each other's way as they jumped for the ball, allowing Stevens to score in off the post.'

This was followed seven days later with a 3-0 home victory over Barnsley, maintaining the usual pattern of inconsistency throughout their season. Three England selectors had been among the 20,000 crowd at Elland Road to take a look at the form of Billy McLeod. He played well, and scored the opening goal after half an hour, a goal disputed by Barnsley who thought McLeod had been offside, but after consulting his linesman, the referee awarded it. Ivan Sharpe scored two, one a penalty, to complete the double over the South Yorkshiremen.

Once again controversy followed City to London, this time against Clapton Orient at Homerton on 2 March 1914. The fixture was set for Monday afternoon with a kick-off time of 4.30pm, to maximise gate receipts. Because there were no floodlights, the game was sure to finish in half darkness. Leeds City did protest against this and the game was moved to a 4.20pm kick off. But then, the officials were late, and a further delay came about when the referee finally arrived; he ordered Scott, in the Leeds goal, to change his jersey, as a league rule of

1909 had stated that the goalkeeper must wear a different coloured jersey to the rest of his team. By the time Scott returned to the field in a different colour jersey, another ten minutes had elapsed. As the game progressed it became increasingly likely that there would not be enough daylight to complete it. Despite the referee only allowing a two-minute interval, the darkness fell quickly and even though the referee had assurances from his linesmen that they could still follow play, it became apparent that the players were having difficulty following the ball. City were 1-0 up thanks to a John Hampson goal, but as the light disappeared, City conceded three goals in quick succession. Scott in goal, deputising for Hogg who was injured, claimed that he could not see the ball for the last two goals. The referee overruled the Leeds keeper's comments and the 3-1 score to Clapton Orient stood.

Herbert Chapman was livid, and complained bitterly to the authorities. City's appeal was recorded in the minutes of the meeting of the Football League management committee on 17 March: 'On behalf of Leeds City it was urged that Clapton Orient fixed the kick-off at an unreasonably late hour of 4.30, notwithstanding a protest by the visiting club that it was too late, that on arriving at the ground they were asked by Clapton Orient to kick off at 4.20, to which they agreed. But the game did not commence until 4.29; that though no interval was taken the game did not finish until 6-7pm; that during the second half the Leeds City players claimed that the light was too bad for football; that the referee himself had considerable doubt as to the light sometime before the end of the game, as he consulted the linesmen; and that it was so dark that when the last two goals were scored by Clapton Orient the goalkeeper and full-backs of Leeds City could not see the ball. The committee decided that there was no rule or precedent entitling them to interfere with result, and therefore the result must stand. The committee were further of the opinion that the time fixed for the kick off was unduly late, and that in consequence the game was played in bad light during the closing minutes. Further, it was clear that Clapton Orient realised that the light was not likely to hold out and shortly before the match suggested an earlier kick-off. Such was contrary to the decisions of the management committee, and the action of the Clapton Orient club in fixing the kick-off so late accounted for all the trouble. The Clapton Orient club, therefore, were fined 25 guineas (approx £26.25) out of which the expenses of Leeds City and the referee and linesmen will be paid.'

The conclusion was of no consolation whatsoever to Leeds City, who had missed out on vital league points, and a week after the Clapton Orient game could only draw at Bury 1-1. For the game at Gigg Lane, Hogg returned between the sticks, Speirs was out injured and other tactical changes were made up front. City should have had two goals inside the first ten minutes, but it was Bury who took the lead – after having a penalty denied for handball by Affleck, they were awarded a penalty when Foley was adjudged to have handled, leaving Perry to convert. Foley made amends a quarter of an hour later, putting Jackson through to score the equaliser. A week later, on 14 March, City destroyed Huddersfield Town, 5-1 in front of a 14,000 Elland Road crowd. Town had dominated the first half hour and taken the lead after ten minutes, but City fought back and Hampson equalised after 30 minutes. Inevitably, Billy McLeod then took charge, putting City ahead just before half-time and in the second half ran away with the game. McLeod completed his hat-trick, and Arthur Price added a fifth for good measure. But the Jekyll and Hyde scenario surrounding City's performances was in evidence yet again just seven days later, and it was beginning to seriously damage their promotion ambitions.

Leeds City arrived at Lincoln City on 21 March confident of victory and of moving further up the table. But, Lincoln, who were struggling near the foot of the division, scored in the first half and that proved to be the winner. However, it could have been even worse for Leeds as the *Yorkshire Evening Post* reported: 'Leeds City were a sadly disappointing team at Lincoln. They were extremely lucky in escaping with such a narrow margin of defeat, for Lincoln City failed to convert a penalty and missed an open goal. Leeds were accompanied by over 1,000 supporters, who could not restrain their disgust at the tame and listless display which their favourites gave.'

The miss of the open goal occurred after Hogg and Affleck both hesitated, allowing Billy Egerton to steal in between them, but with the open net in front of him he unbelievably put the ball wide.

The *Leeds Mercury* said: 'It is now practically certain that Leeds City are not to get promotion this season.'

But, true to form, City bounced back with a victory at Blackpool on 28 March and they seemed to be back in with a chance when the other results of the day revealed defeat for Woolwich Arsenal and only a point for Bradford Park Avenue at Barnsley. The *Yorkshire Post* added: 'Leeds are not the only team among the candidates suffering from staleness just now.' Leeds City's next fixture was at Nottingham Forest, who they had beaten 8-0 previously.

The *Leeds Mercury* said: 'Woolwich Arsenal and Bradford Park Avenue again failed to get on the winning side, but Leeds City lost 2-1 at bottom club Nottingham Forest. Thus they have again greatly jeopardised their chance of promotion. It is perfectly true that they had a certain amount of bad luck in as much as Hampson and Croot each hit the crossbar, but it cannot be said that they were unfortunate to lose.' The *Yorkshire Evening Post* added their findings: 'It appears that once again, Leeds City have shot themselves in the foot.'

Leaders Notts County were without a fixture on Good Friday, 10 April, but the other teams were all in action. City faced a stiff test at Bristol City, a team that had only been beaten once at home all season. They had conceded just eight goals in 11 games at Ashton Gate. Leeds had Speirs back in action after a five-match lay-off with a knee injury. McLeod put City in front after 20 minutes with a fine assist from Foley. But Bristol were on level terms just five minutes later; the score remained at 1-1. Most of the 20,000 crowd were happy, but Speirs had further aggravated his knee injury and needed more treatment.

That injury recurrence forced Speirs to miss the following week's home match against Woolwich Arsenal, a match of great importance to both teams, third against fourth. High, swirling winds enveloped Elland Road, hampering both sides, but City, playing against the wind, were the first to take control, with McLeod and then Price both coming close. Gradually, Arsenal, using the wind to great advantage, got a foothold in the game and pinned City's defence down for long periods. City survived and came out stronger in the second half, even getting the ball over the Arsenal line, only to have it ruled out for what the referee perceived to be a foul on the Arsenal keeper, Lievsley. A second City goal was also ruled out in the dying minutes of the game. Ivan Sharpe appeared to have scored, the ball just crossing the line before Benson kicked it out. Seeing the ball had crossed the line, City players celebrated, but the referee, missing the incident, waved play-on: no goal. The game, which ended 0-0, had also been a benefit match for Fred Croot, City's long serving winger, who received £450 from the gate receipts generated by the 22,500 crowd. The goalless draw, however, had not benefited either Leeds City or Woolwich Arsenal. Notts County had beaten Bury 2-0, to gain promotion as champions; Bradford Park Avenue meanwhile had won, whilst Hull City lost at Wolverhampton. And with a mixture of results on Easter Monday – Bradford lost at Nottingham Forest, Arsenal beat Stockport 3-0 – City had to beat Bristol City at home to have any chance at all of promotion.

Leeds' line-up was once again missing Jimmy Speirs and now John Hampson had joined the injury list. Centre-half Harry Peart was making his debut. After 25 minutes, Neil Turner, who had been drafted in from the reserves, scored the only goal of the game, to give the 12,000 Elland Road crowd a glimmer of hope. Worryingly for City though, Billy McLeod had limped through most of the game, after being kicked by Ware, the Bristol goalkeeper.

The next Leeds City fixture was sure to have bitter connotations. Clapton Orient arrived at Elland Road on 14 April. Because of the events surrounding the corresponding fixture at Orient, and the row over the lack of daylight, several of the home fans offered candles and matches to Orient's goalkeeper, Bower, presumably so he would be able to see the ball. Unfortunately, there was little in the way of humour during the game, which developed into an untidy affair with neither team able to take advantage. Certainly, this would have been one game from which Leeds' players would dearly have loved to get two points.

The draw left City in fourth position, two points behind Bradford Park Avenue and one behind Arsenal. With only two games remaining, promotion was now very much an outside chance for Leeds City.

For the penultimate game of the season at Grimsby Town, Billy McLeod returned after missing the Clapton Orient game through injury and Tommy Lamph made his debut at left-half. A little bit of fortune blew Leeds' way when the strong wind blew a centre straight into the Grimsby net for the only goal of the game. On the same day, Bradford Park Avenue won 3-0 at Lincoln, but Arsenal dropped a point against Orient. City rose to third, but only briefly, as Arsenal then won their game in hand at Grimsby to reclaim third spot.

On the final day of the season, 25 April, Leeds City had 45 points and their two rivals, Bradford and Arsenal, both had 47 points. City had the best goal average of the three teams, but they still needed to beat Birmingham City at home and hope and pray that Arsenal lost at home to Grimsby and that Bradford did the same at home to Blackpool.

Leeds came racing out of the blocks against Birmingham and were one up after ten minutes through Arthur Price after he had been put through by Billy McLeod. However, the visitors equalised, but a determined Leeds City side responded almost immediately when Sampson turned the ball into his own net as he attempted to clear. Then Birmingham equalised a second time through a free kick just before half-time. Yet again Leeds went at the Birmingham defence and minutes into the second half, Jimmy Speirs, back after his knee injury, passed the ball short to Ivan Sharpe who released a fierce shot on the Birmingham goal. The goalkeeper, Hauser, failed to hold the pile-driver and up popped Billy McLeod to score from the rebound. The game remained at 3-2, and all Leeds could do now was wait.

But, Lady Luck, as she would over many years to come, failed to shine on the Leeds club and both Bradford and Arsenal won their respective games, leaving Leeds City in fourth. Looking back over the season, City's poor run in January, the controversial defeat at Clapton Orient, two inexplicable defeats at the bottom two clubs, Nottingham Forest and Lincoln City, certainly hampered the club's progress, but the loss of Jimmy Speirs through injury, proved to be the biggest loss. For nine crucial games during the run-in, Leeds badly missed the intelligence and creativity of Speirs.

The *Yorkshire Post* summed up: 'Promotion has been denied City but taking into account the resources of the club, fourth place should be considered satisfactory. Not only have the club attained a higher position than ever before but receipts and attendances have outstripped any previous record.' The average attendance for the 1912/13 season had been 13,356; by the end of this season it had risen to the region of 17,000.

Leeds City had finished six points behind champions Notts County, but only two behind Bradford Park Avenue and Woolwich Arsenal. Bradford were promoted in second place on goal average over Arsenal. A £10 bonus for each City player for finishing in fourth place was scant reward for a season in which they came so close to achieving their drive for promotion to the First Division.

In summary, Herbert Chapman had recognised the lack of reserves strength as a key weakness: in March he had brought in John Chaplin, former Spurs, Man City and Dundee player, to take overall control of the reserves. Chapman had brought an astonishing turnaround in two seasons with City climbing from struggling in the lower regions of the division to within two points of promotion. City were only defeated at Elland Road twice.

Leeds City supporters carried great expectation for the following season. Herbert Chapman had gone through the summer of 1914 much like any other with his passion for cricket and golf once again dominating the activities involving his players to keep them fit for what promised to be good season. Left-back Jack McQuillan had been recruited from Hull City and a much talked-about acquisition was that of goalkeeper Willis Walker from Doncaster Rovers. With winger Ernie Goodwin joining the ranks from Spennymoor, Chapman was quietly confident of achieving his goal for promotion. But unknown to him, and others, events were unfolding elsewhere in eastern Europe that were to have a profound effect, not just on football, but on the whole world. Never has one bullet led to the death of so many.

Chapter Six

World War One

IN Sarajevo on 28 June 1914, Archduke Franz Ferdinand of Austria was attending a military review with his wife when they were both assassinated by Gavrilo Princip. Nationalist Princip wanted the Austro-Hungarian Empire out of Bosnia. This was the first ripple that cascaded into World War One, or The Great War as it became known back then. Around this time there were a number of different defensive alliances across Europe: Germany was in alliance with Austria-Hungary, Russia with Serbia and France with Russia, whilst Great Britain was in alliance with both France and Russia as well as Belgium. Ferdinand's death was the immediate catalyst for the declaration of war that followed. Austria-Hungary blamed the Serbian Government for the attack on the Archduke and gave a quite unacceptable ultimatum to Serbia. But Serbia refused to accept the demands made to them and Austria-Hungary severed diplomatic relations and immediately declared war on their neighbours. In the event, Austria-Hungary bombarded Belgrade with heavy artillery fire prompting Russia to mobilise. On 31 July, Germany warned Russia to stand down, a threat that was ignored by the Russians and the following day Germany declared war on Russia. In response, France mobilised its forces prompting Germany to attack France via Belgium. Although Britain was less committed to its alliance with France and Russia than the other powers, it had, in 1839, signed a treaty with Belgium which said that it would attack anyone who attacked Belgium. Britain's involvement in the conflict ensued on 14 August 1914 when it declared war on Germany. World War One, despite early indications that it would be over by Christmas, would last for four years, three months and one week. Britain had entered the war without compulsory military service – the only country to do so – but there was absolutely no shortage of volunteers. But as the 1914/15 season approached there was widespread talk of suspending league football for the duration of the conflict; a feeling held vigorously by a very large section of the public and the vast majority of the media.

The suspending of football would allow players and officials alike to volunteer for the war. But amid howls of protest up and down the country, the football authorities made the hugely unpopular decision to proceed as planned with the league schedule despite the angry and patriotic feeling of the public as a whole. The media, also opposed to the plans, declared that they would not report on matches in any form. Letters flooded into the letters' pages of newspapers nationwide. An incensed Mr Croft wrote to the *Hull Evening Telegraph* comparing the Football Association to the Germans, while Mr H. Norris told readers of the *Yorkshire Evening Post*, 'The King should resign as the president of the Football Association.' Mr Potts, in a strong letter to the *Leeds Mercury*, said that 'this should not happen, and I for one shall do everything in my power to see that it doesn't'. Initially, the Football Association stood firmly by its decision and relied heavily on the assumption that the conflict would be over by Christmas. They forced their professional footballers to adhere to their contracts and they could only sign up for the war effort if they were contractually released by their respective clubs. Furthermore, if they refused to honour their contracts, then they would be sued. Then, as tensions reached fever pitch, the Football Association slightly altered their tack and announced that football clubs should release all single, unmarried footballers so that they could join the armed forces if they so wished (over 70,000 footballers joined up). By October 1914 the Football League also announced that 'In the interests of the people of this country, football ought to be continued.' Football Association secretary Fred Wall had announced that legally binding contracts with players, landlords and building contractors rendered any suspension of games in 1914/15 impossible. As league football had begun, amid heavy bombardment and gunfire throughout Europe, newspapers lifted their ban on match reports and although the editions were inevitably dominated by events across Europe, football was covered in the sports pages. Some Leeds City officials and players joined the civilian army, donating 5 per cent of their wages to the national relief fund. The Elland Road ground was commandeered and used for military drill and firing practice. Herbert Chapman bolstered his involvement in the war effort by taking up the role of stores manager at Barnbow Munitions Factory in Crossgates on the outskirts of Leeds, which was dominated by a female workforce. Chapman was in charge of the cartridge department, which detailed the issuing of all explosives, magazines and all aspects of weaponry. Under the circumstances of the war, players found it difficult to concentrate on football and, as a consequence, standards fell; some players became very depressed at having to play in wartime. Gates fell dramatically before the Football League announced a cut of around 15 per cent in wages. Coventry City were the first team to accept the reduction but it was heavily criticised by the Second Division club, claiming that it was unfair in relation to first division players. Leeds City refused to accept the reduction.

Chapman was religious and attended church on a regular basis, and he had signed a church preacher when he signed Evelyn Lintott, a centre-half from Bradford City. Two years after making his Leeds debut at Fulham on 7 September 1912, Lintott joined the 15th Battalion of the West Yorkshire Regiment, better known as the Leeds Pals, being promoted to sergeant a short time later. Having been commissioned – the first professional footballer to do so – Lintott was promoted to lieutenant just before Christmas 1914. On Christmas Eve, on the front line, many German and British troops sang Christmas carols to each other across the lines, and at certain points the Allied soldiers even heard brass bands joining the Germans in their joyous singing. It is reported that at first dawn on Christmas Day, some German soldiers emerged from their trenches and approached the Allied lines across no-man's-land, calling out 'Merry Christmas' in their enemy's native tongue. After first fearing that it was a trick, the Allied soldiers climbed out of their trenches and shook hands with the enemy soldiers. The men then exchanged presents of cigarettes and plum puddings and together they sang carols. It is also said that a football game between the two took place. However, on this very day, Christmas Day, whilst this was going on, Leeds City were playing an away fixture at Glossop. In a 3-0 win, Billy McLeod inevitably scored, but there was a brace from inside-forward John Jackson, who had joined City from Clyde, scoring 12 goals in 58 appearances. And, in fact, during the rest of the war, he played for both Rangers and Celtic.

After being on the Western Front with the Leeds Pals, Evelyn Lintott was with his unit when it became embroiled in fighting for a fortified village called Serre, on 1 July 1916, the opening day of the Somme offensive. Tasked with capturing Serre, they suffered heavy casualties in the attack, losing 222 soldiers, including 13 officers; Lintott was among them. According to Private Spink, who was in Lintott's charge, the officer was struck in the chest and killed by machine gun fire during the advance. This was how the *Yorkshire Evening Post* described that fatality: 'Lieutenant Lintott's end was particularly gallant. Tragically, he was killed leading his platoon of the 15th West Yorkshire Regiment, Leeds Pals, over the top. He led his men with great dash and when hit the first time declined to take the count. Instead, he drew his revolver and called for further effort. Again, he was hit but struggled on but a third shot finally bowled him over. The body of Evelyn Lintott was never recovered and he is commemorated in the Thiepval Memorial to the Missing.'

Despite initially losing Lintott to the forces, new Leeds City signings had bolstered a patched up side and they went on to win the 1914 West Riding Cup, beating Hull City 1-0 thanks to a fine effort by Jimmy Speirs. A crowd of over 1,000 saw a bruising battle between the two sides which saw John Hampson sent off for Leeds.

Another bruising battle was in store for City just two weeks later in a league game at Bury. When the game ended 0-0, the teams were leaving the field when Speirs became involved in a violent argument with a Bury defender, then, as the Leeds players reached their dressing room, they were blocked by a hostile group of Bury fans. Officials eventually cleared a safe a passage through for the players, but both teams reported the referee to the league for 'indifferent refereeing'. Jimmy Speirs had been bought from Bradford City for £1,400; it was something of a coup for Leeds – Speirs had captained Bradford as well as scoring the winning goal in the 1911 FA Cup against Newcastle United. Herbert

Chapman linked him up with marksman Billy McLeod to form a very potent strike force. However, in April 1915 after a 2-0 defeat at home to Barnsley, Speirs left City to return home to Govan in Scotland and signed up for the war with the Queen's Own Cameron Highlanders. After just two months, Private S/18170 Speirs was promoted to lance corporal and posted to the 7th Battalion of the Cameron Highlanders. He was promoted to the rank of corporal a year later, three weeks into the major British offensive north of the River Somme. Speirs was involved in heavy fighting as part of a machine-gun squad on the Somme. He was wounded in his left elbow but after treatment behind the lines, Speirs returned to his unit, and to heavy action during the Battle of Arras, in the spring of 1917. Having sustained significant casualties, the 7th Camerons were finally sent back into reserve to regroup and recover. It was during this period that Jimmy Speirs was recommended and eventually awarded the Military Medal for bravery in the field. Then, after two years of service he became acting-sergeant, then sergeant, before being given home leave, when he would visit his home town of Glasgow and Leeds. During this time, June 1917, Speirs, took part in light pre-season training at Leeds City as his former teammates prepared for the 1917/18 season. Speirs returned to his unit on 12 July. During the first week of August 1917 the British Army launched a major offensive around the Ypres Salient in Belgium. Then on 20 August, the 7th Camerons moved into lines east of St Julien, where they prepared for an attack on a German stronghold at Hill

35. Leaving their trenches at Pommern Redoubt, the battalion made progress only to be held up by heavy machine gun fire. It was here that Jimmy Speirs was killed, but was reported as, 'missing presumed dead'. It wasn't until October 1919 that Jimmy Speirs' wife, Bessie, received news that her husband's body had been found on the battlefield where he had fallen. And it wasn't until the following year, 20 August 1920, that Bessie was informed by the War Office that her husband was now officially recorded as being 'Killed in Action or Died of Wounds on or shortly after 20 August 1917'. On 6 October 1921 Bessie Speirs was informed that her husband's remains had been buried at Dochy Farm Cemetery, north-west of Zonnebeke. To confound Mrs Speirs' grief further, Jimmy's headstone had been incorrectly spelt and it wasn't until 2007 that the headstone was given the correct spelling of Jimmy's name, removing 'Spiers' and replacing it with Speirs.

Another former Leeds City player fought and died in World War One. Gerald Kirk was born in Headingley, Leeds on 14 July 1883, into a wealthy family who owned a great deal of land. In the 1901 census the Kirk family were classed as 'living on their own means'. Kirk was a keen cricketer and tennis player and would go on to become honorary secretary of the Ingleton Conservative Club and of the Ingleton Farmers Association. Kirk only played seven times for City, scoring once, in a 2-2 draw at Leicester Fosse in January 1907; the other goal for City that day was scored, unsurprisingly, by Billy McLeod, who went on to get a season tally of 16. After returning to play for Bradford City, Kirk retired from the game aged 25 and joined the British Army during the first weeks of World War One as a private. He rose to a second lieutenant on 31 January 1915. Kirk sailed for France in February; his unit were the first Territorial unit to be sent overseas. They soon arrived at Bailleul and before too long they moved to the infamous Ypres Salient and on 12 April 1915 the battalion were in the front-line trenches at Polygon Wood. In just five days they lost 14 men and 44 were wounded. The badly battered survivors subsequently moved to St Jean and dug in as Ypres suffered from yet another spell of heavy shelling.

On the afternoon of 22 April 1915, the Germans launched the first gas attack in the history of warfare, at nearby St Julien. It descended on a portion of the front held by French Colonial troops, linked to French North Africa. Terrified by the strange yellow gas that enveloped them, the 'Zouaves' retreated in disarray. Kirk watched as they passed through his own ranks. A Canadian Division managed to plug the gap and checked the ensuing German advance. The following day Kirk's platoon was ordered to support the Canadians, as part of a hastily assembled counter attack. At 1300 hours they moved towards Pilkem and once again dug in. The attack commenced at 1545 and at 1700 the battalion, acting as reserve, joined the fray.

With 'C' company leading, they immediately came under heavy machine gun and rifle fire from three sides. After suffering numerous casualties, they pulled back a couple of hundred yards but with no artillery support, their position was almost hopeless. The colonel in charge witnessed soldiers trying to find cover wherever they could, some behind a pile of manure, but the bullets easily cut through and they were all killed. The colonel made his way to brigade headquarters but was simply told to 'hold his position'. When he returned, he discovered that 'Kirk is seriously wounded'.

The desperate assault had blunted the German attack, but at great cost. Over half the troops involved were killed. The battalion alone lost 26 men and 102 were wounded, one of them gassed. Kirk, leading his platoon forward at Wieltje, was shot through the chest. Badly wounded, he was taken by four of his men to the dressing station behind the lines where he was made as comfortable as possible and he was then the first to be sent off in the motor ambulance. He died the next day at Number 3 Casualty Clearing Station and was buried at Poperinghe Old Military Cemetery. Captain Gerald W. Sharpe wrote: 'He died a noble and gallant death, leading his platoon across an absolute inferno of shot and shell. He was wounded through the chest by a bullet.' Colonel Lord Richard Cavendish said: 'Lieutenant Kirk was severely wounded and died on the night of the following day. He had been mortally wounded when bravely leading his men against a very strong position of the enemy. Although he had been in the Battalion a comparatively short time, he had endeared himself to us all, he will be deeply mourned and long remembered. He had proved himself an extremely efficient officer.' Kirk had died on 24 April 1915; the very day that Jimmy Speirs had played his last game for Leeds City before quitting and joining the armed forces and entering into the war. It was also the last game before all league football was suspended for the duration of the war.

Unfortunately, another former Leeds City player died in battle this same year, whilst with The Thin Red Line. David Murray had been a reliable full-back for City, making 85 appearances and scoring seven goals (six from penalties) between 1905 and 1909. Private S/3845 Murray was killed in action at Flanders, France on 10 December 1915 after his battalion had been sent to the front. He had just turned 33 and is buried in Loos Memorial Cemetery. His guardian and landlady, Mrs Sleight of 13 Garden Street, Mexborough, received his British War and Victory medals.

John Harkins was City's right-half, who made his debut against Blackpool in September 1910 and went on to make 66 appearances. He had joined the Black Watch Regiment – Royal Highlanders, before becoming a professional player, and Middlesbrough bought him out of the Army in 1906. After he left City in 1912, he linked up with his former Leeds manager Frank Scott-Walford at Coventry City. John later joined his old Scottish Regiment as a corporal with F Company, 2nd Battalion and soon found himself dispatched to Basra in Persia (now Iraq) around Christmas 1915. After a ten-day battle with Ottoman forces, the British took Basra. The Black Watch then moved 100 miles north to Amara, and it was here where John Harkins was killed in action on 22 April 1916 – the same day that Leeds City suffered a

2-1 defeat at the hands of Huddersfield in the Midland Section Subsidiary Tournament (Northern Division).

Kathleen Thornton recalls how her great grandad, Cecil, was a big fan of Leeds City: 'He went to a lot of City games, even during the war. My mum told me how he once went on a charabanc to a game in Sheffield and they were stopped by the Army on the way home. Cecil worked at Barnbow Munitions Factory and when the man in charge saw his identity card with his details on, he shook Cecil's hand and thanked him.'

Joe Hargraves was an inside-forward/right-half and had joined Leeds City on 2 September 1905, making 70 appearances. He later joined the British Army as a gunner. He was with the 346th Siege Battery when he was killed in action on 19 October 1917 at Flanders, France. He was laid to rest at the Steenkerke Military Cemetery in Belgium.

Thomas Henry Morris made 109 appearances for City at centre-half from 1909 to 1913. He was the longest serving Leeds City player to die in the World War One. Described as fearless, Tom enlisted in the 2nd Battalion of the Lincolnshire Regiment in 1915, rising to sergeant very quickly. On the night of 18 March 1918, he and his men left the waterlogged trenches of Passchendaele and marched throughout the night to Wieltje, where they joined the 62nd Brigade as part of the 5th Allied Army. The Allies knew that the Germans were set to attack the strategic village of Pozieres, but they had no idea of the huge scale of the invasion. On 21 March gas and explosive shells bombarded the Lincolnshires for four hours as the Germans advanced in thick fog.

The Germans could be seen through the mist carrying stretchers loaded with explosives and ammunition. The British were forced back across the old Somme battlefields by the overwhelming hordes of the German troops and on the last day of fighting Tom Morris, service number 51363, was killed in action at Bapaume on Palm Sunday, 24 March. He is buried at the Pozieres Memorial Cemetery.

Thankfully many of the Leeds City players who served in the war returned. Among them were wartime players such as Simpson Bainbridge, who fought in the Labour Corps 54th Company, Durham Light Infantry and the Lincolnshire Regiment – he made 11 wartime appearances for City, scoring five goals in the process. There was also Richard William Guy, enlisted on 3 March 1908 and signed for Leeds City two months later, making his City debut on the right wing in September, a 2-0 victory over Hull City at Elland Road in front of over 12,000. Norman Holmes fought in the Duke of Cambridge's Own Regiment and the 17th (Service) Football Battalion, He was amongst the first batch to join the conflict in France. But perhaps the most prominent individual in the Football Battalion was a future Leeds United manager. Frank Buckley had fought in the Boer War and in World War One he joined the 17th Middlesex Regiment, then after he was made a major he led the Footballer's Battalion, which consisted of professional footballers.

Major Buckley was seriously wounded when metal shrapnel punctured his lungs. He could never play football again, but he soon returned to the front line and was mentioned in dispatches for his incredible bravery displayed in hand-to-hand combat, but once the Germans released more poison gas, the major's lungs were unable to cope and he was sent home.

Many hundreds of Leeds civilians also fought in the war. William Boynton Butler of Armley, Leeds, was just 22 when he tackled a live shell that had dropped at his feet in a French trench in August 1917. Private Butler, of the West Yorkshire Regiment, grabbed the shell and tried to get rid of it, but at that moment a party of infantry were passing. He shouted at them to hurry past as the shell was going off. He then turned round, placing himself between the party of men and the live shell. He held it until they were out of danger. He then threw the shell out of the trench and took cover, but the shell had exploded almost as it left his hand. It badly damaged the trench, but William escaped with little more than bruising. In December 1917, William was presented with the Victoria Cross by King George V at Buckingham Palace. His citation read: 'Undoubtedly his great presence of mind and disregard for his own life saved the lives of the other men in emplacement and the party which was passing at the time.' On his return to Leeds, William was given a civic reception at Leeds Town Hall and he was given a gold medal by the people of Leeds. William returned to France and survived the war. He died in 1972, aged 78. And in 2017 to mark the centenary of his heroic deed, a commemorative paving stone was laid at Hunslet War Memorial close to his grave in Hunslet Cemetery.

Triplets from Burley all enlisted for the Army in October 1917 and all were accepted. John, James and Thomas Colick were all 6ft and broadly built. They came from a military family; their father, Thomas, enlisted in the Royal Garrison Artillery as a youth and served in the Boer War. His wife went out with him as a lady's maid to General Trotter and the three lads, who were the first children of the marriage, were born in Cape Town. After leaving the army, Mr Colick joined the Leeds Police Force and they had three more children, two boys and a girl. Thomas then served for three years in World War One before being discharged.

The last British soldier to lose his life in action in World War One came from Leeds. George Edwin Ellison fell to his fateful doom on the quagmire of the Western Front knowing that he gave his life for freedom, for his King and for his country. In a cruel twist of fate George died just 90 minutes before the Armistice was called and made the ultimate sacrifice while on patrol on the outskirts of Belgium. He was the last of 886,000 British military personnel to lose their lives in one of the nation's deadliest campaigns. Born in 1876, it is reported that he attended some early Leeds City games with his older brother Frederick. Ellison was working as a barman in a Hartlepool pub when he decided to join the army and the 5th Royal Irish Lancers in 1902. At the start of the war in the summer of 1914 he was one of the 120,000 strong British expeditionary force that was shipped to France. He fought in the Battle of Mons in 1914 and also the Battle of Ypres, the Battle of

Armentieres, Battle of La Bassee, Battle of Lens, Battle of Loos and the Battle of Cambrai. Ellison's squadron of the Lancers were vitally important to the Allies, acting as scouts. At the end of the war, as things opened up, the Lancers, a cavalry regiment, were attached to the Canadian Corps to act as scouts for their advance into Belgium. On the morning of 11 November 1918 Ellison was ordered to advance through Mons and over the canal to secure high ground around the village of St Denis. At around 9.30am Ellison was shot and killed by a German sniper as he crossed the canal. It was such a senseless killing considering that it was pretty common knowledge that they were on the cusp of peace, and despite continuing to push the Germans back, most were generally keeping their heads down. Ellison's grave is situated in the St Symporien Military Cemetery, just south-east of Mons in Belgium. He was 40 years old at the time of his death, and it was just five days short of his son James' fifth birthday.

The first British soldier to have been killed in the conflict was 16-year-old John Parr from London, and he died in very similar circumstances to Ellison. They were both crossing a canal when they were struck, but even more remarkable is where their respective graves stand. The cemetery at St Symporien is surrounded by pine trees and Japanese maples. Ellison's remains had been brought there from a field grave by the British in the 1920s; there was no knowledge at the time of the significance of the plot opposite. Just a few yards of turf stand between the graves of John Parr and George Ellison.

Several guest players had played for Leeds City during wartime and the dispersal of players could in fairness have been a lot worse. Wartime guest players had included Charlie Buchan of Arsenal, Clem Stephenson and Jimmy Stephenson of Aston Villa had made 91 and 36 appearances respectively, but the one guest player that attracted the most attention was undoubtedly Fanny Walden of Tottenham Hotspur. After Jimmy Speirs' departure, Walden offered his services to Leeds City, a decision that enraged his club Tottenham, who protested to the league only to be told that under wartime regulations, it was perfectly in order. Tottenham continued to protest but Walden, who was working in the Leeds area at a motor engineers, made his Leeds debut at Derby County, a 3-1 win, on the opening day of the 1915/16 season – a season in which he played in every single game, including a 7-1 win over Barnsley and a 4-1 home win over Derby, Walden grabbing one of the goals. Fanny Walden was one of Herbert Chapman's earliest discoveries whilst he was manager of Northampton Town. He was just over 5ft tall and a very quick outside-right. His real name was Frederick – Fanny being his nickname due to his 'dainty physique'. On one occasion whilst playing for Chapman's Northampton, Walden was initially refused entry to an away game with his teammates by an official who thought he was a young boy! During the war Fanny served in the Royal Navy Volunteer Reserve as well as the Royal Air Force. After returning to Tottenham after the war and finally coming to the end of his football career, he played cricket for

Northamptonshire before becoming an international cricket umpire. Herbert Chapman had been delighted to secure the services of a player he had long admired, albeit 'on loan'.

During the war, ace marksman Billy McLeod had worked in a local engineering factory supplying parts for the war effort, and Wilson Wainwright worked in a nearby khaki factory. While working at a factory in Hull, Jack McQuillan had his playing career cut short when a grinding machine he was operating exploded. In the middle of the war, just before the beginning of the 1915/16 season, the *Leeds Mercury*, 3 August, reported that the Leeds Rugby League Club was considering 'the question of purchasing the Leeds City Club lock, stock and barrel and transferring it to Headingley'. It caused quite a stir across the city of Leeds. The *Mercury* said: 'The rumour of a proposed transference of the Leeds City Association Football Club from Elland Road to Headingley has caused a sensation in Leeds soccer and Northern Union circles.

'The management of the City club has long been in the hands of Mr Herbert Chapman and Mr Tom Coombs, the Official Liquidator. Second Division of the League is not as great an asset as it once was. When the war is over, and professional football is resumed, however, the league membership will be valuable again, and the players will be an asset again, though not as great an asset as they were. The position as far as the Headingley group is concerned is to buy Leeds City's fixtures at Elland Road, stands etc, if they were to take them and get the league rights to the players on Leeds City's books, plus of course, the position in the Second Division of the league – if the league sanctions the transfer. Given the necessary sanction, the Northern Union game would be banished from Headingley, and soccer would be played instead.

'The Elland Road ground would become waste land, for the time being, and its future would be a matter of doubt. People may ask, "What about the Leeds City shareholders?" The answer to that is, in the circumstances, the Leeds City shareholders don't exist, they have lost their money. And they have no legal right to say a word concerning the future of the club. Fortunately for them there is a distinct chance that the management committee of the league would take the view that the Leeds City shareholders have some moral right in the matter, and they may ask the Liquidator to call a meeting of the old shareholders and ask for their views before disposing of the club to anyone.'

On 4 August, a public notice had appeared in several newspapers announcing an 'Important meeting to be held next week – We are informed that at the request of the Football League Management Committee a meeting of the shareholders of the Leeds City Football Club is being called for Monday next. The meeting which is in connection with the proposal for change of ground, and other schemes affecting the continuity of the City Club and alleged negotiations with the Leeds Northern Union Club, is to be held in the Young Men's Christian Association's Rooms, Albion Place Leeds. At 8pm on the day named.' This Leeds City shareholder wrote to the *Mercury*: 'Sir- The proposed removal of soccer to Headingley cannot be the wish of the thousands of enthusiasts in Holbeck, Hunslet, Armley and Morley, who have supported the club, and will wish to do so again when the times are normal. Who, then, wishes to take soccer to Headingley?

'It cannot be the Northern Unionists, who say they have a better game and seem quite happy and successful. Let all Leeds City shareholders make every endeavour to be present at the meeting which has been called through the press, instead of the usual seven days' notice by letter. They have put their money down and had it thrown away to the mismanagement of the club in its early days. Let them now protest to the English League management committee to see if they will support public opinion against private interests.'

The *Mercury* article continued: 'The Liquidator need not call such a meeting unless he chooses, but his refusal to do so might be followed by a refusal of the management committee of the league to sanction the transfer of the club. In that case the Leeds City club would still exist, but membership of the league would be gone, and it would have no claim to transfer rights in the players.

'It appears that, apart from the Headingley suggestion, there is another scheme afoot to save the Leeds City Club. Several Leeds sportsmen, who desire to see City take their place eventually in the First Division, have offered to buy the Liquidator out at the assessed value of the team and the position in the league. They have offered, it is said, to lease the Elland Road ground with an option to purchase the ground during the next ten years. Compulsory purchase of the ground at the end of ten years has been suggested to them by the Liquidator, but they are not prepared to bind themselves to that in the present, unsettling state of affairs. So far, the offer of these Leeds sportsmen has not been accepted. Apparently, in view of the attitude of the management committee of the league, the old shareholders of the club can play a very large part in settling the future of the club. It should be understood that the management committee can refuse to allow the Leeds City headquarters to be removed from Elland Road to Headingley so long as Leeds City remain members of their body.

'If the shareholders say they do not like the suggested Headingley deal, then it is extremely likely that the committee will insist that if Leeds City wish to play Second Division football when the war is over it must be played at Elland Road. Out of all this arises the question of the views of two sets of supporters, the soccer enthusiasts who with their sixpences have helped build up Leeds City and the Elland Road ground and the rugby followers, who have kept the Northern Union flag flying at Headingley.

'Given a transfer to Headingley, the Leeds City supporters would doubtless be inconvenienced to a considerable extent, while the Northern Union people would be forced to become converts to soccer, something that a great number would refuse to do. Mr J. Connor, president of the West Riding Football Association is entirely opposed to the scheme, which he considers unfair to the supporters of both clubs. He asks if the sporting public of Beeston, Holbeck, Hunslet and Morley, who have been the principal supporters of City, are not to be considered? He would like to see Leeds City and Leeds Northern Union clubs make progress in their respective codes. It would be detrimental to sport to allow one club to sink simply to bolster up the rival code. It would be ridiculous to have only one first class club running in Leeds when football comes to its own again. Mr J. W. Ward, a prominent Yorkshire Northern Union official, regards the scheme as a rash one, seeing that the football section of the Leeds Club is the only section that has made a profit. He is of the opinion that if the scheme is carried out it would mean the ruin of the Headingley ground. "For the moment I would prefer not to go into details" remarked Mr H. Chapman, secretary-manager of the Leeds City Club, "as it is my duty to state the position of affairs to the City club's shareholders at a meeting to be called in the next few days. I shall then be able to give details of the whole proceedings.'"

Luckily for supporters of both the soccer and rugby codes, the ill-thought out plan was thwarted. Joseph Connor had formed a syndicate with J. C. Whiteman, Sam Glover, George Sykes and W. H. Platts. At a special meeting, an agreement was thrashed out with Tom Coombs. The liquidator of Leeds City would sell all assets of the club to the syndicate. In view of the fact that a meeting had been called for the proposed transfer to Headingley, it came as a surprise, albeit a pleasant one to the supporters of both codes. It was also welcome news for the 400 Leeds City shareholders, who represented a capital of around £5,000 in the club, attending the meeting. The general opinion at the meeting was one of appreciation for the syndicate and the overall feeling that the continuance of soccer at Elland Road would be instrumental in furthering the association code in Leeds. Mr Coombs, who presided, said the object of convening the meeting was to place the position of affairs before the Leeds City shareholders. For some time, Coombs had been acting as Receiver and manager on behalf of the debenture holders of the company, as well as the liquidator of the company. About 12 months prior, the club had looked healthy and in a good position, but soon after the 1913/14 season, the country had been plunged into the so-called greatest war of all time. Most likely, Coombs said, there was nothing in the country which had such a serious financial element of business in it as football that had suffered to the same extent, and when the previous season's programme – which had to be carried out – was completed, Coombs stated that he could not act in the capacity of Receiver and manager and to continue the club as a business. He had been endeavouring to dispose of the assets of the club on behalf of the debenture holders with the result that he previously had entered into an agreement for the disposal of those assets.

The shareholders of the club were at liberty to take up the same position as the proposed purchasers under that agreement, that they were prepared to undertake the same obligations and pay the same price as those who had formed the syndicate were preparing to undertake. The shareholders could not have the assets under different conditions or on any better terms, and subject to the approval of the management committee of the English League they could enter into possession at once. The undertaking which the syndicate had entered into was that the management and other current expenses should be taken over immediately. As to the responsibility of the club which had been undertaken by the syndicate, Mr Coombs said the first was the payment of £1,000 unconditionally. Then there was a payment of £250 conditionally upon that amount of money being received by them in respect of the transfer fees of players, who were at the present time on the retail or transfer list of the club.

The syndicate were to undertake all management expenses from the date of the purchase and any existing agreements between the club and the secretary-manager, or between the club and any other clubs in reference to provisional transfers. To lease the ground for a period of five years certain, with an option of a further five years at a rental of £250 a year, and to give satisfactory personal guarantees for the payment of the rent for the first period of five years, with an option to purchase at a price of £5,000. Mr Alf Masser, the Leeds City Alderman and solicitor then appealed to the shareholders to come forward and help the City club, which he stated, had suffered from an initiation owing to being governed by an aristocratic body instead of a democratic one.

The shareholders were, to some extent, to blame for the position the club were in at that time, and it would have been a calamity had the association code been allowed to go to Headingley. Mr Masser said he was glad that the management committee of the Football League had insisted that the old shareholders of the club must be consulted before any transfer could take place, an action which was approved by all sportsmen. He was prepared, he added, to go to £50 or even more, towards the raising of £5,000. Mr Joseph Connor, who was loudly cheered, said when he and his colleagues had approached Mr Coombs with the object of taking over the affairs of the Leeds City club, they did so for the good of the association code, and they had no intention of making any money out of professional football. Mr Connor was then loudly cheered and received more loud applause. He was of the opinion that football ought to take a back seat at the present time, but he hoped that when the war was over, and football came to its own again, that Leeds City would be a successful organisation. A resolution was passed to the effect that the purchase made by the syndicate be confirmed and thanks be accorded to Mr J. Connor and his colleagues for the timely steps they had taken in saving the Leeds City club. For the rest of the war, Leeds City played four seasons in the Midland Section Principal Tournament and the Northern Division of the Midland Section Subsidiary Tournament.

The club used a combination of Leeds City players and 54 war guest players from other clubs as well as the Army; perhaps the pick of these guest players was the much talked about right-winger Fred 'Fanny' Walden from Tottenham Hotspur who played in every game of the 1915/16 season, and was a revelation. A big favourite of Chapman's, the diminutive Fanny mesmerised the crowds with his tantalising displays and the supporters could only wish he was one of their own. City finished tenth in the Principal Tournament, but at the end topped the Subsidiary Tournament. The following season City won the Principal Tournament and reached seventh in the Subsidiary. For the 1917/18 season City finished in fifth position in the Subsidiary and won the Principal for the second consecutive season. Jack Peart of Notts County played at centre-forward in every game, notching up 19 goals. Charlie Buchan of Arsenal made a guest appearance for City, scoring in a 2-0 home victory over Nottingham Forest on 2 February. For this season, the Football League decided that the winners of the Lancashire and Midland sections should play each other over two legs for the privilege of being crowned unofficial league champions. As the winners of the Midland section, City played Stoke City, who had pipped Liverpool for the Lancashire title. The first leg was played at Elland Road on 4 May in front of 15,675 spectators. Billy Hibbert of Newcastle scored along with Jack Peart to take a 2-0 lead into the second leg at Stoke a week later. Leeds had been without Aston Villa's Clem Stephenson, who had starred at inside-right for City in all but a handful of games all season; he had been called away on military service.

The *Leeds Mercury* reported on the game: 'A healthy crowd turned up at Elland Road for this intriguing battle. City had earned the right to participate by winning the Midland Section Principal Tournament. The City were able to take a two-goal advantage for their trip south next week, where they are sure to be followed by a large Leeds contingent of followers.' An estimated 2,000 Leeds supporters saw Leeds lose the second leg 1-0, a very controversial penalty ten minutes from time, but become the wartime league champions of 1917/18. And although Football League president John McKenna congratulated Leeds City on 'the crowning achievement of a season's strenuous and successful football', City's triumph would remain unmarked in the official records of the Football League.

As World War One finally came to an end, City had begun their final war season on 8 November 1918, welcoming back most of their players with a 4-1 home win over Notts County, with County's own Jack Peart scoring for City, added to one from Newcastle's Billy Hibbert and a brace from Rotherham's Tom Cawley. City ended a successful four war seasons with a 3-1 home win over Coventry, McLeod, Peart and Hall scoring to finish fourth in the Principal Tournament. Two goals from Billy McLeod and one from Simpson Bainbridge in a 3-0 win at Elland Road over Bradford City saw Leeds finish third in the Subsidiary Tournament. With Herbert Chapman returning full time from his war work at Barnbow, Leeds City could look forward to resuming league football for the 1919/20 season with great expectation – but whilst World War One was raging, ongoing events at Elland Road had been worthy of a blockbusting movie, and as the players and good citizens of Leeds returned from military service, the Leeds club was about to be rocked to its very foundations.

Chapter Seven

Blackmail and Skulduggery

T HE seeds of what would ultimately kill Leeds City were sown in 1916 when Herbert Chapman quit his job at the club to take over a managerial position at the Barnbow Munitions Factory as part of the war effort. He recommended that his assistant, George Cripps, take over the administrative running of the club but this proved to be a far from popular decision with the players. Chairman Joseph Connor became extremely unhappy with the way in which Cripps was managing the club's books and the club fell into financial difficulties. Cripps was relieved of his accounting duties but was kept on at the club to manage the team. Connor notified the Football League of the financial problems that had been brought about by Cripps' book-keeping, but the club was urged to continue by the league's chairman, John McKenna. Born in Glaslough in Ireland in 1855, McKenna forged out a distinguished career in sport. An ex-professional rugby player, he became Liverpool's first ever manager in 1906, despite being an Everton fan. He had become president of the Football League in 1917 after being chairman. He had a reputation for being fair and understanding as well as being an active Freemason. McKenna served his country as a sergeant major in the 4th Lancashire Artillery Volunteers. He was also vice-president of the Football Association and president of the Central League, devised for clubs' reserve teams.

Meanwhile, though, George Cripps remained at the club in spite of the fact that his relationship with Connor had deteriorated and he had become so unpopular with the team that they threatened to go on strike. The club captain, John Hampson, delivered a letter to the directors stating that if Cripps was allowed to travel with the team for the next match, at Nottingham, then the team would go on strike. Connor managed to persuade Hampson to not carry out their action as it could damage the whole club. Cripps was allowed to travel, but the atmosphere was frosty to say the least. Cripps didn't go into the Leeds dressing room beforehand, or afterwards for that matter. It has been reported that he merely isolated himself.

On the field at Nottingham, the City players were admirable; Leeds won the match, a Midland Principal Tournament game, 1-0, as reported by the *Leeds Mercury* on 11 February 1918: 'At the City Ground, both sides exhibited pace and enthusiasm and while the wind made the ball difficult to control, some brilliant football was displayed. The winning of the toss made all the difference to Leeds; they had the wind behind them, John Hampson made a brilliant solo run to finish with a centre which left Stephenson in possession of half a dozen yards from Johnson. Finding himself covered, however, by Jones, the inside-right deftly touched the ball back to guest player Jack Peart, who found the mark with an irresistible shot. Twice later Peart had possible openings, but he was carefully shadowed by Wightman.

'Once, however, he was only inches wide with a flying header. Forest had more of the game towards the interval, but the City defence allowed them no room. Forest had to fight every inch of the ground, and the only time Hampson in Leeds' goal was troubled was at the end of a sparkling shot from Burton. Peart led the attack wonderfully well, and Stephenson was a great assistant. Both wingers were difficult to hold, but City's real strength was at half-back and full-back. Both defences, in fact, were magnificent. Leeds, however, always held a distinct advantage because of their superior attack. Towards the end Forest rallied with vigour, and it was then that full-back Hewison and company were seen at their best. Hewison was only just checked in time by Millership on one occasion and while Forest's appeal for a penalty was in vain, the honours were worthily won by a fine side.' The coach ride home was buoyant for the players, but it was reported that Cripps remained silent throughout.

At the end of the war, Chapman had returned to the club and was reinstated into his position as manager, with

Cripps being demoted back to his work as his assistant. Cripps was furious with this, and contacted his solicitor James Bromley, a former director of the club, with regards to suing the club for wrongful dismissal. The situation became edgy as the Leeds directors appointed a solicitor, Alderman William Clarke, and during a meeting at the solicitor's offices in the shadow of Leeds Town Hall on South Parade, a so-called agreement was thrashed out between the two parties. Cripps had also charged the club with paying illegal sums to wartime guest players and he supplied evidence to Mr Bromley to support this. Cripps then made a claim against the directors of Leeds City for the sum of £400. City, however, insisted that Cripps give up his cheque book, passbook and all correspondence and documents relating to these club matters, including letters to and from various players. Furthermore, they demanded that all this quite possibly incriminating evidence be sealed in a safe at the Alderman's office under lock and key and not be disclosed. Joseph Connor also asked for a written undertaking from Cripps that he would not disclose any of the club's affairs. A £55 settlement, far short of the initial £400, was paid for Cripps' silence.

According to James Bromley, he then handed over the documents given to him by Cripps to Alderman Clarke to be held in trust and not to be revealed or parted with without the consent of himself and Connor. In addition, one of the conditions of the handing over of the bundle of documents was that City directors make a donation of £50 to Leeds Infirmary. Bromley had asked for a receipt for this donation but was told by Alderman Clarke that Joseph Connor declined to discuss the affairs of Leeds City with him. Since George Cripps had promised not to mention the unlawful payments, and with all the evidence now under lock and key, it seemed to be the end of the matter; but there was another fateful twist in the tale. After the end of the 1918/19 season Charlie Copeland's contract was up for renewal. Copeland had been at the club since November 1912, one of Chapman's first signings, and made his debut against Glossop at Elland Road on 9 November.

Copeland had been a steady servant for the club as a reliable right-back but had recently found himself ousted by the new arrival from Huddersfield Town, Fred Blackman, in February 1914. After Blackman enlisted, Copeland made a comeback in 1915, making 53 wartime appearances. But his appearances once again became infrequent as Copeland was expected to play reserve to Harry Millership, who had arrived from Blackpool, making his City debut against his former club in the first game of the season on 30 August 1919. Before the war Copeland received £3 a week with a £1 increase when he played in the first team. The board had now offered Copeland £3 10s (£3.50) a week for playing in the reserves, and considerably more if he played in the first team. But Copeland demanded £6 and then rocked the directors by claiming he knew of the illegal payments to certain wartime players, and furthermore if his wage demands weren't met, he would report the club to both the Football Association and the Football League. To compound matters even further for City, Copeland said he would employ the services of a certain James Bromley – the same solicitor used by George Cripps – to fight his corner. The only word that could describe these events is blackmail, but Leeds City called Copeland's bluff and gave him a free transfer to Coventry City, who had made enquiries for the full-back two months earlier. Copeland said he had the knowledge of certain documents that would prove his claim against the club and in July 1919 he carried out his threat, reporting City to the authorities. Later, Copeland would deny passing on the information, but the club were certain in their own minds that Bromley had supplied Copeland with the evidence.

Bromley defended Copeland by telling the club that he had served them throughout the war on the promise that his wages would be increased after restrictions were lifted. Copeland said he had asked the directors for a meeting but they had refused and so Copeland put matters in the hands of his solicitor, James Bromley. At the Football Association headquarters, they studied Copeland's evidence carefully, the Football League did likewise, and consequently a joint inquiry was put in place. Chairing the commission was Yorkshireman J. C. Clegg.

Sir John Charles Clegg had been a Sheffield United player (and captain) when they had played neighbours Sheffield Wednesday for the first ever floodlit game on 15 October 1878, watched by 20,000 spectators. Clegg also played for England in their first ever international against Scotland on 30 November 1872. A strict teetotaller, Clegg was a non-smoker, who detested people drinking before a game and disliked gambling intensely. He was known, however, for his wit. He once chaired a disciplinary meeting where a player was up before him on a charge of ungentlemanly remarks towards a referee. When asked by Clegg what he'd actually said, the player replied, 'Well, I said "I've shit better referees."' Clegg thought for a moment before saying, 'I'll give you a week to do just that, but if you can't then I'm afraid you'll have to pay a £1 fine.' The outcome of this little exercise is unknown.

After a brief meeting, the commission, which consisted of 12 members of the Football Association and the Football League as well as an international selection committee, agreed unanimously that the Leeds City club had charges to answer to and summoned them to appear before them on 26 September 1919. Alderman William Clarke, representing Leeds City, was asked to bring along the books for inspection by the committee. When the City delegation arrived, including Joseph Connor, they were asked to produce the club's books and accounts for the years 1916 to 1918. Connor looked across at Alderman Clarke, who said, 'I'm sorry, it is not within my power to do so.'

Earlier, James Bromley had indicated that he was willing for the documents to be shown to the inquiry, but the Leeds syndicate could not agree to this. In their eyes, and with some justification, it would betray the legal agreement drawn up in the Leeds office of Alderman William Clarke. Even taking into account the humorous wit of J. C. Clegg, this proved totally unacceptable to the commission and City were given just two weeks to produce the books, or face the consequences.

Despite the proceedings hanging over the club, and the dark clouds of subterfuge and conspiracy circling above Elland Road, the team began the 1919/20 season away at Bloomfield Road, Blackpool. That morning the *Yorkshire Post* said: 'Leeds City open their season with a visit to Blackpool, where a good test should be forthcoming of the material which the club's new manager Mr R. Hewison, has been able to get together. It has seldom been easy for Leeds City to hold their own on the wind-swept Blackpool ground; one can only wish them success there now.' The *Leeds Mercury* said: 'Troubles never come slightly and Leeds City are experiencing the fore of this. The announcement of the Football Association inquiry into the management of the team during the war takes place today and was a damper on the officials and players alike, though the authorities aver they have an answer to the charges.' The Leeds City players travelled by train to Blackpool and they won't have travelled with too much enthusiasm, and the discomforts of a long and hard journey on a crowded carriage will not have helped lift their spirits, or indeed helped with preparation for the opening game of the season.

The weather in the seaside town was glorious and the crowd of over 10,000, Blackpool's second highest ever attendance, gave their former player Harry Millership a sporting reception. The *Lancashire Daily Post*, on 1 September 1919, carried this take on the game, under the headline 'Strong Leeds City side well beaten':

'Talloch and Fairhurst (Blackpool) were splendid backs, and the wing-halves were always usefully employed, and, generally speaking, the attack for half the game received excellent support, although later the touch between the lines suffered somewhat. The forwards were given vigorous, and, if uneven, their display had distinct possibilities, all the men playing good football. The bouts between City's Millership, Blackpool's old full-back, and Quinn were greatly enjoyed by the home crowd, especially as the latter generally had the better of the argument.'

Once again City seemed to put off-field matters aside and put in a lively performance, but despite two goals from Billy McLeod they went down 4-2. However, the rumblings of the ongoing inquiry were getting louder. The Sheffield sports special, the *Green 'Un*, gave their, not entirely unbiased take on the situation under the headline: 'The sensation of the week. Fra' Sheffield':

'Undoubtedly Leeds City have been the centre of the sensation of the week, with the decision of the football authorities to hold an inquiry into the management of the club during the war period. The joint commission of the Football Association and the Football League, which has to make the investigation will sit in London on Monday. So 'tis said. Of course, there are all sorts of rumours about. The club is stated to have been reported for alleged payments of more than the recognised allowance for players expenses.

'At any rate, the club's directors say there is no cause for apprehension of serious consequences, as they have a complete answer to all charges levelled against them.

Sheffield and district is the soccer nursery of Yorkshire; at least certain West Riding clubs look upon it as such. Leeds City would dearly love to wear their war-time plumes in serious football. The fears of the enforced departures of the Hampsons, the Stephensons, Peart etc might, or might not, be dried by the new talent. Tom Cawley has probably found his right place at Millmoor, he never had what could be termed a regular job at Elland Road.

'The Leeds City management are not a little troubled over the constitution of their half-back line. The Sheffield junior, Wainwright, is an early candidate for first team honours at Elland Road. Fred Blackman, who cost Leeds City a four-figure transfer fee, is stopping with his war-time love, Queens Park Rangers, and City have not got their thousand back. Leeds City would sooner have Millership with them, than against them today at Blackpool. There is not a single Leeds player in the City "probables" or "possibles", so much for "native" talent – or the judgement of the club "watchers". Four lads who were in Sheffield junior football last season appeared in the Leeds City reserves today. Biggadyte, right half-back, Mathews, inside-right, Wainwright, left-inside and Carlton, left-outside.'

Incidentally, the reserve team that this article refers to had made their debut on the same day as the first team fixture at Blackpool, losing 2-1 to Man City reserves at Elland Road, but the *Yorkshire Post* noted, 'the side however was composed of some very promising youngsters, some of whom look set to break into the first team very soon'.

An updated report of league matters released in August 1919, contained very little coverage of the goings-on at Elland Road: 'The management committee of the Football League met at Liverpool yesterday, Mr McKenna presiding. Bristol City asked for assistance owing to the fact that they had failed to get election to the Southern Competition, but it was pointed out that the league was unable to render any assistance. It was reported that the Irish League had decided to drop their usual league competition and to substitute one on the lines adopted by the league clubs in Lancashire, Yorkshire and Nottinghamshire. It was resolved that a player does not cancel any existing agreement by reason of playing as an amateur. Clapton Orient and Bradford were each fined a guinea for non-registration of players.

'The rules of the Lancashire, Yorkshire and Nottingham sections were approved, and Messrs McKenna, Sutcliffe and Bentley appointed to carry out the mutual insurance scheme for all sections. It was stated that Stoke City had appealed against the fine of £500 imposed by the Southern League, and that the entrance fee of £300 would not, during the interim, be enforced. The committee decided to give effect to the resolution that clubs may reckon the coming year's service as one for benefit matches and transfer fees, and that no transfer fees be paid or received during the coming season. The question of the future constitution of the Leeds City Club was left, so far as the league is concerned, to the president and Mr Sutcliffe.'

But any notions that the powers that be weren't treating the situation as a priority were dashed when the *Yorkshire Evening Post* reported on the latest developments from the football authorities on Monday, 1 September 1919: 'A series of meetings of the committee of the Football Association were held this afternoon at their offices in London. Considerable Yorkshire interest was attached to the meetings as it was expected that the consultant committee would receive a report upon an inquiry which had been conducted into the management of the Leeds City Club during the war-time period. The inquiry has relation to allegations respecting the scale of expenses allowed to Leeds City players. It is now nearly a month since Football Association secretary Mr F. J. Wall and director Mr T. Charnley were in Leeds for the purpose of examining the books of the club. Our London correspondent says a meeting is to be held this evening of the commission appointed to inquire into the allegations, at which arrangements will be made for a full inquiry. The facts secured by Mr Wall on his visit to Leeds will be reported to the commission, but no decision will be arrived at on them until a full inquiry has been held, to which both accused and accuser will be invited. It is thought probable that the inquiry will take place in Leeds within the next few weeks.'

The editor of the *Athletic News,* understood to have been communicated with by an aggrieved player, made the following comments on the ongoing situation: 'Certain allegations of improper payments to players and improper treatment of himself have been made by a former full-back at Leeds City Football Club. We understand that he alleges that bonuses for wins were paid during war-time football and that payments exceeding the legitimate amounts were made. Some time ago the Football Association and the Football League appointed a joint commission to inquire, and we believe that the secretaries of both organisations have visited Leeds and inspected the books and the accounts of the club.

'The directors of Leeds City Football Club in welcoming the inquiry, suggest that they are being subjected to what amounts to a kind of blackmail. The charges on both sides are exceedingly serious, and it is essential now that we are returning to normal football and conditions, that those who have been involved in war-time football should have faithfully and loyally carried out war-time regulations:- Messrs J. C. Clegg, C. Cramp and A. Kingscott of the Football League and Messrs J. McKenna, H. Keys and A. J. Dickinson of the Football League, constitute the joint commission.'

City recovered from the opening day defeat at Blackpool the following week with a 3-0 win over Coventry City in front of an Elland Road crowd of over 8,000. McLeod once again bagged a brace, the first of which came from a magnificent first-time, left-foot effort, which flew into the top corner of the net. For his second goal, McLeod pounced on a bad mix-up in the Coventry defence and, after gliding round the floundering defenders, gratefully tapped the ball into an empty net. The game was put beyond Coventry's reach with a fine goal by Simpson Bainbridge. Frustratingly for the home fans, Leeds changed down a gear or two in the second half but still managed to coast home in complete charge with Tom Lamph, Mick Foley and defender Harry Millership in top form. Hogg, in Leeds' goal, was not troubled all evening.

Three days later, City completed their second successive win with a 1-0 triumph over Blackpool at Elland Road. Centre-forward John Edmundson scored the winning goal while at the other end, Willis Walker in City's goal thwarted the 'Seasiders' on more than one occasion, at one point injuring himself after hitting a post as he tipped a goal-bound ball over the bar. City's third win came in the form of an impressive 4-0 rout of Coventry City at Highfield Road. Mick Foley was taken ill during the trip to Warwickshire and Arthur Price had stepped in, as Leeds began against a blustery wind. Once again Billy McLeod capitalised on a Coventry defensive error to take Leeds into the interval 1-0 up. Edmundson put Leeds two up early in the second half, and after McLeod had inevitably registered another brace, Bainbridge completed the trouncing. It has to be noted that, once again, Willis Walker was superb between the sticks.

Two days after the 4-0 demolition of Coventry City, Leeds entertained Hull City in front of a 10,000-strong crowd. There is no doubt that Leeds City were being supported by a staunch following and a letter by Mr P. Bland in the *Leeds Mercury* said, 'I am fairly certain all this disruption at City will be suitably resolved. Right now, we as supporters need to rally to the cause.' It was a very poignant letter and no doubt Mr Bland would have been at Elland Road for the game against Hull, which resulted in a disappointing 2-1 defeat. Bainbridge pegged the visitors back after they had taken an early lead, but Hull City eventually took two points back to the east coast. It is also feasible that Mr Bland also attended the return fixture with Hull at Boothferry Park a week later. It is said that over 3,000 Leeds City fans travelled to this game and they would have been reasonably satisfied with the point City gained from a 1-1 draw, with centre-forward Edmundson registering City's contribution.

Meanwhile dark clouds were gathering over Elland Road as the Football League's deadline came and went without any response whatsoever from Leeds City. For quite a while, the Leeds public, and in particular, Leeds City fans had been unaware of the events that were unfurling within their club behind closed doors; but as more articles appeared in the press startling events became evident and deep concern began to grow. The *Leeds Mercury* announced on 29 September under the headline: 'The Charges of Leeds City. Position of the club said to be critical':

'The editor of the *Athletic News* who is usually well informed as to the inner workings of the Football Association, writes today that the position of the Leeds City Club is extremely critical, he says: "Early in July one of their old players wrote a letter to the Football League alleging illegal practices by the club during war time in paying excessive expenses and bonuses to some of the players who had assisted them. After making some preliminary inquiries, a joint commission of the Football

Association and the Football League was appointed to investigate the charges. The first meeting took place on Friday afternoon.

'The proceedings were conducted behind closed doors, and at once the position of the club became critical. Far be it from us to embarrass Leeds City, but the club was asked to produce certain documents and Leeds City asserted that it was not within their power to do so. The commission thereupon decided to give the club until 6 October to furnish the documents required. If the documents are laid on the table, what then? We leave the case at that.

'Mr J. Connor, the chairman of the Leeds City directorate, who was seen by a *Yorkshire Evening Post* representative, this morning, had nothing to say either in confirmation or modification of this alarming view. "For the present," he says, "I regret I can say nothing!"

'Undoubtedly the charges brought against the Leeds City directors are very serious. It is alleged that they systematically made improper payments to players during the period of war time football. The charges were made originally by C. Copeland, a reserve full-back of the club, who this year had some differences with the directors regarding the terms of his engagement. He has since been transferred to Coventry City, and latterly, the role of prosecuting counsel, as it were, has been assumed by one who a few years ago was a director of the club. That is one of the unpleasant features of the case, and it can readily be understood that the Leeds City directors in the present inquiry are receiving a good deal of sympathy.

They say they have a complete answer to the charges, which well-wishers of the club will hope they prove to be the case, as any contrary result would inevitably be attended by consequences which would gravely endanger Leeds City's future.'

It is difficult to comprehend what was going through the players' own minds as the uncertainty continued to plague Elland Road, and just two days before the aforementioned article appeared in the *Leeds Mercury*, Leeds City had lined up to take on Wolverhampton Wanderers at Elland Road, who, due to a rail strike, arrived by charabanc. City were backed by a crowd of 12,463 and although the visitors had arrived intact, in contrast the home side were in disarray owing to the transport problems within the city. Coming in at the last minute was full-back George Affleck, in for the absent John Hampson. The game was only ten minutes in when a bizarre incident led to a penalty for the home side. Mick Foley over-hit a cross and the ball looked to be heading wide for a goal kick when Wolves defender Garratly dived at the ball with outstretched hands and stopped it on the line.

Momentarily, everybody inside Elland Road was stunned, and the crowd were still talking about the incident as Arthur Price stepped up to tuck the resulting penalty away. Just before the interval, Howell drilled a low hard shot out of the reach of City keeper Willis Walker to level the score for Wolves. Despite City dominating the second half, they were unable to capitalise and the final score remained 1-1. As the crowd dispersed, they would have had no idea that they had just witnessed Leeds City's last ever game at Elland Road.

Two days before an extended deadline granted by the football authorities for City to produce their books, the club arrived at Molineux for their away fixture with Wolverhampton Wanderers, and because of a rail strike they arrived by charabanc just as Wolves had done the previous week. The Molineux stadium was amongst the best in the country at the time, having been built exactly 20 years ago; it was a fitting venue for this dramatic event. Ernest Goodwin had been drafted in for his first game for over 18 months, when he had played on the left wing in a 3-0 victory over Nottingham Forest. Interestingly, that particular game, on 2 February 1918, saw Arsenal's Charlie Buchan, who would later become a Grenadier Guardsman in the war, on the right wing making his only Leeds City wartime appearance as a guest player, and scoring his only goal for City. Hampson returned to the side at centre-half. Reserve Billy Kirton played his only game for the club in the forward line; making his league debut in Leeds City's last ever game. He had been signed from Pandon Temperance, a local club in Newcastle, in 1917, and had showed great promise when guesting for Leeds at inside-right, signing professional terms after the war. Goodwin played on the right flank in place of Simpson Bainbridge.

City started off well, with attempts at goal from both Kirton and Goodwin. But as Leeds became frustrated, it was Wolverhampton who took the lead on 20 minutes. Harrison shot from close range and Walker could only parry and Bates pounced on the loose ball to find the net. Just before half-time Walker was unlucky again when a shot from Brooks cannoned off his leg and into the back of the City net. 2-0 to Wolves. Leeds remained under pressure in the opening stages of the second half and Walker was called upon at least half a dozen times to prevent Wolves from running away with the game. Then Leeds gained a foothold – with Lounds and Kirton leading the attack, Lounds was brought down on the edge of the box, just wide of the goal, and Leeds were awarded a free kick. The free kick was lobbed into the six-yard area and the keeper's punch out connected directly with the head of Tom Lamph and it was 2-1, with 20 minutes remaining. The Wolves defence was showing signs of panic as Leeds surged forward, and three minutes later McLeod, although in an awkward position, swivelled around and executed a brilliant equaliser. City could smell blood as they pounded relentlessly on the home defence, who were by now capitulating. McLeod, receiving strong support from his teammates, put Leeds ahead with ten minutes remaining and five minutes later he completed his Leeds City career with a blistering hat-trick. A quote at the end of the Wolves match report in the *Leeds Mercury* was very striking: 'In both Goodwin and Kirton we shall no doubt see more of in first-class football.'

Chapter Eight

The Beginning of the End for City

AS the joyous Leeds City players showered after their 4-2 victory, allowing themselves a small celebration, they still had no idea of their club's future. They boarded their charabanc for the journey back to Leeds and after about ten miles they spotted a small group of people stood by the side of the road wanting a lift.

Because of the rail strike, they stopped to see if they could help. Among these people was Charlie Copeland, who had just played at right-back for his new club Coventry City in a 1-0 home defeat at the hands of Leicester City. It is unclear how Copeland managed to travel around 30 miles from Coventry heading north-west across the north of Birmingham and on to Walsall, but he did and that's where the Leeds charabanc had pulled up. One can only assume that the City players didn't realise the full implications of what Copeland's actions would mean for the club, otherwise he would almost certainly have been left at the roadside. As it was, they gave Copeland a lift back to Leeds, where he still lived.

Copeland's career at Highfield Road wasn't entirely successful. He played 33 times for Coventry City, and it coincided with the club's longest ever losing streak – 30 August to 11 October 1919 – their longest winless streak – 30 August to 20 December 1919 – and the club's longest non-scoring run – 11 October to 20 December 1919.

On Monday, 6 October 1919, Leeds City arrived at Elland Road at 10am to begin training and preparation for the following Saturday's home game against South Shields.

That same day the *Leeds Mercury* wrote optimistically about the ongoing inquiry: 'Though the announcement of the resignation of the Leeds City directors was a trifle premature, it appears to have been well founded, and the result of the adjourned inquiry today will be awaited with interest. Whether the directors will attend the inquiry today, and whether the documents called for by the commission will be produced, are questions upon which there is considerable doubt. Whatever may be the fate of the present directorate, there is every hope of the club being saved.

'It is understood that a well-known citizen will submit an offer to run the club under any supervision they may suggest for the remainder of the season, and it is probable that the offer will be accepted. Footballers will join in the general rejoicing over the termination of the railway strike. It is astonishing to think that practically all the leading games were played in the last two Saturdays, when no trains were running. Long journeys by road at this period of the year, however, entail a lot of discomforts and dangers, and players and officials will be glad to renew acquaintance with the trains, even though railway travel is not now as comfortable as in pre-war days.'

But despite the *Mercury's* optimism, later that evening, after a meeting of the league inquiry team at the Russell Hotel in London, it was announced that Leeds City Football Club were to be expelled from the Football League and disbanded. The South Shields game was suspended and the city of Leeds was in utter shock. The league chairman, John McKenna, said, 'The authorities of the game intend to keep it absolutely clean. We will have no nonsense. The football stable must be cleansed and further breakages of the law regarding payments will be dealt with in such a severe manner that I now give warning that clubs and players must not expect the slightest leniency.'

McKenna told the *Yorkshire Post* that to have allowed the club to continue would have set a precedent for other clubs to withhold their books, adding: 'Leeds City could not be suspended as a club – we had no power to do that; but so long as they refused to give up those vital documents and papers, we could have no way out save by expelling them. Every member of the commission was sorry that Leeds City had to be dealt with at all. We recognised that they had gone through troublesome times before. We recognised also that they were a new club, and that they had obtained a good holding in a rugby area and that the club certainly had bright prospects, but our case was clear – Leeds were defiant, and could be defiant through one cause – fear of the papers giving away certain secrets.'

The secretary of the Football Association, Sir Frederick Hall, said of the affair, 'The books were never placed on the table. They were not obtained. The inference was that Leeds City had in a broad sense carried on as though no embargo had been placed on their action. It was felt that improper payments had been made and that the books would prove this. The Football Association decided to suspend the club, the directors and the officials for ever.'

So, the club was formally disbanded, leaving players out of work and the City officials facing further punishment. Joseph Connor was banned for life, along with J. C. Whiteman, Sam Glover and George Sykes. Herbert Chapman was also banned for life, but on appeal he was pardoned; he had claimed, rightly so, that he had been working at Barnbow Munitions Factory at the time of the alleged illegal payments. Chapman, however, was angry at the way he had been dealt with by the FA commission and on 16 December 1919 he quit the club, moved from his home in Oakwood, Leeds and took up a manager's position at Joseph Watson and Sons Olympia oil and coke company in Selby, North Yorkshire. Thomas Wood was among the factory staff and his grandson,

Alfred Wood of Cawood, near Selby said, 'My grandad worked at the factory when Herbert Chapman arrived and my mother has told me how he would spend his dinner-time in the canteen talking about football and how he wished he could have guided Leeds City to the First Division and that he believed that City would get there eventually once all these problems have gone. By that I have always assumed that he meant the problems from the guest player scandal.'

Once Chapman's appeal had been upheld the following year, he went back into football management, first with Huddersfield Town and then with Arsenal and he would go on to be one of the game's most successful managers of all time.

Because the requested documents were never produced, it is impossible to know whether Leeds City were guilty or not. The fact remains, however, that other clubs regularly paid wartime guest players. A considerable number of clubs simply had to use guest players if they were going to be competitive in the emergency competitions, and it was widely believed that City were no more guilty than any of these clubs. Wartime rules stated that only token payments and expenses were to be paid, but clubs, just as any employers, can choose their own level of expenses as with wages. There is no doubt that several clubs were hugely relieved when City refused to produce their books. That could quite possibly have taken this saga down another avenue.

Joseph Connor complained bitterly that City were not given a fair hearing and took to the *Yorkshire Evening Post* to address the Leeds public on the matter. 'Old Ebor', chief sports writer for the newspaper, wrote: 'Now that the Leeds City Football Club has met a tragic fate, it seems right that the course of events which have culminated in the suspension of the club, and the assassination of first-class association football from the Leeds district, should be made known. It is due to the recent management of the club, and to the public who support "socker" that certain material facts should be published. I am indebted to Mr J. Connor, the (late) chairman of the club's directors, for a very frank interview on the whole unhappy subject.'

Connor said: 'You will remember that we (the syndicate whom the Football Association with one exception banned for life) took over from Mr Tom Coombs, what could be called be called loose effects of the club – the players, transfers and membership of the League. This was after the First World War, when the club had been left in such a perilous condition that had we not assumed the responsibility of running it, a collapse may have occurred at that time. We have kept the game going. Leeds City won the League War Championship, twice, and we leave the club in a much healthier state than before we were installed. £700 in transfer fees and credit in the bank. Not bad for four years work.

'Mr Chapman had to go to Barnbow on war work and recommended that Mr George Cripps be appointed to act in his stead. Mr Cripps has been Mr Chapman's personal employee, and therefore Chapman considered him well acquainted with the work. I personally preferred Mr R. Fenwick, treasurer of the West Riding Football

Association, to be appointed – but the choice had fell on Mr Cripps who was given the charge of secretarial work whilst the responsibility of choosing the team was shared by Mr J. C. Whiteman and myself.

'At the end of Cripps' first season, the books were in such a hopeless state that I told my co-directors that unless there was no alteration I should resign. The result was that a competent accountant's clerk was appointed to take charge of the accounts, and Mr Cripps was placed in charge of the team and the club's correspondence.

'Friction was created that season between the players and directors, and also between the directors and Mr Chapman. At the end of the 1917/18 season the football aspect was so bleak owing to the war that the directors felt it would be better to close the club down altogether rather than take the risk of losing what little money we had left and they would have done so but for the persuasion of Mr McKenna the chairman of the league.

'The directors had so much disagreement with Mr Cripps that they became sick of the trouble and called upon Mr Chapman, once again to take charge of the club's affairs and to place Cripps in the position that he occupied when he was previously his assistant. An arrangement was made that one director, and not Mr Cripps, should travel away with the team, unless under special instructions. The result was that before a match at Nottingham, which Mr Cripps attended, a letter written by John Hampson was sent to Mr Chapman stating that if Cripps was allowed to travel with the team, they would go on strike. Mr Chapman interviewed Hampson and pointed out "the foolishness of the letter" and the position the players had taken and eventually they agreed to play under the conditions laid down by the directors and overall for the sake of the club.

'Towards Christmas of last year, the friction between Cripps and the directors had become so bad that they decided to sever his connection with the club. The result was that Cripps made a charge that directors had paid players improper sums on account of expenses and supplied evidence on this point to Mr J. W. Bromley a former director of the club. He also made a claim of £400 against the directors which in legal hands was settled at £55. One of the terms of the settlement was that Cripps should deposit all documents relating to the affairs of the club, including his cheque book and passbook and all correspondence with the players with the solicitor retained by the directors, Mr W. H. Clarke. Reluctant at first to comply he was persuaded to do so by Bromley, which he did in the presence of Mr Whiteman and myself. Mr Cripps gave a written undertaking not to disclose any of the affairs of the club and accordingly Mr Bromley gave his word of honour that, so far as he was concerned, the documents should never be revealed. These were the documents that were to become prominent in the whole case. Mr Bromley wanted to make a stipulation that the club should give £50 to the Leeds Infirmary, we could not agree to this. In December last year Mr Chapman intimated that owing to having secured an important commercial appointment he would have to resign his secretaryship of the club and he did so on New Year's

Eve. Until the end of last season the affairs of the club had been conducted by Whiteman and myself, with the assistance of other directors and Mr R. Hewison was then appointed secretary-manager.

'I now refer to the case of Charlie Copeland. In fixing up players for the present season, 1919/20, the case of Charlie Copeland had to be dealt with. Before the war began, he was receiving a salary of £3 a week rising to £4 when he played for the first team. City offered him £3.10s (£3.50) a week for the second team and a substantial amount when he played in the first eleven; and the club intimated that if he preferred instead, he could be given a free transfer. Copeland refused these terms and wrote a letter to the directors that unless he received £6 a week he would report the club and the directors to the Football Association for making illegal payments during war time to guest players. The club ignored Copeland's threat, other than to place him on a free transfer with immediate effect, so that he was able to go where he desired. The club stated, through myself, that they didn't think of Copeland as a first-class player, and certainly not such a player that the club needed, and that his previous experience with the club backed up my statement. After placing Charlie Copeland on the transfer list, the club chose to refuse all the threats and instead decided to permit matters to take their course. Copeland had got hold of copies of certain documents, or their contents, and he carried out his threat. At a first hearing of a joint Football Association and Football League inquiry the City club was very surprised to find present not only six members of the commission, but at least a dozen members of the Football Association and the Football League, including members of the selection committee. This did not appear exactly a fair proceeding. It was the only occasion on which the directors met the commission, and we were simply asked, "where are those documents, have you come prepared to produce them?" The club replied that it was not in our power to do so.'

The *Yorkshire Evening Post* concluded: 'Mr Connor, in the course of a conversation as to the future policies of the suspended directors, said that he could not see that any good would now be done by producing the documents as they might simply do more harm. If payment not strictly proper under the war regulations of the Football Association was made to players, they were not of such a nature as fully to compensate them for the time and wages lost in playing the game. But even small illegalities carry punishment – when discovered or exposed – and the directors appear to have definitely made up their minds to sacrifice themselves rather than let punishment fall on the players who had been loyal to them, and whose suspensions now might be a serious matter for the clubs which they are now connected. The directors leave the club in a very different position, both financially and in a playing sense from that in which they found it, when indeed, it seemed probable that but for their intervention it would have gone under.'

Bromley's version of events was quite different to that of Joseph Connor, and George Cripps also responded to Connor's statement with his own account in an open letter to the *Yorkshire Evening Post* on 17 October 1919; the very same day that Leeds City players were sold by auction at Leeds' Hotel Metropole.

'To the editor of the *Yorkshire Evening Post*.

'Sir, with reference to the prominent report you gave in your issue of Tuesday evening last of the interview by "Old Ebor" with Mr J. Connor, regarding the affairs of Leeds City Football Club. My name largely figures in the report, which contains so many inaccurate statements that I would ask you to give me an opportunity of correcting them, so that the public may be under no misapprehension as to my position in the matter.

'In the first place, I was not appointed to act in the stead of Mr Herbert Chapman, but to assist him to carry out his work, as he had to spend so much of his time at Barnbow. My position was that of corresponding secretary, and this position I took up in August 1916. I did not wish to undertake the book-keeping of the syndicate, as I considered it no part of my duties, but it was thrust upon me for certain reasons, which need not be entered into here. Mr Connor is said to have stated that, at the end of the first season, the books were in a hopeless state. This I emphatically deny. The books were audited by Messrs W. H. Platts and Co and I had followed the system of book-keeping adopted by Mr Chapman. At the end of this season the syndicate gave me an extra grant of £30 as an acknowledgement for the able manner in which I had carried out my work with the club. This is hardly consistent with the allegations that I had got the books in a hopeless state.

This first floor meeting room in the Griffin Hotel is the actual room in which Leeds City Football Club were formed in 1904. (Steve Riding)

Boar Lane, Leeds, the Griffin Hotel is on the left. The bay window of the meeting room can be seen on the first floor. (Martin Jackson)

The Football League Management Committee 1903/04. John McKenna is back centre. (Tony Winstanley)

This is thought to be the only image of Leeds v Burnley 1906. City's David Wilson (heading the ball third from right) left the pitch shortly after this was taken and died minutes later. (Mark Ledgard)

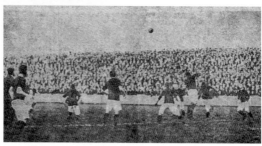

David Wilson's home in Beeston, Leeds. His body was carried up these stairs and into his house just hours after collapsing at Elland Road. (Author)

In 1907, Leeds City came from two down to beat high flying West Brom 3-2. This is how the local media saw it. (Dave Tomlinson)

Leeds City 1905/06 featuring Roy the City Dog laid in front of manager Gilbert Gillies. (Tony Winstanley)

Leicester Fosse (later renamed Leicester City) during a League Division Two match against Leeds City, 7 February 1914.

City manager Herbert Chapman 1912. After a life ban in 1919 was overturned he went on to become one of the best managers that Britain had ever seen. (Andrew Varley, Official Leeds United FC Photographer)

Perceived to be the villain at the centre of the Leeds City scandal in 1919, former City right-back Charlie Copeland. (Mark Ledgard)

George Cripps, assistant to Chapman, featured heavily in the scandal of 1919. (Victoria Wooldridge)

William Street, Castleford, home of Walter Cook who returned to the area in 1920 to play for Castleford Town. (Author)

Jack Hewitt of Leeds City 1919. Inscription written on back by his daughter Mary: "My lovely Dad, played for Leeds City and his County". (Mary Hewitt)

Walter Cook, former Brighton keeper, was a WW1 guest player for Leeds City. (Luke Griffiths)

The Hotel Metropole, Leeds, where the infamous auction took place in October 1919. (Author)

The Grand Hall of the Metropole where every Leeds City player went under the hammer. (Author)

Salem Church, Leeds, with the distinctive curvature. The birthplace of Leeds United Football Club, 17 October 1919. (Keith Barber)

A rare image of the meeting hall (curvature to the rear) inside Salem Church where supporters laid the foundation for United. (Keith Barber)

A wintry image of Leeds United's first ever game, against Yorkshire Amateur FC at Elland Road in 1919. (Neil Roche)

Harry Dodsworth. A member of the first ever Leeds United team in 1919/20. (Jon Dodsworth)

The first known photo of Leeds United. Dodsworth is the second player from the right, in the middle row. Matt Ellson is second from left, front row.

Matt Ellson (left) scored Leeds United's first ever goal against Rotherham Town in November 1919. (Tony Hill)

The first ever known metal badge of Leeds United. (Martin Jackson)

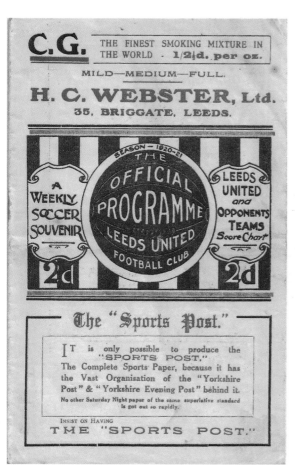

Match programme from United's first League season, v Barnsley 1920/21. (Michael Hewitt Programmes)

Leeds United players relaxing in Blackpool before a cup-tie at Bolton in 1923. Left to right, Duffield, Frew, Morrell (trainer) Swan and Baker. (Mark Ledgard)

United's Harry Duggan was an Irish international. This is his shirt from his debut v Italy at Lansdowne Road in 1927. (The Duggan Family)

When United won promotion in 1931/32 each player was awarded a watch by the club. This one was given to Harry Duggan. (The Duggan Family)

Don Revie made his football debut for Leicester City in 1944. He went on to transform Leeds United into one of the best sides in Europe. (Duncan Revie)

'During season 1916/17 I had a break-down in health and about August 1917 an accountant's clerk was appointed by Mr Connor personally to keep the books of the syndicate during the season 1916/17. The accountant's clerk was paid £16 per annum for his work and had also to assist me at Elland Road on match days, and the fact that this was only a fraction of the salary I had been paid and continued to receive, as well as the fact that as "an incompetent man" I was retained, seems to me to speak for itself.

'Mr Connor is then reported to say that the directors had so much disagreement with me that they became sick of the trouble. As a matter of fact, during the course of my engagement with the Leeds City syndicate, I never had any trouble with any directors, except Mr Connor, and this latter only after the end of the 1916/17 season, for in the season of 1917/18 certain minutes were passed by the directors which probably accounted for the disagreement. At the end of the 1917/18 season I again received an extra grant of £30 for the successful working of the club, which again, I say, is hardly consistent with anything but satisfaction of my work by the directors, and I was never told by anyone that the directors were dissatisfied with my work or me, and it was not as a result of any such disagreement that Mr Chapman came back again.

'As Mr Chapman had more time to give to the affairs of the club, apart from his work at Barnbow, he again took over the financial affairs of the club. Mr Chapman merely told me that the club could not afford to pay both of us, and I said I would go if I were paid the sum due to me under my year's agreement. Eventually, I had to place the matter in the hands of my solicitor Messrs Bromley and Walker, through whom I claimed the sum of £150 for money which I had expended on the syndicate's behalf out of the salary voted to me, and as to a further £150 for damages for wrongful dismissal. It will be seen that this is not the £400 as stated by Mr Connor. After considerable negotiation I withdrew my claim for the first £150, as it was of a technical nature, and all parties concerned in the matter having decided to avoid the scandal which would result had the claim been persisted in.

'Eventually the second claim was, after considerable negotiation, settled for a sum of £55 and payment of my solicitor's costs which were a considerable sum, and it was arranged that I could proceed with my journalistic work without interference, the contemplated loss of which was one of the items in making up the claim of £150. I think this puts an entirely different complexion on the statements made by Mr Connor. On one final matter I would mention that Mr Connor is stated to have said that one of the terms of the settlement was that I should deposit certain documents with Mr W. H. Clarke. This was not so, as I had some time previously parted with same to Mr J. W. Bromley and I was no party to any such arrangement. My own private pass and cheque books were not included in the documents, and merely a pass and a cheque book of an account in my name, but relating to the club's affairs which I opened at a Leeds bank on the introduction of Mr Connor. Yours, etc, Geo H Cripps, 13 Belvedere Mount, Dewsbury Road, Leeds.'

In October 1979, George Cripps' son posted a letter in the *Yorkshire Post* regarding the inquiry of October 1919 and his comments were interesting: 'The remarks of John McKenna make me smile when I remember some of the things my father told me about the machinations by various member of the then Football League, which have certainly led me to believe that they were not so simon pure as the image they presented to the public.'

Many protests were voiced at the severity of the punishment handed out to Leeds City, and Port Vale – who were to replace City in the league – were accused by many of putting undue pressure on the commission in an attempt to replace City as quickly as possible. But the protests were in vain, as the inquiry having made by their decision, made it abundantly clear that they would not to be swayed otherwise.

After just eight games of the 1919/20 season, Port Vale inherited City's playing record of: played 8, won 4, drawn 2, lost 2, goals for 17, goals against 10, points 10. Port Vale took over City's fixtures with that game against South Shields, eventually finishing 13th in the table. Port Vale had begun life as Burslem Port Vale and were founder members of the Football League Second Division in 1892, but had been forced to resign from the league after the 1906/07 season and subsequently liquidated. They were widely expected to replace City owing to the fact that the previous season they had failed to enter the league, when they lost by just one vote in the election at the Annual General Meeting of the Football League. Much later, in 1967, Port Vale themselves were expelled from the Football League for making illegal payments to players in contravention of Football Association rules. On 31 December 1967, the *Football League Review Magazine* wrote:

'The sensational events of this season, involving Port Vale, have brought many sweeping and inaccurate comments. It must be remembered that the actions taken against the club were the result of deliberations by a joint commission of the Football Association and the Football League. The members of the commission must be given credit for knowing something about the rules and regulations.

'At this stage let us state emphatically that the breaking of the rules in any sport does not in any way brand those concerned as criminals – any more than those who break the laws on the pitch are criminals. But in the same way that offending players must be dealt with under the rules and regulations of sport, so must the clubs. The fact that some might get away with rule-breaking unnoticed cannot detract in any way from the working of any disciplinary commission, on or off the pitch. If any sport is to prosper then its rules must be observed. Those who take the risk of breaking them – however unwittingly – must realise that there can be no cause to complain if they are found out; even though there are few of us who would contend that, at some time or another, we have not transgressed some law, rule or regulation. We have never yet heard a successful defence made out on the grounds that everyone else is committing the same offence – but have yet to be discovered. The lesson must be this: minor infringements which are allowed to go unchecked can lead to bigger offences ... and if the big offence becomes widespread it can lead to the collapse of the whole foundations of the sport concerned.

'No governing body derives any pleasure from investigations of this kind. The modern trend in all walks of life is for the extraction of the biggest possible benefits without any actual rule breaking. If it occurs then a plea of ignorance of the rule cannot in any way be accepted. The decisions which have been taken, and the punishment inflicted, have been fair. They have been taken with the future of professional league football very much in mind.'

This statement is remarkably similar to the one regarding Leeds City ... except for the fact that Port Vale were readmitted to the league later that season on appeal.

Leeds City were expelled despite the intervention of the Lord Mayor of Leeds, Alderman Joseph Henry, who had been a director of Leeds City under the chairmanship of Norris Hepworth, and who had made contact with the Football Association and the Football League offering to take over the club from the directors. His pleas had been in vain, however, and he wrote in the *Yorkshire Evening Post* that there was no supporter of association football in Leeds more disappointed than he was at his failure to preserve the Leeds City club.

'I know full well when it started,' said the Lord Mayor, 'the non-production of the documents and the fact of the club being under suspension were very awkward points to overcome. I was quite sure that if the documents could not be produced it was useless making any effort to prevent heavy punishment being given to the person who had control of the club at the time the alleged irregularities were committed and I made no effort to do so. I, therefore, made my appeal in the direction of having the suspension of the club removed, and to keeping down the fine (if any) which might be imposed. At my first interview with Mr J. C. Clegg, the chairman of the Football Association commission and Mr A. J. Dickinson of the Football Association council, I urged them to call the commission together to consider my statement; he kindly fell in with my suggestion, and it was arranged to meet at Sheffield on the following Wednesday. On the morning of that day I invited the members of the club's syndicate (J. Connor. J. C. Whiteman. S. Glover. G. Sykes) and their solicitor, Alderman William Clarke, to meet me to talk over the whole question. At that meeting, there was presented to me, by Alderman Clarke, an agreement between the acting members of the syndicate and Mr Platts (Leeds accountant and lessee of Elland Road) whereby the acting members retired and all the assets of the club were transferred to Mr Platts with he paying them the money they had advanced the club. I was advised that this was desirable in order to preserve the legal continuity of the club, in view of the resignations of all the members of the syndicate.

'When we met the commission in the afternoon, the case was very ably handled by Alderman Clarke.

I then made my appeal on behalf of the supporters of the game in Leeds and for the city itself, and I am sure that the case, as put by me, had some influence on the commission. The chairman of the Football League, Mr J. McKenna, was a member of the commission, and pointed out that no decision should be given until he had consulted the league committee, and with that object the meetings were adjourned to London. Subsequently we met with the league commission at the Russell Hotel in London, where I at once found my greatest difficulty. The chairman had been fully informed as to the situation with the Leeds City management, of which I was totally ignorant, and, after a long and friendly interview, we were told that their report would be presented to the commission that afternoon. We met the commission in the afternoon and I was asked if I had any suggestions to make. In reply, I again appealed for the removal of the suspension, pointing out that if a new club was formed we would have to apply for admission to the league; and I added that without league membership it would not be possible to run a club. Mr Clegg then gave us the decision that refers to the club. He did not say to us what penalty was to be passed on to the alleged offenders.

'After a night of very careful thought I have come to the conclusion that, but for the actions of the league, the commission would have let the club off with a fine. But the league committee were very firm for expulsion. I am sure, also, that Burslem Port Vale did not act in a sportsmanlike way in pressing for their claim before that final decision was arrived at. I was also very much handicapped by several local people sending letters to members of the league, making suggestions, of which no copy had been sent to me. I am deeply indebted to Alderman Clarke for the services he rendered to me in all legal matters, and for his explanation as to his instructions not to produce the documents that had been demanded by the league commission.

'The supporters of the club and the game owe a deep debt of gratitude to Mr Platts for his action in shouldering the whole financial position of the club and his promise to help in future. I am sure that I am expressing his views and Mr Clarke's and indeed my own when I say that there are no persons in Leeds more sorry that we are at our failure, after our great hopes at one period of the negotiations.'

The Leeds public were learning more about this saga with each passing day, with letters and opinions flying in from all directions.

'To the editor of the *Yorkshire Evening Post.*

'Sir, as a supporter of the Leeds City Club, I think we have a right to know more of these mysterious documents. Why should a clique of say half a dozen men hold up the public from seeing first-class football in Leeds? The Lord Mayor is to be commended for the way he tried to keep the ball rolling, but all his efforts have been in vain. Now, Leeds supporters, let us see this through. Why let it rest at this stage? The players concerned knew they were breaking the rules of the FA. Why should they get off scot-free?

'Yours etc ... Another, Harehills. Leeds Oct 16, 1919.'

Then, on the same day that the auction of the Leeds City players was to be held, James Bromley, who had acted on behalf of Charlie Copeland, had his say on the matter. Under the heading of 'Copeland's Case – His connection with the Leeds City Club' he wrote this in the *Yorkshire Evening Post*:

'Sir, our client, Mr Charles Copeland, who entrusted me, has reported the Leeds City Football Club to the Football Association and the Football League, has seen us today with reference to the interview which you published on Tuesday last, by "Old Ebor" with Mr Connor, a member of the Leeds City syndicate. The statements alleged to have been made by Mr Connor under the sub-heading, "The Case of Copeland", are so inaccurate and incomplete, that our client has requested us to place before you the exact position from his point of view, so that the public may be under no misapprehension as to what has occurred, so far as he is concerned.

'During the war Mr Copeland gave his services loyally to the club, often at a financial loss to himself, on the promise that after the war he would receive every consideration on the question of wages, etc. Under the rules of the Football Association, a player was allowed to receive a 50% increase for the season 1919/20. Mr Copeland's pre-war wage had been £176 for the year. On May 7, 1919, Mr Copeland was offered a wage of £3.10s per week for 39 weeks and no summer wages, therefore being £136.10s for the year, and thus a reduction, and not an increase on his pre-war wage. He was asked to consider it and meet with members of the syndicate at Elland Road on the following Saturday with his reply.

'Mr Copeland asked for 50% increase on his pre-war wage, which the members of the syndicate refused. The syndicate members were not at Elland Road to meet him as planned, but he saw them later at Bradford, and refused to accept the reduced wage offered him. He then saw Mr Sykes, a member of the syndicate, who told him that he (Mr Sykes) would be willing to give him £5 a week all the year round, but, told him that two other members would not agree; and at Mr Sykes's suggestion, Mr Copeland then wrote a letter offering to accept £4.10s per week. In reply to this, Mr Copeland then received a letter from the club stating that as he had refused an offer of 50% advance in wages, it had been decided that nothing further should be done. That he had had any such offer was entirely untrue, and he immediately wrote back to the club saying so, pointing out the correct facts, and expressed himself as quite agreeable to sign on for a 50% advance.

'Mr Copeland then saw Mr Sykes, who characterised the club's statement as untrue, as he was present when the first offer of £3.10s per week had been made. Mr Copeland wrote to the club for an interview, but they refused him one.

'Being unable, therefore, to get any satisfaction whatsoever out of the club, Mr Copeland consulted us and placed in our hands certain information, with instructions to make the necessary report to the Football Association and to the Football League.

'In his interview, Mr Connor is alleged to have offered Mr Copeland a free transfer and to have subsequently placed him on the free transfer list. Your report is the first intimation of this which Mr Copeland has received, although he had been in correspondence with the secretaries of both the Football Association and the Football League on the subject.

'With regard to the allegation that Mr Copeland had got hold of certain documents, we are instructed to state that he has not now got and never had any copies of the documents deposited with Messrs W. H. Clarke and Co.

'Yours, etc., Bromley and Walker, Greek Street, Leeds, Oct 17 1919.'

'Sir, the letter from Mr Bromley makes very interesting reading. There are, however, one or two rather pertinent questions which Mr Bromley will perhaps be good enough to answer. Whence came the parcel of documents to which he refers to in his letter? As it is fairly obvious that they were not sent with the approval of the Leeds City directors, would it not have been more sportsmanlike to have handed them back to the directors as being their property, instead of holding them up as ransom?

'As the documents were apparently forwarded by the sender with the hopes of ousting Leeds City from the football world as a personal revenge, and not any desire to keep the game clean, the part played by Mr Bromley appears to me to be decidedly mean.

'Yours, etc, W. C. G. Beeston, October 18 1919.'

'Old Ebor' reflected on the sorry aftermath: 'Neither condemnation of the late Leeds City directors or the criticism of the action taken by the Football Association or the Football League will repair the disaster that has overtaken the association game in the Leeds district this past week. It is quite true that the league's action in expelling the club and electing Port Vale to its place seems to have certainly been unreasonably hurried, and even ferocious, but it may be useful to remember that if the game is to be resuscitated in this district, abuse of the powers in office will not assist in the process. Personally, I deeply regret what happened; the more so that seeing it coming was powerless to prevent the catastrophe. Now, the ruins of Leeds City Football Club are a monument – to what? Some may say to the championing of purity in association football, but do they believe it? Does anyone really think that Leeds City are the only club that made allowances to players for the loss of work when playing football in the war period? Was Elland Road the only ground which men from a distance found it possible to travel for football purposes?

'The reader must not assume that I am justifying breaches of the law, temporary though the enactment was; far from it; I only suggest the possibility that anyone seriously seeking purity in war-time football might wander a long way from Elland Road without finding it. It is also possible that some clubs were more skilled in the art of concealment than the Leeds City directors – or more justified in expecting the confidence of those around them. It is further possible that those who have deliberately brought the club to ruin may not in the times to come feel specially proud of their performances.'

Mr Platts, the Leeds accountant acting on City's behalf, made a statement in which he told Leeds City season ticket holders that they would be kept informed once the financial position of the club was ascertained. He said, 'Whilst there may be no legal obligations towards them, I recognise that there is a moral obligation for redemption in what they will miss. The published statement that there is £2,000 in the bank, however, is not correct.

'The club has a lease on the Elland Road ground for ten years, but with the option determining same in five years. This term of five years will be up on 8 August 1921 so there will be two years left on the lease. Pending further developments for the reorganisation of the club or the "socker" game in the district, there is a suggestion that the Yorkshire Amateur Association Football Club might find a suitable home at the Elland Road enclosure.' Which they duly did.

Despite making an annual profit of £122 in their first season, Leeds City made a loss in every one of one of the following seasons: 1906/07 a loss of £338; 1907/08 – £728; 1908/09 – £1,200; 1909/10 – £1,904; 1910/11 – £1,060; 1911/12 – £1,805; 1912/13 – £1,803. After a fairly successful season City made a profit of £353 in 1913/14, but the following season, the first season of the war, the club made a loss of £1,568.

The intriguing thing about this whole saga is those vital documents, that were so instrumental in the downfall of Leeds City Football Club, may still lie, covered in several inches of thick dust, locked away deep beneath the Alderman's old offices in South Parade, Leeds.

Chapter Nine

The Auction.
A Sale of Flesh

THE Hotel Metropole stands yards away from South Parade and just around the corner from Leeds Railway Station, on King Street. It was built in 1897/98, ironically around the same time that the third club called Leeds went out of existence.

It had been designed by local architects Chorley and Connor and at six storeys high made an instant impact on the Leeds city skyline, with its distinctive ornate Victorian facade and pink terracotta cupola, all of which remain today, along with the original hotel signage.

At around 10.30am on the morning of 17 October 1919 the hotel was the setting for the only auction of a full team of professional footballers anywhere in the world, as the whole Leeds City team went under the hammer. It is reported that that the first player to arrive was Willis Walker, the goalkeeper; he was soon joined by Billy McLeod. One can only imagine what they discussed as the players entered the hotel through the front doors greeted by the Leeds coat of arms, and walked up the three steps leading into the heavily carpeted reception area and main lobby. Directly ahead of them were two large floor-to-ceiling screen doors with glass frames atop. To the side of the right-hand door stood an easel with a sign on it that read, 'Leeds City Sale. Messrs S. Whittam & Sons, Auctioneers.' Through these doors was the large central hall where the auction would take place. The giant entablature high above supported by giant moulded marble columns went unnoticed by the players, 24 in all, as they arrived with clearly other things swirling around inside their heads. The players had been asked to arrive early, and just before 11am, they were all present and the large screen doors were closed behind them.

They were shown into a smaller meeting room off to the right of the main hall, where they were briefed as to the events that would be taking place later. Over an hour was spent discussing the methods of the procedure. The players sat in silence the whole time as they were informed that everything that was being done today was being done in the interests of the players themselves. It was explained to them that in no case would a player be required to go where he would not feel comfortable. In other words, the players would have the option of exercising their own choice between the clubs who were showing an interest in obtaining their services. With regard to the manager

Mr Bob Hewison and the trainer, Dick Murrell, it was explained that special arrangements were being made either to secure their future, or to compensate them for any loss that they might sustain by the winding up of the club.

As well as Billy McLeod being the obvious choice for most clubs, there was plenty of other talent around. John Hampson had been Herbert Chapman's trusted captain at both Northampton Town and Leeds City, John Edmondson's brief appearances for City had shown him to be a reliable goalscorer and Harold Millership had only recently joined City, but already commanded a fee in the region of £1,000, and he would later become a Welsh international. Simpson Bainbridge had been brought in as a youngster on trial, but went on to shine for the club, making over 70 appearances; he too would command close to £1,000. City had somewhat of a star in goal too: Willis Walker, despite fighting in the war, had put in several reliable shifts between the sticks for City, when the situation allowed. Twenty-year-old Billy Pease was born at 7 Roxborough Place, Hunslet, but initially played rugby and only learned to play football, on the right wing, after joining the Northumberland Fusiliers. When he returned from World War One, he joined Leeds City as an amateur – unfortunately, just in time for the auction.

Meanwhile, managers and their representatives from over 30 clubs were starting to arrive, some dressed in dark three-quarter-length coats, others in blazers, waistcoats, white shirts and ties, or bow ties, smart trousers, highly polished shoes and most of them sporting a bowler, although a few flat caps and bare heads were evident. They were scattered around the lobby area, smoking pipes and cigarettes, creating a huge fug of smoke; with cups of tea on various tables, they looked through the list of items for sale. Members of the press could be seen strategically positioned around the lobby and entrance, acribbling everything down. The *Yorkshire Evening Post* later described the auction as 'a melancholy spectacle'.

After the players had been before the committee, they were seated at the back of the main hall around three large tables, on which were jugs of water, all of which were topped up on a regular basis. Then, the representatives from over 30 English League clubs entered the hall and took their places towards the front, facing the auctioneer's podium which had a gavel and block resting atop, in readiness. Each club had been instructed to place their sealed bid for the players they wanted in the envelopes provided.

Members of the local and national press and selected members of the public then began to file in and take their places. The Leeds accountant Mr W. H. Platts, in charge of the club's affairs, had decided to also dispose of the effects of the club including, nets, goalposts, balls, kit, the shower baths, physiotherapy equipment and billiard tables, but the Elland Road Ground itself would not form part of the sale.

Mr Platts instructed auctioneers Messrs S. Whittam and Sons to arrange the sale. It was decided that the committee would fix the opening transfer fees to be paid for the respective players, the various club managers could then take the name of the players in whom they were interested and it would then be for the players themselves to decide which clubs they should join. The following transfers were fixed:

Billy McLeod, Harold Millership, John Hampson and Simpson Bainbridge £1,000 each; Willis Walker, Tom Lamph and John Edmondson £800 each; Arthur Price £750; George Affleck and Billy Hopkins £600 each; Ernest Goodwin, Billy Kirton and Billy Ashurst £500 each; Mick Foley and George Stephenson £400 each; John Jackson £300; Fred Linfoot and Herbert Lounds £250; Arthur Wainwright and William Short £200 each; and Francis Chipperfield £100.

The club managers present were from, among other clubs, South Shields, Stoke City, Aston Villa, Everton, Liverpool, Nottingham Forest, Lincoln City and Notts County. The County manager was Albert Fisher, who had been an inside-forward for Aston Villa as well as a host of other clubs before going into management. Sitting on the end of the second row was Glasgow man George Ramsay, the celebrated manager of Aston Villa, wearing a light tweed jacket and matching waistcoat with a black bow tie. He had served Villa as player, manager and secretary for 59 years and he guided them as manager to six league titles and six FA Cups. Another famous manager of the time was there too: Arthur Dickinson had become Sheffield Wednesday's first manager in 1891 and remains the longest-serving and most successful manager of all time for the club, overseeing two league title wins and two FA Cups. He was known to be interested in John Edmondson and Arthur Price, depending, of course, on the price. Preston North End manager James Vincent Hayes arrived late and as he sat down and lit a cigarette, he was handed a list of the players on offer, which he studied carefully. Hayes had been a player with a number of clubs, including Brentford and Bradford Park Avenue, but he excelled in management; coaching Norway in the 1912 Summer Olympics in Stockholm, Sweden as well as Wiener SC from Vienna, Austria. Four years after this auction he would become the manager of Atletico Madrid.

The players in greatest demand were McLeod, Millership, Walker, Hampson, Price, Hopkins and Bainbridge. In regard to Billy McLeod, it was well known that three weeks previously, Aston Villa had offered £1,000 for his transfer, but City had wanted to keep him, obviously hoping the cloud hanging over them would disappear and they could continue as they were. McLeod's overall goal tally for Leeds City was 177 in 289 appearances. At the auction, Aston Villa would be challenged by Stoke City, and no doubt others, for McLeod's signature. Full-back Millership had only joined City from Blackpool for £600 at the beginning of the season. City's captain, Hampson, was badly wanted by Nottingham Forest, whilst one of the Sheffield clubs was interested in inside-forward Arthur Price.

Apart from McLeod and Millership, none of the players had been very costly to Leeds City. Willis Walker, the goalkeeper, had been obtained from Worksop two seasons before war broke out. A £50 transfer fee in each case secured Hopkins from Sunderland, and Lounds from Gainsborough Trinity. Bainbridge, who was probably the most promising outside-left the club ever had, was brought in at very little outlay from Darlington. Short, Linfoot and Kirton, from the Tyneside area, all cost the club practically nothing. The same may be said of Tommy Lamph, who came from Spennymoor, Ashurst, formerly of Durham City, Wainwright from the Sheffield district, Edmondson, from Leyland in Lancashire, and Goodwin from the south-east.

Suddenly the auctioneer introduced himself and explained the proceedings ahead. Then things got under way. As the gavel came down with each transaction, Billy McLeod was sold. Then it was Harry Millership and John Hampson, and then it was down the line, Bainbridge, Edmondson, Walker and so it continued. Most of the players were sold for their fixed transfer price, but there were a couple that caused small bidding wars. One of them, unsurprisingly, was marksman, Billy McLeod. Villa, as mentioned, were very keen on signing him, but Stoke took the bidding over the £1,000 fixed fee, which the committee agreed to, and so Villa then bid higher than Stoke, but in the end, it was Notts County who won the race for McLeod, with a fee of £1,250. Simpson Bainbridge went to Preston North End for £1,000 while Harold Millership was also sold for £1,000 to Rotherham County. Another £1,000 was paid by Aston Villa to secure John Hampson. Sheffield Wednesday paid £800 for the services of centre-forward John Edmondson and

Willis Walker was sold to South Shields for the same amount.

Arthur Price went to Sheffield Wednesday for £750 and Billy 'Pop' Hopkins moved to South Shields for £600. There were three players who were each sold for £500 each: Billy Kirton to Aston Villa, Billy Ashurst (who would later play for England) to Lincoln City and George Affleck to Grimsby Town. Kirton would go on to finish that season by scoring Aston Villa's winning goal in the FA Cup Final against Huddersfield Town. He also went on to play for England. Four City players sold for £250: Ernest Goodwin to Man City, Fred Linfoot to Lincoln City, Herbert Lounds to Rotherham County and George Stephenson to Aston Villa. He later became an England international. Arthur Wainwright went to Grimsby Town for £200 and Francis Chipperfield joined Arthur Price and John Edmonson at Hillsborough, for a mere £100.

Walter Cook, who had deputised for Willis Walker in goal whilst the latter fought in the war, moved to Castleford Town and just three months later Cook would face new club Leeds United in goal for Castleford. William Crowther went to Lincoln City, Billy Pease went to Northampton Town for basically nothing but in 1926, Middlesbrough would pay £2,000 for his services, and he played for England. Tommy Lamph moved across the Pennines to Man City and the last man standing was Robert Wilkes who joined Billy Hopkins and Willis Walker at South Shields. In *Leeds United: A Complete Record 1919-1989* by Martin Jarred and Malcolm

MacDonald, Willis Walker said, 'It was a sad day because we had a fairly good side. It was a great shame for the city of Leeds. I had been lodging with a policeman in Beeston, Leeds, and on the day of the auction, I walked down to the Metropole. It was during the day, I think the bids were put into sealed envelopes and we were sold to the highest bidder. After Leeds United were formed I trained with them, Leeds were very good to me and I was happy there. United had the same trainer as City – Dick Murrell.'

After been bought by South Shields, Walker – who also played cricket for Nottinghamshire, scoring 1,000 runs a season for ten seasons – continued to live in the Leeds area and travelled to home games by train, a long and tortuous journey via Newcastle. He would catch the 7.25am train to his native north-east and often would not return home until midnight on match-days.

Walter Cook had been a war guest player for City, as well as also serving himself with the Scottish Border Regiment. Born near Midsomer Norton, Somerset in 1894, Walter was one of nine children (two sisters and six other brothers), although before Walter was born, his brother George died in his infancy after he drowned in a flooded stream behind the family home in Somerset. When he was five Walter headed north with his parents, Joseph and Helen, so that Joseph could work down the mine near Castleford, and at 23, after plying his trade in West Riding local football, Walter made his debut as the goalkeeper for Leeds City away to Notts County. It was the final season of the Wartime League and Cook was deputising for the first team goalkeeper Willis Walker, who was serving with the Royal Naval Depot in London. Walker had played for City in the first game of the 1918/19 season against Notts County at Elland Road in a 4-1 win, but his latest call up for duty meant that when City played County again the following week on 14 September, Cook was between the sticks. Although City were beaten 5-2, Cook received glowing reports and rave reviews from the media with the *Yorkshire Post* declaring, 'Some of Cook's saves were brilliant'. Cook retained his place for the following five games and on the 19 October after a narrow 1-0 defeat at Lincoln City, the *Leeds Mercury* reported, 'Along with his defence, it was the really brilliant goalkeeping of Cook that prevented a far worse situation for Leeds City.' And once again the *Yorkshire Post* was full of praise for Cook's 'fine custodianship'. Cook played less than a dozen games for City but he was back as the reserve keeper after Walker was demobbed.

Then, following the expulsion of Leeds City, Cook joined Castleford Town, living on William Street off Lock Lane. Cook's debut for Castleford was an FA Cup tie against Hednesford Town in January 1920. The year after, he returned south to play for Plymouth Argyle, a club new to the league. However, Cook did find it difficult to break into the first team on a regular basis due to the consistency of regular keeper Fred Craig. In his final appearance for Plymouth, Cook had been outstanding in a 0-0 draw at Millwall, but his major breakthrough came when he moved along the south coast to join Brighton and Hove Albion in 1923. But, after 52 games for Brighton, Cook had to have a major operation on his cartilage and unfortunately in those days it was a very serious injury. He had surgery at St Thomas's in Brighton and although the club paid for it, they felt they had to release him. Walter's daughter, Vera, recalls, 'It was all very sudden for dad, the club paid his train fare back up to Yorkshire and that was it.' To further compound the situation, it was during the great strike of 1926, the year Vera was born, and transport was very limited. Vera added: 'Dad had to stand up all the way back to Yorkshire on an overcrowded train – on crutches. And because it was during the strike, the train had to be driven by a director of the rail company.' After recovering from his cartilage procedure, Cook spent a season at Stockport County before going back across the Pennines to North Yorkshire in 1929, playing the final two seasons of his career between the posts at Harrogate Town. Walter died in Harrogate in 1973.

Another former City player at the auction, though not directly involved in the sale, was a local man, John Ernest Hewitt. Many players of this era preferred the amateur scene to the professional game. 'Jack' Hewitt was one such player. His career with Leeds City was short-lived, comprising only a handful of games, and is largely undocumented, but he did also represent City at left half-back for the Yorkshire League side in a fixture arranged against the Irish Intermediate League on 7 March 1919. Along with Jack, two other City players represented the Yorkshire League, J. Woodcock and

H. Whitehead. The rest of the Yorkshire team that day consisted of: N. King (Methley Perseverance), H. Church (Castleford and Allerton United), A. Blackburn (Goole), F. Pollard (Methley Perseverance), R. Burton (Methley Perseverance), H. Raynor (Selby), S. Ranby (Selby), B. Johnson (Brodsworth Main) and W. Burton (Wakefield City). Mary, or Molly as she is known, is Jack's daughter. Molly was a very accomplished dancer in her day and is still active even now in her 90s, living in Crossgates, Leeds. She told how Hull City tried to lure Jack to the east coast and offered him the princely sum of 10s 6d a week. 'Dad was a staunch family man,' said Molly, 'and he decided to stay with his family in Leeds. He felt that a move to Hull would be abandoning his family.' After politely turning down Hull's generous offer, Jack went on to enjoy an extremely successful career in amateur football. He was born the youngest of eight children in Garforth in 1899 and lived at Strawberry Avenue for several years.

The Hewitts were a huge sporting family with their interests ranging from football to rugby and cricket. Much later, Jack's brother-in-law, Philip Parkinson, had trials at Leeds United at the same time as John Charles. Unfortunately, Jack's brother, Harold, was killed at the Battle of Arris in the first World War One in 1917. Molly said: 'Dad always considered Harold the best footballer in the family and my uncle Harold's death affected him deeply. It was so sad to lose such a great sportsman at such a young age.' Jack was a very modest man; he worked down the mines and he was considered a local sports hero in his beloved Garforth, playing for several local teams. Molly recalled how her dad would often be carried around Garforth shoulder high by adoring local fans. Many newspaper articles from that era certainly support Jack's popularity. Molly worked in the canteen at Barnbow Munitions Factory in Crossgates, where incidentally, the author's grandma, Minnie Kilbride, had been a crane operator. Molly went on to marry Bob Sherburn from Kippax and they had a son, Colin. Bob and Colin became avid supporters of the newly formed Leeds United Football Club, and would follow the team home and away. Molly told me proudly, 'They were amongst the first supporters to obtain season tickets at the club and they always clapped the opposition onto and off of the pitch.' Jack Hewitt died in 1973.

So, the curtain came down on the auction at the Hotel Metropole and indeed on Leeds City. Mr J. C. Clegg, the chairman of the council of the Football Association, and a member of the commission which suspended Leeds City, said afterwards, 'Whilst I cannot express any personal opinion as to the unfortunate position in which lovers of the association code in Leeds find themselves, or in regard to the prospects of any new club which may be formed in the city, I can say that much sympathy is felt with the Leeds public, who, innocent of any offence, are being deprived of their sport. There can of course, be no objection, either on the part of the association or the league, to the formation of a new club in Leeds, but it must be a new club under new management, and not merely a reconstruction of Leeds City under another name. It cannot spring at once into the position held by the City club, the players of which have been disposed of today. It must begin at the beginning.'

Almost immediately after the auction, City supporters and members of the Leeds public sprang into action.

Chapter Ten

A City is United

LESS than three hours had elapsed since the players' auction at the Hotel Metropole, and with many of the club's supporters stunned and totally shell-shocked, word quickly spread around the town that a meeting had been hurriedly arranged at Salem Church to discuss the possibility of forming a new football club from the ashes of Leeds City Football Club. Groups of men began meeting all over the city and the public houses were doing good business. The White Horse, housed above Fairburn's chemist on Boar Lane, was doing very well with the more select of the supporters tucking into pork chops with mashed potato and carrots and it was standing room only at the Scarborough pub around the corner from the Griffin Hotel, where Leeds City had been formed 15 years earlier. Men spilled outside into the alley and street as the Whitelocks pub became too full and boisterous as the possibility of a new club was discussed vigorously. Around 6.30pm a large body of men left the Golden Lion Hotel on Lower Briggate and made their way over Leeds Bridge.

This was the very bridge where it is said that the world's first ever moving pictures were filmed by French artist Louis Le Prince in 1888. And because of its strategic position at the south of the city, Leeds Bridge was effective in the defence of Leeds during the English Civil War in 1643. Now another historic occurrence was about to take place nearby. As the entourage from the Golden Lion crossed the bridge, a group of around 50, who were stood outside the Adelphi pub, immediately drained their tankards and bottles and joined the growing movement for the remaining 100 yards to Salem Church, all no doubt with the hope that something could be salvaged from a very sad day. Hundreds more were already at the doors of the church. One man unbuttoned his jacket and placed it over his arm, 'Thank you for coming gentlemen, please follow me.' That man was Alf Masser, a Leeds solicitor and former vice-chairman of Leeds City, who had been elected to preside over matters for the evening.

Among the estimated 1,300 to walk through the doors that evening was a frail, 69-year-old John Bennett. By his side was his nephew Harry Bennett, who after completing a good amateur soccer career with Leeds Northern as well as representing the West Yorkshire League on a number of occasions, had retired from playing aged 41, and was now manager at Yorkshire Amateur AFC. Salem Congregational Church began life in Leeds in 1791 and is still today the oldest surviving chapel in the city. With the industrialisation of the 19th century, Salem became a focal point for Hunslet's working classes, hosting weddings, christenings and Sunday school classes, as well as having two large ballrooms, a woodwork shop and facilities for billiards, snooker, table tennis, cricket and a gymnasium. Keith Barber was christened at Salem Church in 1940 and Margaret Fynes was christened there two years later. Keith married Margaret at Salem Church on 30 March 1963 and they were advised, many years later, by their church registrar, Jack Fuller, that they were the only couple to have ever done that. Sadly, Jack died in May 2018, aged 100. Keith Barber's knowledge of Salem Church is extensive, and as a speaker and presenter of 1940s, 50s and 60s nostalgia he has given over 700 lectures. During their existence, Leeds City Football Club had held many meetings in the large hall which was now filled with hundreds of people hoping that another association football club could fill the void.

Salem Church was in very close proximity to Tetley's Brewery, which opened there in 1822. Salem was staunchly against the manufacture, sale and use of alcohol, even going so far as serving non-alcoholic Holy Communion wine; so an inevitable conflict of interests existed between these two neighbours. However, it's pretty certain from all accounts and documents, that there were people there on 17 October 1919 from both sides of the persuasion. The message was that the people of Leeds were 'united' in wanting an association football club in Leeds as soon as possible.

Despite being a meeting of such huge importance, it lasted for little under an hour, by which time it had been proposed by Mr Smart and seconded by Mr Leggott, both supporters of City, that a professional football club be formed in Leeds. It was carried unanimously and the new club would be called Leeds United.

The minutes for the meeting read: 'Public meeting held at Salem Central Hall, Hunslet Lane, Leeds, Friday October 17th 1919. By a unanimous vote Mr Alf Masser was elected to take charge of the meeting. It was proposed by Mr Smart, seconded by Mr Leggott that a professional football club be formed in Leeds immediately which was carried unanimously. Proposed by Mr Leggott and seconded by Mr R. E. H. Ramsden that a limited liability company be floated carried unanimously. The meeting appointed the following gentlemen to act as a committee to formulate a scheme and place before the next meeting a report of the progress made. Committee: Messrs Alf Masser, Joe Henry jnr (whose father as Lord Mayor of Leeds had done so much in trying to save Leeds City from expulsion), Mr Barker, C. Morgan, Dick Ray, Charles Snape and R. E. H. Ramsden. Signed, Joseph Henry Jnr, Oct 31st 1919.'

Grade II listed Salem is arguably the most significant monument in the city of Leeds (aside of course from Elland Road itself) to Leeds United's 100-year history. A Blue Plaque on the front of the building confirms this.

Chapter Eleven

The Emergence of Leeds United

L EEDS United Association Football Club was now established and they were duly invited to join the Midland League by its secretary Mr J. Nicholson, thus replacing Leeds City Reserves, and United appointed long-serving Dick Ray as the club's first manager. Ray had been captain of Leeds City, playing 44 times, and was on the committee that got United on its feet. He had served in World War One in the Royal Army Service Corps. The committee funded the club's early operating expenses out of their own pockets and several adverts were placed in local newspapers and national paper *Athletic News* asking for players. Ray steered United through their Midland League season on a shoestring budget very admirably, until Arthur Fairclough arrived from Huddersfield Town to take up the managerial reins with Ray as his assistant.

Yorkshire Amateur Football Club had moved into Elland Road after the demise of Leeds City and graciously moved out to allow United to move in, for a fee of £250 – it is said that Yorkshire Amateurs still have the original bill of sale.

United's first ever game was on 15 November 1919 against Yorkshire Amateurs in a friendly, fittingly at Elland Road. Amateurs remained at Elland Road for that season, playing on alternate weekends to United. United's team for this historic game was: Hird, in goal, although he wasn't a regular goalkeeper; Fagan, Dodsworth, Parsons, Heslop, Rodgers, Wilson, Hunt, Batley, Moiser and Mill. Lining up for the Amateurs were: Jeffrey, Mathers, Pickard, Thomas, Stirling, Anstead, Keen, Payton, Booth, Walton and Hale. Seven of United's line-up were from local clubs. As the game got under way, snow was falling heavily, on to the already snow-covered pitch, creating hazardous conditions. Herbert Dodsworth, who played right-back in this game, died relatively young. His great grandson, Jon, told me: 'He passed away in his forties of heart failure. I have a 1919 medal from when he played for Leeds United.'

Hunt scored after 17 minutes, to become the first ever to score a goal for United. Then goals by Payton and Keen sent the teams in at half-time with Amateurs leading 2-1. Moiser soon equalised in the second half and a quarter of an hour later Heslop put United ahead from a penalty conceded for handball. Leeds put the game beyond doubt with two late goals; Rodgers getting one and the other was scored by Hird, who had made his way upfield in a clear attempt to emphasise to the spectators that he wasn't a goalkeeper.

Leeds United opened their league campaign a week later with a home game against Barnsley Reserves. Just over 4,000 were at Elland Road to witness a hard-fought 0-0 draw. The honour of scoring Leeds United's first competitive goal fell to schoolmaster Merton Ellson. Matt, as he was known to his teammates, started playing for Frickley Colliery before joining United in July 1920. It was a historic goal for the club but the game finished a disappointing 2-2 draw against Rotherham Town.

Ellson played the whole season, making 37 appearances and scoring eight goals. He returned to Frickley the season after, before joining Halifax Town. He then became a schoolteacher and taught at Blenheim School, Leeds. By all accounts, Matt was a very colourful character. Trevor Chorley is now in his mid-80s and is a member of the Crossgates Methodist Church in Leeds: 'I was about 11 years old and I remember Mr Ellson very well. He used to tell us that he had played for Leeds United and that he had scored their first ever goal. I remember he swore a lot; he used to call us "fucking wicked urchins". Once, when he went out of the class, we took his cane out of his desk and broke it and put it back in his drawer.' Another of Matt's pupils was Les Harrison, who lived on Burley Lodge Road, Leeds. Now 83, he told about how Ellson would often say that he had played a lot for Leeds United and had scored lots of goals. 'We used to like him talking about football as we didn't have to do lessons, but it wasn't until later that I realised how important Mr Ellson had been at the club. He used to call us reprobates, but we didn't know what it meant. He would use the "f" word a lot when addressing us and sometimes we would get a clip round the ear, but it was never anything untoward. My son and grandson go to Elland Road and often mention to anyone who will listen that one of Leeds United's first ever players taught their grandad at school.' Mrs Alice Beesley, who lived on Kirkstall Road, close to where ITV's Yorkshire Television Studios stood, recalled: 'Mr Ellson used to scare me, and so did the school. It was also a school for blind children and in the basement was a three-foot deep swimming pool which was used by the blind children learning to swim. It was dark and horrible down there, and sometimes if we had been naughty, Mr Ellson would threaten to send us down there on our own, until he told us we could come back up. As far as I can remember though, they were just threats, but it was scary at the time.'

Ellson was on the scoresheet twice in United's second game, one a penalty, in a 4-3 defeat to Worksop. Riddick got Leeds' third. Ellson would finish the season as top scorer with eight goals. United had to wait until the 20 December 1919 for their first ever league victory, and it came by way of a 2-0 home win over Lincoln City Reserves, Birtles and Bedford getting the goals in front of a crowd of 4,322. Five days later, United entertained Halifax Town on Christmas Day. With the sides level at 2-2 at half-time (Buckley and Parsons), they emerged for the second period and 15 minutes in, United edged in front through right-winger George Mason – but Town equalised from a penalty by Birtwhistle. The draw left Leeds sitting precariously near the foot of the table with only Gainsborough Trinity and Hull City beneath them, and only one point separating all three teams.

Leeds travelled to the east coast the day after and in a Boxing Day friendly they drew 0-0 at Scarborough, before beating Bradford Park Avenue 3-2 at Elland Road the day after. They resumed their league campaign on New Year's Day with a 2-1 defeat at Barnsley Reserves. It was the first of three consecutive defeats; 4-0 at Lincoln Reserves and 4-3 at Chesterfield Municipal, who would go on to win the league in May 1920. On 24 January Leeds played Castleford Town at Wheldon Road in front of 3,546 spectators. Castleford should have been lining up against Notts County, but they were unable to fulfil the fixture and Leeds, who were without a game themselves, stepped in at the last minute. A strong Castleford team put United under the cosh for lengthy spells and even when they broke free, United found Castleford full-back Bert Duffield in excellent form. Likewise, in goal for Castleford was Walter Cook, who had been bought at the Leeds City player auction at the Hotel Metropole three months earlier. He would have walked the short distance from his home in William Street, off Lock Lane, Castleford, to Wheldon Road. With a strong wind blowing throughout and a very heavy pitch, the bar was struck at either end of the field and Eastwood headed off the line for Leeds and in the end Leeds were happy with a point in a 0-0 draw, especially, as the *Leeds Mercury* said: 'Castleford Town are a particularly hard nut to crack on their own ground.' Eric Mattison was a United fan at that game. His grandson James said: 'Grandad Eric used to tell us how he saw Leeds United's first games. He lived on Lock Lane, Castleford and I recall him telling us how he saw the great Bert Duffield play at Castleford before signing for Leeds United. Grandad Eric once sat on a wall at the end of Princess Street close to Castleford's ground talking to Bert after a game.'

When Castleford finally played their re-arranged game against Notts County, Duffield was standing in at centre-forward and found the back of the net four times, closely watched by a Leeds United representative. Castleford Town later joined the Yorkshire League before disbanding in 1937 and Castleford Tigers RLFC moved into the stadium in 1927, where the rugby club still plays today. When Leeds played Castleford in February at Elland Road, their form was somewhat on the up, and they romped home with a 6-0 victory.

After a disappointing 5-2 defeat away at Sheffield Wednesday, United appointed Arthur Fairclough as their manager, and Dick Ray became his assistant. Two days after taking charge, Fairclough oversaw a 1-1 draw at Notts County Reserves.

As the end of their first season drew closer, United entertained Rotherham Amateurs in a friendly on 6 April. The *Yorkshire Post* said: 'Leeds United concluded their holiday programme yesterday before around 3,000 spectators at Elland Road. Out of four matches played in five days, three have been won, their goal record being 16 goals for and three against. An interesting game was witnessed with the Amateurs proving themselves capable of playing good football, but they were no match for their robust opponents. Early in the game Rodston, at outside-left, put across a fine centre from which Booth opened the scoring for United. Five minutes later a flag kick from the left was accurately placed in the Rotherham goalmouth by Rodston, which was smartly headed into the net by McGhee. Just before the interval, Enzor at outside-right, tried to penetrate the home defence, but was finally bundled off the ball. Halfway through the second half United went further ahead. Following an attack on Amateurs' goal, Booth scored from close range. Result: Leeds United 3 Rotherham Amateurs 0.'

Earlier on the same day, United had played a league game at Grimsby Reserves (because they joined the league late, they sometimes played league matches on the same day as friendlies until they caught up with the fixtures they had missed), watched by the *Sheffield Independent*: 'Leeds United visited Grimsby yesterday, and carried off both points as the result of good play. Butler dashed between the backs, Spendiff pushing the ball away, but before he could recover Bedford rushed up and scored. Later, Huxford of Grimsby struck the cross-bar, but failed to gather the rebound. Crossing over a goal in arrears, played up much better, but Rounds was safe in the visitors' goal, making excellent saves. George Mason, who had joined Leeds from Frickley Colliery alongside Merton Ellson, was constantly in the picture at outside-left, with smart runs and centres. Before the end Butler put in an easy goal for United. Almost on the stroke of full-time, Spendiff, the Grimsby goalkeeper, struck Fawcett as the latter was trying to get to the ball, and was promptly ordered off, the whistle sounding for time as Spendiff was still leaving the field.'

The *Leeds Mercury* carried a similar story: 'Leeds United journeyed to Grimsby yesterday and carried away the points by a victory of two goals to nil. Leeds displayed plenty of dash, and in the initial stages the home goal had a narrow escape, O'Kelly putting in a neatly placed centre to Butler. The latter got his head to the ball, but it struck the cross-bar. Twenty minutes from the start Bedford scored for Leeds. Grimsby did more of the pressing, but all attempts at goal were spoilt by bad footwork. Huxford with one of his cross-shots suffered hard lines. There was little of note in the second half, and Leeds did not get their second goal until Butler scored just before the final whistle sounded.'

United wrapped up their ten friendlies on 10 April at home to Halifax Town. Over 12,000 fans filed into Elland Road to see Robinson give the visitors a 1-0 lead at half-time. But as the *Leeds Mercury* noted, the playing conditions weren't ideal: 'Rain had been falling for almost 24 hours when this friendly fixture commenced at Elland Road, this afternoon. It was still falling; but in spite of this drawback, quite a goodly number of spectators assembled. Of course, the ground was a perfect quagmire, and although the men tried hard to surmount their environment, play was by no means brilliant. Leeds' equalising goal was a snap affair and the Halifax goalie didn't appear to make an attempt to save. Maybe he was stuck in the mud.'

The *Halifax Courier* took this perspective: 'On Leeds United, Butler, a local production, played a really good game and was well seconded by a good pair of wing men in Mason and Bedford, but I wasn't over-struck by the goalie, Broom. The lad made but one mistake, however, he didn't shape up to my satisfaction. It was the friendliest of friendly games, and, with honours easy, was a most satisfactory result. Leeds United are making a plunge for the Second Division next season, but should they fail, these home and away matches should be real "Derby" days.'

During their season in the Midland League, which was a well-established and credible league having being founded in the Maypole Hotel in Nottingham in 1889, United had been constantly scouting for new and reliable players and after finishing 12th they were elected to the Second Division, with Leeds United reserves taking their place in the Midland League, before entering the Central League the following season.

Just along the A62, Huddersfield Town were struggling and getting really low gates, leading to a poor income. Four wealthy brothers, the Crowthers, along with other wealthy local sportsmen, had been injecting massive amounts into the club, but to no avail. When Huddersfield beat Fulham at home in November 1919, a crowd of only 2,500 paid receipts of just £90 – this was the final straw, and with the club still owing the benefactors over £40,000, Hilton Crowther, who was also the club's chairman, made known his intentions to amalgamate with Leeds United, a move that had the full backing of the United directors and also a number of Town players. On 7 November 1919 at the YMCA Hall on Albion Street in Leeds, Alf Masser presided over a meeting, supported by the city's chief magistrate and Lord Mayor, Alderman Joseph Henry. It was well attended by Leeds supporters and shareholders and a proposal to transfer Huddersfield Town to Elland Road was carried unanimously. It was put forward that Leeds take over Town's remaining fixtures for that season under the name of Leeds Trinity. But this was rejected and the club kept the name of Leeds United, who would now wear the blue and white stripes of Huddersfield Town as opposed to the traditional club colours of blue and gold. All the players signed by Leeds United, and all liabilities incurred, would be the responsibility of the new directorate. The proposal would need endorsement from the league, but that was considered a formality. What they hadn't taken into consideration, however, was the opposition mounted by the Huddersfield public. The day after the Leeds meeting, Huddersfield reserves played Nelson in a Central League game and supporters invaded the pitch and protested loudly in front of the directors' box.

As a result, an emergency public meeting was held the next day. The realisation that they could lose their club if they didn't support it, had finally dawned on the

Huddersfield folk, and they turned up in huge numbers to the meeting at Leeds Road. After months of legal battles concerning the money owed by Huddersfield, the Football League negotiated several deals and, with substantial amounts of money now coming into the club, Huddersfield Town were saved. Their secretary-manager Arthur Fairclough moved to Elland Road as United's new manager, with Hilton Crowther, who set his heart on building the new Leeds United, also moving to Elland Road as the club's chairman. Former United manager Herbert Chapman went the opposite way to Leeds Road.

Meanwhile, following a league meeting on 31 May 1920, Leeds United were successfully elected to the Football League, Second Division by 31 votes. Cardiff City, with 23 votes, were elected in second place.

Among the new recruits for the 1920/21 season was full-back Bert Duffield, who Leeds had finally captured from their neighbours, Castleford Town. When he signed for United, Duffield was convinced they had bought him as a centre-forward: 'When Leeds United had watched me play, I was deputising at centre-forward and scored four goals against Notts County reserves. And until I saw my name on the Leeds team sheet for my first match, I was under the impression that they had signed me as a goal-getter.' Duffield, originally from Lincolnshire, had lived locally for most of his life and had friends and family living in Leeds, Garforth and Kippax, where his great nephew, Mick Duffield, still lives. After fighting in the World War One war and getting wounded as a bombardier in France, Bert made his United debut against the team who had become an enemy of Leeds, Port Vale, after controversially taking the place of Leeds City in the Second Division. Also making his debut for United that day was the experienced Jim Baker, who became the club's first ever captain.

The new secretary-manager, Arthur Fairclough, never played the game at a high level, owing to ill-health, but still excelled as a manager, taking Barnsley to two FA Cup finals in 1910 and 1912. They lost the first one to Newcastle, but beat West Bromwich Albion two years later to give Barnsley the only FA Cup in their history. Also a Football League referee, Fairclough left to join Huddersfield Town in 1912, where he laid the foundation for Herbert Chapman's success at the Terriers. Jim Baker had played under Fairclough at Leeds Road and jumped at the chance of joining him at Elland Road. Fairclough also reintroduced former Leeds City players Tommy Lamph and Ivan Sharpe, who despite playing very few games, became the only two players to play for both Leeds City and Leeds United.

The eleven chosen to play in that opening Football League game were extremely young and inexperienced. They lined up thus: goalkeeper Billy Down, 20-years-old, brought from Ashington; Bert Duffield, 26, right-back; Arthur Tillotson, 17, left-back from Castleford Town; Robert Musgrave, 27, at right-half, from Durham City; Baker, 28, at centre-half; left-half was 16-year-old Jimmy Walton from West Stanley; George Mason, 19, on the right wing; inside him was 22-year-old Ernie Goldthorpe from Bradford City; at centre-forward was

Robert Thompson, 25, from Durham City, but formerly of Preston North End; inside-left was Jack Lyon, 26, from Hull City, and outside him on the wing was 19-year-old Jerry Best, recruited from Newcastle United. United took to the field in blue and white stripes.

It would have been very satisfying to put one over Port Vale in that opening game of the 1920/21 season, but unfortunately United went down 2-0. And a couple of days later United suffered a 2-1 home defeat against South Shields, watched by just short of 17,000, a match which was remembered only for the fact that Len Armitage went into the history books as the first United player to score in Second Division football. The following weekend Port Vale were the visitors to Elland Road, and the club badly wanted to win. The 15,377 crowd felt every bit the same. That man Matt Ellson grabbed a brace whilst Jerry Best added another to stage a 3-1 win and exact just the smallest piece of revenge.

Leeds United's first season in the league had its ups and downs and they finished 14th in the table. Bob Thompson became the first player to score a hat-trick for the club, in a 3-0 win over Notts County on 12 December, watched by over 12,000 spectators. But the ten goals that the club scored away from home is still a record low for the club. Leeds did, however, score seven goals in one game. In an FA Cup tie on 25 September 1920, they beat Leeds Steelworks 7-0. The defence, with Duffield, Baker and teenager Ernie Hart, a very stylish centre-half who had made his United debut in the second half of the season, was formidable. Goalkeeper Billy

Down was an ever-present. This defence, reinforced by left-back Jimmy Frew from Hearts, would grow to be the backbone of the club and would concede just 38 league goals for the season of 1921/22. A new goalkeeper, Fred Whalley, was drafted in from Grimsby Town to replace Down, and Harry Sherwin, who made 91 wartime guest appearances for Leeds City, came on board from Sunderland. Leeds' priority had been a goalscorer and to that end, Fairclough swooped once again on Leeds Road and persuaded centre-forward Jack Swan to join him at Leeds in November. Swan would go on to score 47 goals in 108 appearances for the Elland Road club. United also signed Welsh inside-forward Billy Poyntz from Llanelli.

Amazingly, the next season's first opponents were, once again, Port Vale. A bumper crowd of 18,787 squeezed into Elland Road on 27 August hoping that they could inflict further damage on a club who certainly wouldn't have been on the club's Christmas card list. Tommy Howarth, playing at centre-forward, and left-half Jimmy Walton (it would by Jimmy's only goal of the season) were on target for United in a 2-1 win. A 0-0 draw at Bristol City followed, before yet another encounter against Port Vale away. Tommy Howarth scored the only goal of the game to ensure a very happy journey back to Yorkshire.

After a relatively slow first half of the season, United had to wait until February for the first win of the New Year, a 2-0 home win over Bury. But the following week, Leeds travelled to Bury and suffered a 2-1 defeat, in a game that saw the first Leeds United player to be sent off; Billy Poyntz was dismissed just before half-time. Poyntz bounced back the following week with a superb hat-trick in a 3-0 win over Leicester City at Elland Road – just three hours after his wedding. Leeds entered the run-in with a 5-2 victory over Coventry City at Elland Road in front of a 10,876 crowd, Armitage getting two and Swan notching up a hat-trick. The *Yorkshire Post* enthused: 'This was a hurricane finish – four goals in ten minutes. Better forward play has not been seen on this ground for a long while.'

Leeds followed this with another fine home performance, beating Yorkshire rivals Barnsley 4-0. The *Leeds Mercury* said: 'In atrocious conditions, with turf soddened, almost the whole of the second half was played in a violent sleet storm. Leeds United triumphed over their surroundings in great style.'

But, unfortunately, after looking like promotion hopefuls, Leeds slipped away and a poor end to the season saw United score only one goal and one win (away at Fulham) in their final five games. They finished in eighth place, three points behind West Ham in fourth.

The season of 1922/23 once again saw United at great strength in defence. Three new faces had also been added. The first was a Scot, Joe Harris from Bristol City. Harris, a right-winger, had been suspended for 12 months whilst at Bristol and fined £50 after being paid while on amateur forms. Just before he left Bristol City to join Leeds United, Harris was given a £600 benefit game. The second newcomer was another winger, Alan

Noble from Brentford. Noble made his debut for Leeds in a 3-1 home win over West Ham on 4 November 1922 alongside the third new face, inside forward Percy Whipp, who opened his new Leeds account with a hat-trick. Glaswegian Whipp joined Leeds from Sunderland. He quickly became a favourite with United fans who nicknamed him 'the Arch General'. Leeds also signed their first ever player from outside the British Isles. John Armand was born in Sabathu, India and signed for United in December 1922. Leeds had made a slow start to the campaign, but Whipp's arrival had kick-started United's season and a fine 2-0 win at South Shields on 25 November sparked a run of five wins in a row and it wasn't until the end of January that they suffered a defeat. After a spell of inconsistency United recovered and ended the season in fine style, winning the final three games, to finish a credible seventh in the league.

After the season had drawn to a close, Dick Ray left Elland Road to manage Doncaster Rovers and Arthur Fairclough replaced him with Blackpool manager Dick Norman, who had worked with Fairclough at Barnsley before World War One.

The end of the season also saw the FA Cup Final move to Wembley Stadium. The capacity was 127,000 but an estimated crowd of 250,000 saw the pitch engulfed in a sea of spectators. It became known as 'The White Horse Final' as PC George Scorey, sitting upon his 13-year-old horse Billy, became the focal point of attempts to calm matters. The final, between Bolton Wanderers and West Ham United finally got under way 45 minutes later.

Leeds United kicked off the 1923/24 season with a 1-1 draw at Stoke City followed two days later with an emphatic 3-0 win over Crystal Palace in front of an Elland Road crowd of over 10,000. The summer had seen a clear-out of many fringe players: Alf Dark, Jimmy Walton, Len Armitage, George Mason and Joe Potts all moving on, and former Leeds City winger Ivan Sharpe retiring. Four new recruits joined the club. Bob Fulham, Lawrie Baker and George Speak were joined by new goalkeeper Bill Johnson, but Billy Down had regained the keeper's jersey from Fred Whalley, which in turn restricted Johnson's appearances between the sticks to just three. The defence would be as tight as ever with Duffield, Hart and Baker dominant throughout. In addition, the attack became much more effective with forwards Joe Richmond, Percy Whipp and Jack Swan efficiently supplied by wingers Joe Harris and Alan Noble. But United got off to a slow start. The 3-0 win against Crystal Palace was followed by four games without a win. But then seven consecutive wins saw United surge to the top of the division. At the end of October, United fans were especially pleased to witness two successive victories over Port Vale, home and away. But a poor Christmas was in store and through December United went five games without a win, eventually beating Oldham 5-0 with goals from Swan (two), Richmond and Whipp (two). Leeds were then defeated 2-0 on 5 January at South Shields, but then went on a morale-boosting run and after a goalless draw at Hillsborough, they notched up six consecutive wins to remain sitting at the top. But Leeds just couldn't maintain this run of form and following a 2-0 away win at Fulham, they went another five games without winning. Leeds still only needed two points to secure promotion and they came with a decisive 4-0 victory at home to Stockport County.

The crowds at Elland Road had been disappointing over the previous weeks, but they returned in style for this famous victory as reported by the *Yorkshire Post*: 'The holiday crowd, officially returned at 22,145, was more demonstrative than perhaps any that has been assembled since the war. Though cleverer teams have won promotion, no set of players have tried harder or trained more conscientiously. The extraordinary tenacity of the home players and their effective tackling was too much for Stockport in the second half.'

With promotion secured, it was now time to go for the title, which required two more points from the remaining two games; both were against second from bottom Nelson, the first one at home. United fans were confident of becoming champions, but for much of the first half United's defence were pinned down by a lively Nelson attack that belied their lowly position in the table. And United came very close to conceding just before half-time when, with goalkeeper Billy Down beaten, Duffield headed off the line. After a stern word or two from Fairclough, Leeds United emerged for the second half and eventually worked their way into the game.

On 28 April 1924, the *Leeds Mercury* reported: 'Footballers are very, very human. And the tempestuous and sustained roar with which the great crowd at Elland Road on Saturday thundered its appreciation of Leeds

United's success in the struggle for promotion must have rushed to the heads of the team like strong wine. It left the side unsettled throughout the first half and the determined defenders of Nelson never allowed them time to recover their composure. So, it was not until 86 minutes of the game had passed that Coates scored the goal that assured United of the Championship; and, it seems likely, thrust Nelson back into the Third Division. Nelson were not a brilliant team, and although in the first half they often threatened the Leeds goal, their chief aim was to prevent Leeds from scoring. Their backs had one fixed notion – to keep the ball as far from their goal as possible, without wasting much thought on its destination. They put this theory into practice with such direction and vigour that it seemed they would win the priceless point for which they were striving. To their skill and restless energy can be ascribed the reason for the dearth of goals. They erected a barrier around goalkeeper Abbot, and it was not until the last quarter of an hour that it was overcome, and the keeper had to deal with many troublesome shots. Leeds were strong on the left wing, where Harris dribbled very cleverly. Richmond played one of his best games of the season. He was thrustful and ever ready to shoot, and, moreover, he distributed the ball with intelligence, and drew the defenders with a subtle cleverness which at times deceived not only his opponents, but also the crowd. It was well that the Leeds defence had not to face a faster, more formidable line of forwards, for they showed an unusual hesitancy when hard pressed, and now and again the lack of effectiveness caused palpitations among the crowd. The lapses, which occurred mainly in the first half threw into vital prominence the capable goalkeeping of Down, who is not a spectacular goalkeeper, but he possesses the gift of intuition and a safe pair of hands, worth much more than a tendency to perform acrobatic feats.'

So, with three minutes left, Joe Harris took a corner on the left with such precision that it fell at the feet of Walter Coates, who composed himself and fired home the goal that sent United fans wild and United into the First Division for the first time ever. After the final whistle, thousands of fans poured on to the pitch to mark this momentous occasion. The fans remained on the pitch to celebrate with the players and hear speeches of congratulations and appeals for financial help. Even at the height of success, United's cash problems were never far away.

Meanwhile, the *Yorkshire Evening Post* reflected on the run-in at all levels: 'The position of the Football League has become all the more exciting as a result of the week-end happenings. In Division One Cardiff City and Huddersfield Town have not settled the championship, and a heavy defeat in Division Two at Leicester has impaired Derby County's prospects of promotion. Bury are two points in front and have the better goal average. Leeds United have assured themselves of the championship of this division, and Portsmouth seem most likely to carry off the honours in the Southern Section of the Third Division, but Wolverhampton Wanderers and Rochdale are still running neck and neck for the title in the Northern tournament. Though they won handsomely, Chelsea's fate in the First Division was sealed by Nottingham Forest securing a point from Huddersfield Town.'

The following week, United lost their final game of the season 3-1 at Nelson, but United won the league with 54 points and Bury went up in second place, pipping Derby County on goal difference with 51 points. Nelson, meanwhile, were relegated after just one season in the Second Division. Everywhere the United players went around Leeds they were treated like kings.

For the record, Herbert Chapman's Huddersfield Town emerged victorious over Cardiff City on goal average by 0.024 of a goal.

After just four attempts, United began the 1924/25 season in the top flight. It had been a busy summer for Fairclough and his backroom staff and directors. Displaced goalkeeper Fred Walley left the club as did Jimmy Frew. In total, there were 11 new arrivals, but only two of these, forward Cuthbert Robson and half-back Josh Atkinson, made any real impact. And although it was inevitably tougher in the First Division, the prolific trio of defenders, Duffield, Hart and Baker, would once again more than hold their own. Bill Menzies had been drafted into the first team in place of Jimmy Frew at left-back. Menzies, known for his brain rather than brawn, had been at United since joining from Mugiemoss FC Youth team from the suburb of Aberdeen in March 1922, and he made his debut at Oldham on Christmas Day 1923. Menzies played a big part in helping United to promotion and would become almost a permanent fixture, making almost 260 United appearances.

Sunderland were one of the strongest clubs in the country and they were United's first opponents in the First Division. A total of 33,722 fans crammed into Elland Road on 30 August, which was a club record at the time. The *Yorkshire Post* described the events of the day: 'A knowledge of the training methods led to the expectation that United players would lack nothing in physical fitness, but the speed and alertness of the whole side and the incisive methods of the forwards astonished even the most fervent admirer... the Sunderland half-backs ... were overwhelmed by the whirlwind attacks.'

Jack Swan sparked wild celebrations from the crowd when he headed Leeds in front and despite a Sunderland equaliser minutes later, a final score of 1-1 had convinced the fans that United would more than hold their own in the top flight. But the club still needed more funds.

After the game against Sunderland the club began a 'Lend us a Fiver' campaign to urge supporters, and anyone else for that matter, to help raise much-needed financial assistance. Chairman Hilton Crowther had invested heavily into the club since his arrival from Huddersfield Town, providing over £58,000. Now though, Crowther wanted to step down as chairman, and wanted £35,000 of his money back. Chapman's successor, Major Albert Braithwaite, had instigated the 'Fiver' campaign and at a packed meeting at Leeds Town Hall 24 hours later Braithwaite said, 'Unfortunately many people appear to be oblivious to the obvious advantage of Leeds United retaining the position they have won. The Sunderland game brought business worth £15,000 into the city. Hilton Crowther has acted as a sort of fairy godmother to this club and if 7,000 rank and file supporters interested in the maintenance of high-class soccer subscribe a £5 note each, then the problems would disappear.' Crowther would remain on the board until his death in Blackpool in 1957.

In the meantime, United followed the draw with Sunderland with three more games without a win before recording their first victory with a 4-0 thumping of Preston North End in front of over 20,000 spectators. Four days later United beat Everton 1-0, giving the 22,786 Elland Road fans some optimism. However, by mid-October United had only secured eight points from their first ten games, but had seen the record crowd at Elland Road rise to 41,800 for a 1-1 draw with Huddersfield Town. Nevertheless, United were struggling somewhat to adapt to life in the top division.

Three successive victories over Tottenham Hotspur, Blackburn Rovers and West Ham United again gave the Leeds faithful new hope, but they then went six more games without a win. That run was ended in emphatic style, though, on Christmas Day at home to Aston Villa. With the score 0-0 at half-time, the 24,235 crowd was growing frustrated, but in the second half, an amazing hat-trick from Percy Whipp, a brace from Jack Swan and one from Ernie Hart gave United a staggering 6-0 victory. But after a 4-1 win at Preston, an 11-match run without a win saw United spiralling down the table. Four wins from their last eight remaining games ensured United's status in the division, but after finishing 18th, everyone at Elland Road was left in no doubt that it was tough at the top. Arthur Fairclough had already strengthened the side before the season had ended, capturing three top names: Tom Jennings was a recognised goalscorer with Raith Rovers, and very difficult to compete against; the brilliant inside-left Russell Wainscoat signed from Middlesbrough for £2,000; and Willis Edwards, from Chesterfield, joined for £1,500, right from under the nose of Aston Villa who had been tracking Edwards for several months. These three players, coming in just in time for the run-in, played an integral apart in ensuring United's survival. Two wingers joined in the summer: Billy Jackson and Jackie Fell, plus right-back Jimmy Allen. Moving the opposite way to finance the imports, were 13 players, including Walter Coates, Jimmy Down, Alan Noble and Jack Swan. The club were now set for their second season in Division One. The offside rule had been changed, reducing the number of men who had to be between attackers and the goal line from three to two.

Two months into the 1925/26 season, Bert Duffield, after 211 appearances, left the club and joined Bradford. After retiring three years later, Bert entered into the licensed trade, before becoming a greengrocer. He then became involved at Elland Road greyhound stadium on the catering and licensing side. A couple of years later he moved to Rawcliffe, near Goole, to run a poultry farm; here he also coached the village football team. Bert died in Beeston in 1981, aged 87.

Despite losing on the opening day, 1-0 at Notts County, United won five out of their next eight games, but it proved to be somewhat of a false dawn. Crushing defeats at Everton, Arsenal and Burnley on Boxing Day saw Leeds limp through the Christmas period in the lower regions of the division. The departures of Down, Swan, Harris and Duffield had severely impacted the side but a new signing from Falkirk, centre-half Tom Townsley, had cost £5,000 and would prove to be an essential asset to the team. Winning the first three games of the New Year against Sunderland, Notts County and Leicester City respectively, United edged slowly out of danger, albeit briefly. Despite a glorious 4-2 home win over high-flying Arsenal, United's form in the final few months of the season was pretty much abysmal, and after winning only once in the six games, the final game of the season, at home to Tottenham Hotspur, was absolutely crucial to United's hopes of escaping relegation to the Second Division.

Going into the Spurs game, United were level with Burnley on 34 points, Man City were just above them on 35 points and Notts County, rooted to the foot of the table, completed the bottom four clubs. By half-time on this final day, Burnley were three goals up against Cardiff City while Leeds were level 1-1 against Spurs. In thick Elland Road mud, the two teams struggled to get the ball out to the wings, but after Spurs seemed to be getting on top, United rallied tremendously and ran out 4-1 winners. The win, however, did not guarantee the safety of United, as they waited nervously for news of the other two games. Burnley had won and all eyes now focussed on the Man City game at Newcastle United. City had been 3-0 down, but had clawed one back, before missing a penalty. There were anxious moments for Leeds fans as City pulled another back and chased the equaliser that would relegate Leeds. Fortunately, the score remained at 3-2 to Newcastle, relegating Man City along with Notts County. Leeds and Burnley clung on to 19th and 20th positions respectively, level on points. Twenty-six goals by Tom Jennings set up a new club record.

In the summer of 1926 Jim Baker left the club and joined Nelson, leaving a massive gap in United's defence. Baker had played 209 times for the club, 149 of those consecutively. And after a brief spell at Nelson, he returned to Leeds to run the Smyths Arms pub on Gelderd Road, close to the Elland Road ground. He then ran another pub, the Mexborough Arms in Chapeltown, Leeds. Baker would join the Leeds board in 1959. He died, aged 75, in 1966.

Meanwhile, the change in the offside rule the previous season had thrown many defences into disarray and there was a significant increase in goals conceded; United were no exception. Tom Jennings in attack, however, continued to flourish, scoring 35 goals, 19 of which came in just nine games, with four goals on two occasions and two hat-tricks. But sadly, Jennings would be the only shining light in a fateful season.

A 5-2 hammering at home by Bolton Wanderers on the opening day set the tone for the long, hard season ahead. Six weeks into the season saw the debut of Harry Duggan, who had been signed the previous May. Born in Dublin on 8 June 1903, Harry was an outside-right, but played only played nine games that season, at inside-forward. It would be a couple more years before he commanded a regular place in the team. He was described as a 'livewire, enterprising and enthusiastic individual who did not stand idle or wait for things to turn up'.

After winning just two games out of their opening seven, United hit a bit of good form with three straight wins. They beat Arsenal 4-1 with a hat-trick from Jennings, had a 4-2 win at Liverpool, with all four goals coming from Jennings, and beat Blackburn Rovers at home. The *Yorkshire Post* reported on the Blackburn game, a 4-1 victory, saying: 'A personal triumph for Jennings with all four goals, but United had much the stronger half-back line, and Townsley was masterful in his straight runs and low passing up the field.' Tom Townsley had signed for Leeds in December 1925, originally replacing Ernie Hart the centre-half. Townsley was eventually converted, very successfully, to full-back, allowing Hart to continue in the centre of the defence. But for all that, it was the defence that had been found wanting, and they were conceding goals at an alarming rate. Week in, week out, United continued to struggle and despite paying Hearts £5,600 for the services of inside-forward John White in February, it made little difference in terms of results and United continued in a downward spiral at an alarming rate. Even though they beat West Ham in their penultimate game by six goals to three, they were relegated before their last game, a 1-0 defeat at Hillsborough. The end-of-season statistics did not make happy reading for United fans. Although they had created a club record by scoring 69 goals, they conceded a record 88 goals. They accumulated just 30 points with only five of them away from Elland Road. Before the last ball of the season had stopped rolling, Arthur Fairclough, who had been in the managerial chair almost since the formation of the club, resigned his position.

Dick Ray was the directors' choice to replace Fairclough and he returned with the task of taking United back to Division One. Ray's duties began in earnest and Percy Whipp and Billy Jackson were sold and new signings Charlie Keetley and Joe Firth came to Elland Road. Firth was equally at home at half-back or inside-forward. The *Yorkshire Post* noted: 'The enforced return of Leeds United to the Second Division has awakened a new spirit among the management and players alike. There is a feeling that United's set-back is only temporary, the utmost confidence is felt that a team which includes players of such outstanding merit as Townsley, Edwards, Jennings and White will make a bold strike for a return to the top flight.'

Initially playing in the reserves, Keetley learned from Tom Jennings and in one Central League game, he scored seven goals against Bolton Wanderers. Making his debut on New Year's Eve 1927, Keetley scored in a 3-0 home win over South Shields. Leeds had begun their season at South Shields in August and blew the home side apart, winning 5-1. Wainscoat, White (two), and Jennings all opened their accounts; Mitchell got the fifth. The *Yorkshire Post* was suitably impressed: 'The effect on morale of such a victory is incalculable. With confidence restored, Leeds should stand out in the Second Division.'

The three central attackers continued in top form, and White and Jennings were on target in a 2-2 home draw with Barnsley, while the week after, United beat Southampton at home 2-0 with Wainscoat getting both goals. Jennings scored four when United beat Chelsea 5-0 at Elland Road on 10 December, and it sparked off a run of seven consecutive victories. Even when the effects of blood poisoning put Jennings out of action, Charlie Keetley stepped up to take the lead, adapting to league football from his previous role in the non-league with little effort. He tucked away 18 goals in United's final 16 games. During the run-in United beat promotion rivals Chelsea 3-2, watched by a Stamford Bridge crowd of 47,562, the *Yorkshire Post* noting: 'The exchanges were extraordinarily fast and keen and reached a high standard of cleverness.' The *Yorkshire Evening Post* said, 'Leeds United are showing a high degree of class as they home in on promotion at the first attempt.'

The win in the capital placed United three points ahead of third-placed Chelsea with just two more games remaining. On their return to Leeds railway station the team were met by hordes of supporters, including the Lord Mayor and Mayoress, who greeted their heroes ecstatically. Leeds lost their two remaining games, one of which was at home to their title rivals Man City. A record Elland Road crowd of 49,799 saw United go down 1-0 in a match that had they won they would have been crowned champions, but as it turned out they went up in second place. Nevertheless it had been a tremendous achievement by Dick Ray's men, who would once again compete at the top table in the 1928/29 season.

United began that campaign with a 4-1 trouncing of Aston Villa at Elland Road, Charlie Keetley recording a hat-trick. This team was easily the best that Leeds United had produced and two days later they beat Bury 3-1, with Wainscoat (two) and John Armand finding the net. This was followed by a pulsating 4-4 draw at Leicester City and by the beginning of November, United found themselves as potential contenders for the title with eight wins from the first dozen games. But a poor run of form away from home, including an 8-0 thumping at West Ham in February, saw United slip down to mid-table, where they remained for the rest of the season. A 2-2 draw at home to Liverpool on 2 February saw Tom Jennings back in the team and on the scoresheet after several bouts of blood poisoning. But a 2-0 win against Sheffield United on 2 April proved to be United's last victory as they failed to win any of their remaining seven matches. After initial signs of a title challenge, Leeds had to settle for 13th place, but it had been an altogether satisfying season and they could look forward to next season with confidence.

That confidence took an early blow in the first game of the 1929/30 campaign when Arsenal romped home 4-0 in front of a Highbury crowd of almost 42,000. But United bounced back in good style with a 4-1 victory over Aston Villa, who had finished third the previous season. Right-back Harry Roberts scored two from the penalty spot. Roberts, who was from Crofton, near Wakefield, had signed for United from Castleford Town in February 1925, but had had intermittent runs in the side before attaining a sustained run in the first team in the 1926/27 season. He would leave for Plymouth Argyle in November 1930. The other two goals against Villa were from another Yorkshireman, inside-right Eric Longden, and one from Tom Jennings, who was still suffering from bouts of blood poisoning. Two indifferent results followed at Everton and then at Huddersfield with just one point gained, but then United embarked on a tremendous run of seven straight victories, starting with a 2-1 win against Everton and culminating in a 1-0 home win over Birmingham City. At the start of this remarkable run of wins, Jack Milburn made his debut. He was one of three Milburn brothers to play for Leeds, George and Jim being the other two. They were all full-backs. Jackie Milburn, who was a legend for Newcastle and England, was the uncle of a future Leeds centre-half, Jack Charlton.

Leeds' winning streak was punctuated by a 2-2 draw at Leicester, but a week later a 6-0 win over Grimsby in front of an Elland crowd of over 25,000 seemed to have steered the ship back on course. Leeds now sat on top of the league with 20 points out of a possible 26. The defence was strong, with a formidable half-back line of Willis Edwards, Ernie Hart and George Reed, who was from Altofts near Wakefield, and had been a steady fixture of the side for three seasons. The attack was equally as formidable, with sterling performances by Wainscoat and Turnbull, who scored six goals apiece, while Dave Mangall – who, along with Keetley, deputised when needed for Jennings – had hit five. Mangall was a young centre-forward who had scored ten goals in a 13-0 win over Stockport County in a Midland League, Northern Section game for Leeds in September 1929. He was a natural, prolific goalscorer, but after he scored six goals in his first nine consecutive league games, many Leeds fans were extremely angry when the club allowed him to join Huddersfield Town at Christmas. After scoring 33 goals for Huddersfield in the 1931/32 season, Mangall was struck by multiple injuries and after moving to Birmingham, he played for several southern clubs including West Ham and Queens Park Rangers and guested for Millwall in wartime whilst a member of the Civil Defence. After four years in management at QPR where he took them to the Third Division title in 1947/48, he was replaced by Jack Taylor. He died in Penzance in 1962, aged just 52.

Meanwhile, Leeds were having a tough winter and at the end of 1929 they suffered five successive defeats. However, they began the New Year with wins at Arsenal and Aston Villa, and then trounced Crystal Palace 8-1 in the FA Cup third round. They did suffer the odd defeat along the way, but United remained focussed right to the finish. Sheffield Wednesday won their second successive league title, but at least United had the satisfaction of beating them home and away, both convincingly, and they had crossed swords with and won against the previous year's top four teams. Leeds had reached an outstanding fifth place and if they had won their final match at Portsmouth instead of drawing 0-0, they would have finished an incredible third. But Dick Ray was determined not to rest on his laurels.

By the time Leeds United entertained Portsmouth for the opening match of the 1930/31 season, John White had left for Hearts for a fee of £2,350. But with Leeds seemingly strong throughout the team, their fans didn't blink an eye. And despite a 2-2 draw with Portsmouth followed by two defeats at Derby County and then at Herbert Chapman's Arsenal, Leeds fans were confident of their team challenging for the coveted Football League championship. That confidence appeared justified when two emphatic 4-2 victories against Man City and Blackburn Rovers, both in the top six the previous year, seemed to have arrested the slide. And with the young Wilf Copping benefiting from the experience of Willis Edwards and Ernie Hart and establishing himself as an accomplished left-half, there seemed no cause for alarm. The attack looked as potent as ever and three days after a 1-0 defeat at Maine Road, United travelled to Blackpool and trounced them 7-3. Even the following four consecutive defeats did not seem to have too much significance, especially when United recovered with a 7-0 thrashing of Middlesbrough with Tom Mitchell opening the scoring followed by two each from Harry Duggan, Russell Wainscoat and Tom Jennings. In between the two wars, outside-left Mitchell had been a very popular player with the United fans. Excelling in the promotion year of 1927/28 he played in every game. In later years he coached in Norway and became an RAF pilot there and was actually married in Oslo Cathedral. In over 150 appearances for Leeds he scored 51 goals.

But Leeds United were becoming erratic. Leeds beat Birmingham away 1-0 on Christmas Day 1930, then on Boxing Day they beat Birmingham again, 3-1 at Elland Road. But it would be their last win until 7 March. In between, Leeds went further in the FA Cup than any Leeds City or United side before them by beating First Division teams Huddersfield Town 2-0 and Newcastle United 4-1 to reach the fifth round where they inexplicably crashed out3 -1 at Third Division Exeter City. Leeds' poor league form continued and they hurtled towards the bottom of the division. During April, they were in the mix for relegation. The club from Old Trafford were rooted to the bottom with no means of escape, whilst Leeds and Blackpool fought to avoid the remaining relegation place.

Leeds suffered two defeats, against Bolton and Aston Villa, which put them in serious jeopardy. On the last day of the season Leeds had 29 points and Blackpool had 31, but with a much inferior goal average. Therefore, Leeds had to beat Derby County, who were in the top six, and hope that Man City, who were in eighth position, beat Blackpool, who had one of the worst defensive records in the league, at Maine Road. Leeds kept their end up by convincingly beating Derby 3-1; however, Blackpool snatched a late equaliser to secure the point they needed to survive, sending Leeds down despite being nine points above the bottom club. Once again Leeds United would have to dust themselves down and pick themselves up.

Dick Ray knew he had to take action and disposed of several players: George Reed, Bill Johnson, Ben Underwood and Tom Mitchell all left, but the saddest departure was that of Tom Jennings to Chester. Jennings had set a goalscoring record at Elland Road with an aggregate of 112 goals and a seasonal best of 35. Overall, he scored 119 goals for Leeds United in 147 appearances. In *Leeds United – A Complete Record* by Martin Jarred and Malcolm MacDonald, Jennings is named as a member of the Raith Rovers team in 1921 that was shipwrecked en route to the Canary Islands.

Dick Ray had always considered that United had been unlucky to be relegated and to that end, he stuck mainly with the men he had the previous season. Although he brought in two more goalkeepers in Stan Moore and Reg Savage, he kept faith in regular keeper Jimmy Potts, as well as full-backs Jack Milburn and Bill Menzies. He installed his usual half-back line of Edwards, Hart and Copping and saw no reason to change his forwards, Firth, Keetley, Cochrane, Furness and Duggan.

Ray was convinced his side were well equipped to launch an immediate return to Division One and the fans were also convinced when United started the 1931/32 season with a bang. Two successive away wins at Swansea and Port Vale respectively got United under way, but then they stumbled with two home defeats on the trot, against Barnsley and then Millwall, but they then embarked on a remarkable 15-match unbeaten run, which lasted right up until a few days before Christmas when they were beaten by Southampton 2-1 at the Dell. The defeat at Southampton had seen Willis Edwards carried off injured. Edwards, who by now had played 16 times for England, was sorely missed in Leeds' defence, and his absence heralded a severe dip in the team's overall performance, but they recovered thanks to a concerted effort from the attack. Following the departure of Jennings, Charlie Keetley was finally establishing himself as first choice centre-forward. He was ably assisted up front by Billy Furness and Joe Firth. A 3-2 home win over Bradford Park Avenue on Boxing Day sparked off three consecutive wins, the third of which, on 16 January, saw the debut of one of the new goalkeepers, Worksop-born Stan Moore making his debut, in a 2-0 win at Barnsley. The competition for the goalkeeper's jersey was fierce and Moore would play the next ten games before Potts fought his way back into the side. Moore had been signed by Leeds after they played a pre-season friendly at Worksop Town, who had Moore in goal. Leeds were so impressed with the young keeper that they signed him straight after the match. The goal tally from United's impressive forwards gave United enough points to ride a series of poor displays as they entered the run-in still near the top of the table, and more importantly still in with a chance of promotion. Leeds' main two rivals were Wolverhampton Wanderers and Stoke City but United had taken four points from Stoke and three from Wolves, and that proved enough to carry United back to the First Division in second place, two points behind Wolves and two points in front of Stoke. Keetley was top-scorer with 23 goals from 37 games.

United began their return to Division One the following season with an unwelcome 2-0 home defeat by Derby County, but then went on a 14-match unbeaten run that took them all the way to 26 November, when they suffered a 3-1 defeat at the hands of Newcastle United, before continuing on another unbeaten run up to New Year's Eve. This unbeaten run included two massive games against Herbert Chapman's Arsenal. On Boxing Day, thousands of United fans descended on London for the game at Highbury and, as part of a 55,876 crowd, they were rewarded by a sterling performance from Leeds United. Charlie Keetley bagged a brace and despite Arsenal pulling one back, Leeds came away from the capital with both points. The *Evening Standard* was suitably impressed: 'This Leeds United team look a fine side indeed. They have strength in defence and in attack with possibly the best inside-forward in the country in Billy Furness. Arthur Hydes, who was plucked from obscurity, was prominent.'

The next day saw the return fixture with Arsenal at Elland Road. A crowd of unprecedented proportion flocked to the ground from all directions, many arriving four hours before kick-off. Thousands were locked out as a record crowd of just under 57,000 assembled inside. The *Yorkshire Post* reported: 'Had proper packing been possible, it could have held many more especially behind the goal at the Gelderd Road end of the ground. The crowd overflowed onto the roof of the newly covered part of the popular side, scores were seen watching from the roof of an inn and so great was the crush that gates had to be opened to relieve some of the pressure.'

Order was restored as the game finally got under way and United attacked. It was an intense game as the *Yorkshire Post* later confirmed: 'It was a game worthy of the occasion, fought at a tremendous pace.' Both sides came close and Harry Duggan, after cutting inside, hit the post with a low drive and Hydes, following up, put the rebound inches wide. Potts made two brilliant stops and as both the teams shut up shop in the closing stages, one fan was seen being taken away on a stretcher in front of the main stand as the referee blew the final whistle. *The Times* was impressed by United: 'Leeds were only kept from success by the familiar concentration of the eight members of the Arsenal side within or near their penalty area, and the tackling of Hart and the brothers Milburn was too strong for the Arsenal men.'

The game had finished 0-0, but it was three priceless Christmas points taken from Arsenal, who would go on to win the league. One major disappointment for the club was that following on from the huge Christmas crowd, the game at home against Blackburn on 7 January attracted only 14,043 supporters for a 3-1 victory. Apparently, 42,000 fans had vanished, most of them never to be seen again. But United continued to show their potential by beating Newcastle United 3-0 in a third round FA Cup tie at St James' Park, with Hydes providing a hat-trick. In the next round United triumphed over Tranmere before losing in the fifth round at Everton. The win

over Blackburn was United's last league win until 18
March, when they trounced Liverpool 5-0. An own goal
made way for two goals from Johnny Mahon and one
apiece from Hydes and Duggan leading to a convincing
win. But the poor run after the Blackburn game had
left United too far away from the top teams and they
lethargically crossed the line in May in eighth position,
but on reflection it wasn't too bad, and Leeds seemed to
have finally adjusted to life in the fast lane, reflected by
Dick Ray's reluctance to make any major adjustments to
his squad for the following season.

In the West Riding Senior Cup Final against
Huddersfield Town on 26 April, Ernie Hart was sent
off for swearing at the referee. Hart complained about a
Huddersfield goal, which was the only goal of the game,
with such vigour and expletives that the referee Mr
Harper dismissed him. The game was at Valley Parade,
Bradford and most of the 2,700 crowd were incensed
when a Huddersfield player appeared to handle the ball
before scoring from close range into Stan Moore's net in
the first half. The sending off resulted in Hart missing
the first five games of the 1933/34 season. The Football
Association also banned Hart from an England tour
to Italy and Switzerland a month later. Willis Edwards
deputised for Hart for Leeds' opening game at Blackburn
Rovers. Charlie Turner played the next four games at
centre-half in Hart's absence. Leeds lost at Blackburn
but triumphed in the next two home games, 5-2 over
Middlesbrough and 3-0 over Newcastle. As well as Hart's
suspension, injuries hampered Leeds throughout and

Willis Edwards only played 15 games because of injury and Hydes didn't play again after a 2-0 loss at Newcastle on 6 January 1934. At Christmas, Leeds had plunged as low as 17th place but four wins through February resuscitated their season and a good run in March saw them thump Liverpool once again by five goals to one with a goal from Mahon, and a brace each from Firth and Duggan. Then, on 7 April, Leeds United played host to Leicester City and slaughtered them 8-0. The *Leeds Mercury* on 9 April 1934 told the full story:

'Scorers: Leeds United – Duggan (2), Mahon (2), Furness (2) and Firth (2) – eight goals. Leicester City – Nil. It was not a new Leeds United that inflicted this staggering defeat on Leicester City at Elland Road, but the old United with a new finish. All those who have seen the side regularly and wish to be fair to the men will admit that there have been games when the side has played just as brilliantly as in this match and when their play has been as attractive to watch and as full of promise. But sometimes the shooting of the Leeds forwards has been poor; sometimes it has been unlucky. And so, opponents have escaped the slaughter they looked like getting. Leicester were not so lucky on Saturday. The Leeds attacks were finished off with shooting as deadly as I have ever seen. I doubt if McLaren in the Leicester goal had a real chance with one of the shots that beat him. The scoring shots were fired in at great pace, well out of reach of the goalkeeper's arms. They were the result of attacks carried out at a pace that left the Leicester defence gasping.

'The Leeds team, for an end-of-the-season match with nothing at stake, and a heavy and disappointing holiday programme, showed astounding freshness, speed and enthusiasm. The exhibition was a tribute to the work of those behind the scenes at Elland Road. Every one of the forwards did his share in the open, swinging attacks made on the Leicester goal, and it was good to see the men overcome their old fault of bunching too closely together when the scoring chances came along. Duggan was all fire and eagerness as leader. One of his goals came after a great burst for 25 yards on his own. Mahon's speed was altogether too much for his opponents, and he, too, obtained a spectacular goal. Furness gave another fine display, and Firth was particularly forceful and effective at inside-right. To their international half-back line, Edwards, Hart and Copping, the Leeds United forwards owed much. The occasion was historic, for it was Leeds United's biggest league victory. It was fitting that Willis Edwards, one of the club's greatest players – some say the greatest – should return to share in such a notable triumph after a long absence from the side. We were all happy to see this great artist in his happiest mood again, "killing" the ball as no other player can, lobbing it into the opposing goalmouth with all his old accuracy, and pushing through ground passes to his forwards that made their work easy. What a player!

'Leicester started promisingly, but after Stan Moore had had some rather fortunate adventures in the Leeds goal, their attack fell away, and it will be kinder to draw a veil over the sufferings of their defence in the later stages of the game, A time-table of the scoring on this memorable occasion will be interesting: first half: Duggan (25 minutes); Mahon (34); Furness (36); Mahon (44); second half: Furness (three minutes); Duggan (16); Firth (17); Firth (32). It will be noted that all eight goals came within a period of just over 50 minutes, so that the 12,000 spectators during that time enjoyed a goal every six minutes. Good going!'

Two players in the Leeds team that day had close family ties in Leeds: Harry Duggan and Stan Moore. Born in Dublin on 8 June 1903, Duggan became a stonemason after leaving school, and played for Dublin junior club Richmond United, scoring 49 goals in 1924/25. His progress was closely watched by Leeds United who signed the 19-year-old in May 1925, and he made his Leeds debut against Aston Villa on 15 September 1926. Goalkeeper Stan Moore made 83 appearances for Leeds United and would no doubt have made more but for a broken leg sustained at Huddersfield Town in February 1935, which lost him his place in goal before being transferred to Swansea.

Harry Duggan was a private and quiet man, who would never boast about the fact that he played for Leeds United. Harry married Doris on 22 December 1926; they had five children, Harry junior, Terry, Patrick, Doreen and Kath, who all went to St Anthony's Catholic School in Beeston, Leeds. He was a proud family man; a family that is very large and rightly proud of Harry and his achievements. His youngest son, Patrick (Paddy), lives in Morley with his wife Ursula and, pride of place on a wall in their home is a painting of the man himself in the green of Ireland. In 1952 Harry junior married Margaret, whose uncle was Stan Moore, the United goalkeeper. At the same time that Harry Duggan was transferred to Newport County in October 1936, Stan signed for Swansea. Both would return to live in Leeds in 1939, just after Harry had skippered Newport to the Third Division South title. Harry was an ARP warden during World War Two and later worked for the Moorhouse Jam Factory and then a glass merchants in Leeds, and Stan Moore joined the police force. Harry and Doris settled in Cross Flatts Drive with two of their children, Terry and Kathleen, and their door was always open, and the house was always full of family and friends. Margaret said: 'Anyone was welcome to call and the first time I met Con Martin was at the house and John Charles often dropped in and would play table tennis with the boys. The Milburn brothers also lived nearby as did Jimmy Dunn and Jack Charlton later on. Harry was a lovely man, loved by all he met; if you called in on him, he would be sat near the fire with a large pot of tea.'

Harry junior and Margaret moved into their first home together in the Highfields in Beeston, before moving to Wesley Street, which is very close to the Elland Road ground. Con Martin, from Dublin, was a Leeds United player from 1946 to 1948; he was a centre-half but was equally at home in the left-back position. Like Harry Duggan, he was a dual Irish international with 36 caps. Martin was formerly a Gaelic footballer, winning the Leinster title in 1941 with Dublin before going on to play football for Drumcondra on the outskirts of Dublin, and headlong into controversy. The Gaelic Athletic Association was opposed to foreign sports and withheld Martin's winners medal, only giving it to him 30 years on. Con Martin is regarded as one of the pioneers, along with several other notable Dublin footballers who had successfully switched codes. He signed for Aston Villa in 1948 for £10,000 where he enjoyed considerable success for eight years.

Harry Duggan's granddaughter, Ann, said, 'Grandad took the pledge and never drank, not even at weddings. He was very generous, giving away some of his international caps (Harry was capped eight times for Northern Ireland and four times for the Republic of Ireland at a time when you could represent both countries) and he would give regularly to the church. He was a proud family man and was very proud of his Irish roots.' Harry's great grandson, Mike Oldfield, added: 'Harry had interests outside of football including his garden/allotment, which was always immaculate with no sign of weeds anywhere. He was colour blind, so used to bring flowers into the house and say "these smell lovely, don't they … what are they?" Harry was a keen golfer and a member of South Leeds Golf Club. He loved his food, especially a nice dish of mutton. He also liked a little flutter on the horses and would fill the pools in, much like everyone else at that time, every week. He strikes me as someone who was very meticulous in everything that he did. He did quite well with the pools, one of his wins paid for a trip to Ireland for the family. My grandma says he never drank and didn't even have a sherry at their wedding.' He played 196 times for United, scoring 50 goals.

Leeds' 1933/34 season petered out, however, and although Leeds had left it too late to make any sort of challenge at the top, they finished in ninth position, which was more than satisfactory. Leeds United had now played in the First Division for eight of their last ten years, but there was still a concern over the lack of support for the club. The attendance for the final home game against Chelsea, a 3-1 win, was barely 7,000, which was pretty poor by any standards, especially considering the huge strides that Leeds United had made since their formation just over 14 years before. Sadly, also, this season had marked the death of Herbert Chapman, in the early hours of Saturday, 6 January 1934. Chapman had gone to watch a player he was interested in at Bury the week before and then went on to watch Arsenal's title rivals Sheffield Wednesday. He had developed a heavy cold and against the club doctor's advice he then went to watch Arsenal's third team. Eventually, the cold developed into pneumonia and by 3am on Saturday morning, Chapman had died.

Herbert Chapman had coveted Leeds' Wilf Copping for many months and following Chapman's death Arsenal swooped on Elland Road and took Copping to Highbury for the princely sum of £6,000. Leeds United were devastated to lose a player of such high calibre and were unable to fill the gap in the half-back line that had served United so well. It proved to be a dismal season for United and on 5 March Dick Ray ended a

30-year association with Elland Road by resigning his
£1,000-a-year job to join Second Division Bradford
Park Avenue. The directors installed former Leeds City
wartime guest player Billy Hampson as replacement to
Ray almost immediately, but a 7-1 defeat at Chelsea on 16
March emphasised the massive problems facing United,
who were now lying sixth from bottom, precariously
hovering above several clubs only a point or two below
them. A 2-0 win at Preston in the penultimate game
ensured United's safety with goals by Duggan and
Hydes, and they finished off the season with a 4-3 win
over Tottenham Hotspur on 4 May to settle into 17th
place, five points clear of relegation, but Hampson clearly
had work to do over the summer of 1935.

Seven players left the club, including John Mahon
and keeper Stan Moore. The incomers were mainly from
lower leagues, with the exception of former England
internationals Albert McInroy, a veteran goalkeeper from
Sunderland, and centre-forward George Brown from
Burnley. Brown had played in Huddersfield's dominant
team of the mid-twenties and Hampson hoped some of his
experience would rub off on some of his less experienced
players. Hampson, himself, wasn't the most experienced
manager, but whilst at Carlisle United he had discovered
a young Bill Shankly. Hampson continued signing players
during the autumn as United struggled to get to grips
with the season. Sammy Armes, who had played under
Hampson at Carlisle, was drafted in from Blackpool
and, along with several young Irish players, 16-year-old
full-back Jim Milburn was brought in, uniting him with

his brothers George and Jack. Hampson worked closely with right-back Bert Sproston, who had been at the club for two seasons, and Sproston won the first of his 11 England caps in October 1936. Sproston's emergence ousted George Milburn. United's start to the season, however, was poor and it wasn't until 21 September that they recorded their first win, a 1-0 home win over Liverpool, thanks to a penalty by Jack Milburn who had become the club's regular penalty-taker; in October he scored three penalties in three games.

But it wasn't a brilliant season for United and although they managed the odd victory, they never really looked like reaching anywhere near the top of the division. More importantly, though, they managed to stay well clear of the lower regions. On 9 November they achieved a welcome win over Sheffield Wednesday. Another penalty from Milburn and a hat-trick from Harry Duggan contributed towards a 7-2 romp for the home side. Duggan scored in the next home game during a 5-2 win against Bolton Wanderers. Vital wins in the New Year saw United improve on last season's final position and a 2-2 draw at Arsenal ensured 11th place.

A 3-2 home defeat by Chelsea opened the 1936/37 season and heralded what was to be a pretty dire campaign. There had been some departures, notably Harry Duggan, now 33, moved to Newport County and George Brown, also 33, went to Darlington. Stan Moore went to Swansea. The big-name departure was Ernie Hart, who left Leeds with a club record of 472 appearances in total. He joined Mansfield Town but would return in later years to become a scout for United. Leeds also paid Oldham Athletic a whopping £12,500 for winger Arthur Buckley, and more recruits were brought in as the season progressed: 21-year-old centre-forward George Ainsley swapped Bolton for Leeds, Hampson signed Aston Villa's burly South African centre-forward Gordon Hodgson, who was almost 34, and Barnsley centre-half Tom Holley replaced Hart in the Leeds defence. Eric Stephenson had signed professional terms for United in September 1934, but this season saw the inside-left finally get a decent run in the side and he chipped in with half a dozen goals in 22 games. The new players made a positive difference but the season was spent flirting with the drop zone and their survival was only confirmed with a final day 3-1 win at home to Portsmouth and other results going right, to ensure 19th place for United, five points clear of the bottom club Sheffield Wednesday.

Gordon Hodgson had proved to be an astute signing by Billy Hampson, and for the 1937/38 season Hampson kept more or less the same set of players, with the exception of the outgoing George Milburn, Albert McInroy the veteran keeper who had lost his place to Reg Savage – who had signed alongside another keeper, Stan Moore, in 1931 – and Billy Furness, who departed for Second Division Norwich City after nine years' service at Elland Road. United reserves had won the Central League the previous season and many of those youngsters were brought into the Leeds team for this campaign. In the 1-1 opening draw at Charlton Athletic, United's team consisted of just three players over the age of 24. United then beat Chelsea at home, 2-0, with goals from Sammy Armes and an own goal. They failed to win in the next three games, but then a hat-trick of victories gave the United team and fans alike some much-needed confidence. Eric Stephenson was proving to be a great discovery and continued to justify the faith Hampson showed him, scoring a hat-trick in a 4-3 home win over Sunderland on 4 December 1937, and his seven goals in seven games included one in a Christmas Day 5-3 win over Middlesbrough at Elland Road. Leeds, however, had a disappointing second half to the season, winning only five games from a 3-0 win at Huddersfield on 29 January up to the end of the season. The only highlight was a 4-4 home draw with Everton, which saw all United's goals dispatched by Hodgson. Despite the poor run of form, United had banked enough points to reach ninth position in the table. Leeds lost their remaining two games of the season away at Man City and Portsmouth, who were both in the bottom four; had they won those two games, United would have finished in fourth. Some of the promising youngsters had been given a taste of the action, young Irishman David Cochrane making his debut in March while young Irish keeper Jim Twomey had been between the sticks after replacing regular keeper Reg Savage. Leeds United's future looked in good hands.

David Cochrane had signed for Leeds when he was just a teenager. He was only 17 when he scored 14 Irish League goals in 13 games, persuading Leeds to give Portadown £2,000 for the speedy winger's services. He made 12 appearances for Northern Ireland and four for the League of Ireland; only World War Two prevented him making further appearances. After the war, he returned to Leeds, which is where Tony Winstanley, a Leeds fan since the early 1960s, first met 'Davy' Cochrane: 'He was only 5ft 4in tall and when he first arrived at Leeds, many people thought he was a jockey. During the war he guested for Linfield and Shamrock Rovers, scoring 50 goals in one year for Linfield. He came back to Leeds after retiring at the age of 30 in 1951. He ran a newsagent's on Lodge Road in Beeston, and I moved into nearby Stratford Avenue in 1970. I used to see this wee guy on his bike or walking past our house, sometimes kicking the ball back to the kids. I was told by a neighbour who he was, so I introduced myself as the greatest Leeds United fan in the world. He chuckled at that but he would always stop to have a chat and comment on how the team were doing. Running a newsagent's in those days meant being up and about long before the rest of the world, but Davy always seemed to be cheery and have a smile on his face. One day he passed by and patted my son, also called David, and his friend on the head. I had visions of my lad one day wearing the Leeds shirt.

However, the only time he does this is on the Kop. In 1977 we moved from Stratford Avenue to be nearer Elland Road. I looked around a house in Sunnyview Terrace and I could see the ground from the bedroom window, so I bought it. I only saw Davy once after we'd moved, but he still asked how we all were. He was a lovely bloke who must have been a great sight in full flow on the wing.'

Leeds started the 1938/39 season without their prize asset – Bert Sproston was sold to Tottenham for £9,500 – but United started strongly, winning nine of their first 15 matches. On 1 October United kicked off a hat-trick of victories with an 8-2 triumph over Leicester City; Hodgson continued his outstanding form with five goals, added to by another Jack Milburn penalty and one apiece from Cochrane and Hargreaves. The five goals by Hodgson is still a United record to this day. Billy McLeod had also scored five times in one game for Leeds City. United surged up the table, reaching third place, but following a 2-1 victory at Blackpool on 19 November, they only managed one win in their next 15 games. 'Iron Man' Wilf Copping returned to Leeds United just in time to play against his former club, Arsenal, and Leeds finally hit a winning streak with a 4-2 win. The return of Yorkshireman Copping proved very welcome indeed: he put the fear of God into his opponents; he rarely shaved before a match, giving him a menacing appearance. His crunching tackles brought him fame, but despite the destructive side to his game, he was scrupulously fair, he made excellent use of the ball and was an expert of the long throw. Inside-forward Aubrey Powell had by now returned to top fitness and top form. The Welsh international had broken a leg in March of the previous season and had been told he wouldn't play again, but he defied all odds to strike up a highly-effective partnership with David Cochrane. The win over Arsenal was followed by two successive wins over Brentford and Blackpool, but United had suffered too much damage to mount any serious challenge to those at the top end of the division and they had to settle for 13th position in the table. However, Leeds, with a combination of youth and experience, looked more than ready for the new season ahead. But the threat of war was hanging over the country.

Chapter Twelve

World War Two and the Future of Leeds United

A YOUNG Adolf Hitler had been decorated twice for bravery in World War One and had been injured twice, once in 1916 when he was hit by an exploding shell and again near the end of the war when he was temporarily blinded by mustard gas. The surrender of Germany at the end of that conflict had deeply affected Hitler. He had tried unsuccessfully to overthrow the German government in 1923 before becoming chancellor of Germany in 1933. He abolished democracy and began a massive rearmament in Germany and introduced conscription, and when the president, Paul von Hindenburg, died, Hitler appointed himself as Fuhrer – the supreme commander of every Nazi paramilitary organisation in the country. The Nazis had only just annexed Austria, in May 1938 when the England team arrived in Germany at the start of their end-of-season tour of Europe. Before the match the England team obeyed orders in giving the Nazi salute to Hitler's henchmen despite misgivings from most of the players. England, who had Leeds' Bert Sproston in the team, beat the Germans 6-3. The 1938 World Cup finals were held in France and the holders Italy retained their title, beating Hungary 4-2 in the final in Paris, but the British nations refused to play despite desperate pleas from FIFA.

The rise in prominence of Germany, combined with weak and divided states around its borders, had provided the perfect opportunity for Germany to make a second bid for European domination. And on 1 September 1939 they made an unprovoked attack on Poland. Hitler claimed that the invasion of Poland was a defensive action, but in truth it is widely recognised that Germany's main intention was to create more space for German people. But this was only the beginning as the Germans moved throughout Europe.

After just three games of the 1939/40 season – United had lost twice to Charlton Athletic and once to Sheffield United – on 3 September, Prime Minister Neville Chamberlain declared war on Germany, and so began what would be the most destructive conflict in human history, ending with the death of 80 million men and women worldwide. A halt was called to all sports in the country, with emergency regulations forbidding the assembly of large crowds. The Football League and FA agreed on a temporary suspension of both fixtures and players' contracts. A few weeks later permission was given for matches to resume, subject to approval by the local police and strict crowd limits. Clubs were restricted to paying a maximum of 30 shillings per player and were allowed to use guests to replace those who were away on national service. Many teams had already volunteered en bloc and six clubs decided to close down for the duration of the war: Aston Villa, Derby County, Exeter City, Gateshead, Ipswich Town and Sunderland.

Those clubs who chose to continue were organised into ten regional leagues to avoid the need for lengthy journeys, with travel restricted to journeys that could be completed on the day of the game. Leeds were members of the North East Division along with the two Bradford clubs, Darlington, Hartlepool, York and Newcastle. Leeds finished fifth out of 11 clubs, winning half their fixtures. Many of the old guard were still around, albeit intermittently, including Ken Gadsby, Jim Makinson, Wilf Copping, Tom Holley, Jack and Jim Milburn, Gordon Hodgson and Eric Stephenson.

This was the most organised of the wartime seasons and United's most successful. As the conflict dragged on, understandably, things became more chaotic. Leeds' performances deteriorated. Crowds rarely got above 5,000, and many teams remained undecided until they were about to kick off because of the uncertainty over who would be available. On Christmas morning, Brighton travelled to Norwich with only five players, hoping to recruit more on the way. They made up their team with some Norwich reserves and soldiers from the crowd of 1,419, but were beaten 18-0. This set the scene for pretty much the duration of the war. Wilf Copping played most of the second half of the season for Leeds whilst on leave from the Army. Jack and Jim Milburn alternated in the right-back spot, and the best player by far was Eric Stephenson, who was at his peak.

But the war raged on and Stephenson became a major with the 3rd Gurkha Rifles. Eric had moved to Leeds from East London with his family when he was very young, going to Oakwood school in Leeds. He had worked his way up through the ranks at Leeds United and had done the same in the services. Four days after his 30th birthday in September 1944, Major Stephenson was operating as part of a guerrilla force behind enemy lines. In Japanese-held Burma territory he was engaged in jungle warfare and was killed. Leeds centre-forward Alan Fowler also died in action. In 1934 Fowler had signed for Swindon Town, but returned to Leeds as a wartime guest player and on his return to Swindon he enlisted in the Dorsetshire Regiment. On 10 July 1944 Fowler's battalion were fighting for a strategically important hill in France. During the very first raid Fowler died in battle. The youngest United player to die in the war was 20-year-old centre-forward Maurice Lawn. Trooper Lawn was part of a reconnaissance party clearing an area in Calet, France when they came under heavy machine gun fire and Maurice, providing cover for a withdrawal, was hit in the stomach. He was taken on board hospital ship SS *Amsterdam*, but tragically on 7 August 1944 the ship hit a mine and Lawn was one of 55 men who drowned along with 11 German prisoners of war. Later that month, tragedy struck another Leeds United player. Left-half Leslie Thompson was only a youngster at Elland Road and on the ground staff. He never played for the first team before the war, but made his debut for the juniors in a 3-0 win over Bradford City. On the night of 26 August 1944, Leslie, a wireless operator and a gunner, was returning from a flying mission with another five crew on board when they were shot down by enemy fire. Their Lancaster ME650 of RAF 630 squadron crash landed in a Danish field in Skarrild, killing all on board. Denmark was under German occupation and as a German working party were digging a grave for the men, a remarkable act of kindness and gratitude occurred. Constable Egon Christiansen persuaded the military to allow the bodies to be buried in the local churchyard rather than a field. Christiansen borrowed a horse-drawn carriage and with the bodies on board he covered them with a Danish flag and took them to the churchyard. *Leeds United: A Complete Record* by Martin Jarred and Malcolm MacDonald, says: 'A grave had been prepared and two large coffins had been placed in it. Constable Christiansen climbed down the grave as the bodies of the men were passed down to him and placed in the coffins. Each year on the evening of 5 May, the day of the liberation of Denmark, a ceremony is held at Skarrild Cemetery in honour of the fliers.'

Promising United forward Robert Montgomery was killed when leading a bombing raid on a vital German ball bearing factory at Schweinfurt on 27 April 1944. And two players who guested for United in the war, Birmingham's Tom Farrage and Harry Goslin of Bolton, were killed in action. Several other United players saw active service during the war. Tom Holley was Leeds' centre-half before, during and after the war and he saw service in India. On retiring, Holley went on to become a very successful sports journalist with the *Yorkshire Evening Post* and then the *Sunday People*. Also in India was Billy Heaton, an outside-left who had signed for United from Whitkirk in December 1937, making 60 appearances for the club. He was the cousin of the author's grandmother. Goalkeeper Alex Lee was awarded the Air Force Medal during the war, while Bob Kane, who was competing with Holley for the position of centre-half, served with the Royal Artillery in Gibraltar. Jim Milburn was injured in Belgium where Aubrey Powell was also stationed. While serving in Italy, Albert Wakefield turned down a number of offers to join Italian clubs. Wilf Copping inevitably was involved in action and served with the Army and was trainer to the Army XI in Dusseldorf in in 1945. He even found time to turn out for United when on leave. And according to *Leeds United: A Complete Record*, Alf and Bill Stephens turned out for United in wartime games; they were both with the Royal Engineers and were both captured, ending up in the same PoW camp.

Perhaps the most famous of United's connections with World War Two was the club's future president and cousin of the Queen, the Earl of Harewood. A captain in the Grenadier Guards, he was wounded and captured after D-Day and held captive in the dreaded Colditz in November 1944, after direct orders from Adolf Hitler, who because of his royal connections saw him as a bargaining chip. In March 1945 Hitler signed the Earl of Harewood's death warrant, but on realising that the war was lost, the SS General in Command of all PoW camps refused to carry out the sentence and he was released into the care of the Swiss.

On 6 May 1945, Adolf Hitler committed suicide in a bunker beneath his headquarters in Berlin, and just days later, Germany unconditionally surrendered to the Allied Troops.

Eric Drummond came home from France as a decorated World War Two veteran. His father had taken him to his first Leeds game, a 2-0 home win over Sheffield United, when he was eight years old. Eric told the *Yorkshire Evening Post* in 2012, 'At that time the Kop had no roof with railway sleepers and cinders to stand on and there was a boys' enclosure behind the goal. He plonked me in there and said, "you sit there until I come back". I have been hooked on football ever since.' Eric lived in Scarcroft, Leeds until recently, but even when he moved to Dorset with his late wife, Betty, for several years, Eric regularly made the 12-hour round trip to watch his beloved Leeds – even suffering a heart attack outside the ground after a match failed to keep him away. But, in recent years, arthritis had forced him to watch the Whites from the comfort of his armchair. Sadly, Eric passed away in a care home in Colton, Leeds on 12 March 2019. He was the uncle of Carol Smith, who lives in Kippax with her husband Ken.

Leeds United's form during the war had been nothing short of abysmal, virtually living in the nether regions for the duration. And any glimmer of hope the fans had, once the Football League resumed, evaporated very quickly. Almost immediately, Leeds were on the back-foot – and they stayed there. Con Martin was brought in from Glentoran in an attempt to halt the slide, but after winning just six games all season, Leeds were relegated with just 18 points. Hampson was relieved of his duties in April and Willis Edwards, who by now was assistant trainer, was appointed manager. Sadly, it didn't work out for Edwards, and World War One veteran 'Major' Frank Buckley took over the managerial position for the 1948/49 season. United managed to finish three points above their position the previous season, but on a plus note, the Elland Road crowds had been encouraging and continued to grow. Major Buckley was a bit eccentric to say the least. He was known for injecting his players with monkey-gland extract, which he believed would sharpen their thinking. And it wasn't long before a mechanical kicking machine was installed at Elland Road. It was designed to pump footballs out at different heights and speeds to improve heading, trapping, volleying and goalkeeping. Leeds improved greatly the following season and Buckley's major contribution had come when he had introduced 18-year-old John Charles the previous April. The young Welshman played at centre-half in every game in the 1949/50 season and United finished in a very satisfying fifth place – a position they also attained the following season.

In August 1946, 19-year-old Donald George Revie made his Football League debut for Leicester City. Revie was born on 10 July 1927 and lived at 20 Bell Street in the shadow of Ayresome Park, Middlesbrough. He was obsessed with football. As a six-year-old, he would constantly kick a small round bundle of rags against his back-yard wall. He captained Archibald School team three years later and on leaving school he signed for Newport Boy's Club. Six months later he was transferred to a prominent club in Teeside, Middlesbrough Swifts, for five shillings. In November 1949 Don Revie left Leicester and joined Hull City for £20,000; two years later he moved to Man City for £25,000. It was here where Revie became synonymous with introducing the so-called deep-lying centre-forward plan to England – a plan adopted from the famous Hungarian side of 1954. The 'Magyars' dominated football at the time and tore other teams apart using centre-forward Nandor Hidegkuti in a deep-lying role, operating just behind the forward line. In England it became known as 'the Revie Plan' and was widely recognised as being a contributing factor in Man City's FA Cup win at Wembley in 1956.

Don Revie had a distinguished playing career, moving to Sunderland for £22,000 before arriving at Elland Road in 1958. He came as a player, but became manager in 1961 and this was the messiah that Leeds fans, both City and United, had been awaiting for 57 years. Don Revie went on to transform a team at the bottom of the

Second Division in to one that would consistently take on and beat almost every team in front of them, and that included across Europe. Leeds had at long last found their man.